INSTITUTE OF PACIFIC RELATIONS

INQUIRY SERIES

THE INSTITUTE OF PACIFIC RELATIONS

The Institute of Pacific Relations is an unofficial and non-political body, founded in 1925 to facilitate the scientific study of the peoples of the Pacific Area. It is composed of National Councils in ten countries.

The Institute as such and the National Councils of which it is composed are precluded from expressing an opinion on any aspect of national or international affairs; opinions expressed in this study are, therefore, purely individual.

NATIONAL COUNCILS OF THE INSTITUTE

American Institute of Pacific Relations

Australian Institute of International Affairs

Canadian Institute of International Affairs

China Institute of Pacific Relations

Comité d'Études des Problèmes du Pacifique

Netherlands-Netherlands Indies Council, Institute of Pacific Relations

New Zealand Institute of International Affairs

Philippine Council, Institute of Pacific Relations

Royal Institute of International Affairs

U.S.S.R. Council, Institute of Pacific Relations

INTERNATIONAL SECRETARIAT AND PUBLICATIONS OFFICE
1 EAST 54TH STREET, NEW YORK 22, N. Y.

JAPAN'S EMERGENCE AS A
MODERN STATE

JAPAN'S EMERGENCE AS A
MODERN STATE

Political and Economic Problems of the Meiji Period

By

E. HERBERT NORMAN

I. P. R. INQUIRY SERIES

GREENWOOD PRESS, PUBLISHERS
WESTPORT, CONNECTICUT

Library of Congress Cataloging in Publication Data

Norman, E   Herbert, 1909-1957.
  Japan's emergence as a modern state.

  Reprint of the ed. published by International
Secretariat, Institute of Pacific Relations, New York,
in series: I. P. R. inquiry series.
  Bibliography: p.
  1. Japan--Politics and government--1868-1912.
2. Japan--Economic conditions--1868-1918. 3. Japan--
Economic policy. I. Title. II. Series: Institute of
Pacific Relations. I. P. R. inquiry series.
DS882.N6 1973   952.03'1   72-9092
ISBN 0-8371-6573-3

Originally published in 1940 by the International Secretariat,
Institute of Pacific Relations, New York

Reprinted in 1973 by Greenwood Press, Inc., 51 Riverside Avenue,
Westport, Conn. 06880

Library of Congress catalog card number 72-9092
ISBN 0-8371-6573-3

Printed in the United States of America

10 9 8 7 6 5 4 3

TO MY MOTHER

FOREWORD

This study forms part of the documentation of an Inquiry organized by the Institute of Pacific Relations into the problems arising from the conflict in the Far East.

It has been prepared by Mr. E. Herbert Norman, formerly research associate of the International Secretariat, Institute of Pacific Relations and at present in the Department of External Affairs, Ottawa.

The Study has been submitted in draft to a number of authorities including the following, many of whom made suggestions and criticisms which were of great value in the process of revision: Dr. John K. Fairbank, Dr. Hugh Borton and Mr. Jack Shepherd.

Though many of the comments received have been incorporated in the final text, the above authorities do not of course accept responsibility for the study. The statements of fact or of opinion appearing herein do not represent the views of the Institute of Pacific Relations or of the Pacific Council or of any of the National Councils. Such statements are made on the sole responsibility of the author. The Japanese Council has not found it possible to participate in the Inquiry, and assumes, therefore, no responsibility either for its results or for its organization.

During 1938 the Inquiry was carried on under the general direction of Dr. J. W. Dafoe as Chairman of the Pacific Council and in 1939 under his successor, Dr. Philip C. Jessup. Every member of the International Secretariat has contributed to the research and editorial work in connection with the Inquiry, but special mention should be made of Mr. W. L. Holland, Miss Kate Mitchell and Miss Hilda Austern, who have carried the major share of this responsibility.

In the general conduct of this Inquiry into the problems arising from the conflict in the Far East the Institute has benefited by the counsel of the following Advisers:

Professor H. F. Angus of the University of British Columbia

Dr. J. B. Condliffe of the University of California

M. Etienne Dennery of the Ecole des Sciences Politiques.

These Advisers have co-operated with the Chairman and the Secretary-General in an effort to insure that the publications issued in connection with the Inquiry conform to a proper standard of sound and impartial scholarship. Each manuscript has been submitted to at least two of the Advisers and although they do not necessarily subscribe to the statements or views in this or any of the studies, they consider this study to be a useful contribution to the subject of the Inquiry.

The purpose of this Inquiry is to relate unofficial scholarship to the problems arising from the present situation in the Far East. Its purpose is to provide members of the Institute in all countries and the members of I.P.R. Conferences with an impartial and constructive analysis of the situation in the Far East with a view to indicating the major issues which must be considered in any future adjustment of international relations in that area. To this end, the analysis will include an account of the economic and political conditions which produced the situation existing in July 1937, with respect to China, to Japan and to the other foreign Powers concerned; an evaluation of developments during the war period which appear to indicate important trends in the policies and programs of all the Powers in relation to the Far Eastern situation; and finally, an estimate of the principal political, economic and social conditions which may be expected in a post-war period, the possible forms of adjustment which might be applied under these conditions, and the effects of such adjustments upon the countries concerned.

The Inquiry does not propose to "document" a specific plan for dealing with the Far Eastern situation. Its aim is to focus available information on the present crisis in forms which will be useful to those who lack either the time or the expert knowledge to study the vast amount of material now appearing or already published in a number of languages. Attention may also be drawn to a series of studies on topics bearing on the Far Eastern situation which is being prepared by the Japanese Council. That series is being undertaken entirely independently of this Inquiry, and for its organization and publication the Japanese Council alone is responsible.

The present study, "Japan's Emergence as a Modern State," falls within the framework of the second of the four general groups of studies which it is proposed to make as follows:

I. The political and economic conditions which have contributed to the present course of the policies of Western Powers in the Far East; their territorial and economic interests; the effects on their Far Eastern policies of internal economic and political developments and of developments in their foreign policies vis-à-vis other parts of the world; the probable effects of the present conflict on their positions in the Far East; their changing attitudes and policies with respect to their future relations in that area.

II. The political and economic conditions which have contributed to the present course of Japanese foreign policy and possible important future developments; the extent to which Japan's policy toward China has been influenced by Japan's geographic conditions and material resources, by special features in the political and economic organization of Japan which directly or indirectly affect the formulation of her present foreign policy, by economic and political developments in China, by the external policies of other Powers affecting Japan; the principal political, economic and social factors which may be expected in a post-war Japan; possible and probable adjustments on the part of other nations which could aid in the solution of Japan's fundamental problems.

III. The political and economic conditions which have contributed to the present course of Chinese foreign policy and possible important future developments; Chinese unification and reconstruction, 1931-37, and steps leading toward the policy of united national resistance to Japan; the present degree of political cohesion and economic strength; effects of resistance and current developments on the position of foreign interests in China and changes in China's relations with foreign Powers; the principal political, economic and social factors which may be expected in a post-war China; possible and probable adjustments on the part of other nations which could aid in the solution of China's fundamental problems.

IV. Possible methods for the adjustment of specific problems, in the light of information and suggestions presented in the three studies outlined above; analysis of previous attempts at bilateral or multilateral adjustments of political and economic relations in the Pacific and causes of their success or. failure; types of administrative procedures and controls already tried out and their relative effectiveness; the major issues likely to require international adjustment in a post-war period and the most hopeful methods which might be devised to meet them; necessary adjustments by the Powers concerned; the basic requirements of ,a practical system of international organization which could promote the security and peaceful development of the countries of the Pacific area.

EDWARD C. CARTER
Secretary-General

New York,
February 15, 1940

AUTHOR'S PREFACE

One word of apology is due the reader, and that is for the excessive number and length of the notes. Since the footnote has become the bane of modern academic writing some justification may be called for. The chief plea is that this study is something in the nature of a pioneer work in Western languages. Hence it was difficult or rather impossible to dismiss many of the minor, but no less interesting problems by a mere reference to works already existing in European languages. Rather than follow each digression to its logical end within the text itself, and in order not to break the thread of the chief argument too often, it was considered more fitting to relegate them to the comparative obscurity of a footnote. As some of the more controversial questions also appear in these notes, it is hoped that the reader who has the patience to consult them will gain an inkling of a few of the historical problems which are exercising Japanese scholars.

The titles of all Japanese works have been translated into English when they appear for the first time and afterwards are cited only in transliterated Japanese. Japanese names appear in the conventional manner—that is the family name preceding the given. Unless stated otherwise all quotations from Japanese sources have been translated by the author who thus accepts full responsibility for any errors and crudities in the English approximations.

The author would like to take this opportunity of expressing his warmest appreciation for the patient help and fruitful suggestions which his colleagues on the International Secretariat of the Institute of Pacific Relations have so generously contributed. To Mr. R. Tsunoda and Dr. Hugh Borton, both of Columbia University, the author is deeply indebted for the many corrections and valuable references which they have so kindly offered from time to time. A similar debt has been incurred to Mr. S. Tsuru of Harvard University whose penetrating criticism has been of the greatest aid especially in matters relating to Japanese economic history.

Ottawa, January 1, 1940   E. H. N.

CONTENTS

xv

JAPAN'S EMERGENCE AS A
MODERN STATE

ABBREVIATIONS

JGD   Japanese Government Documents (see Bibliography under McLaren)

KUER Kyoto University Economic Review

TASJ Transactions of the Asiatic Society of Japan

CHAPTER I

INTRODUCTION

This study is an attempt first to select and analyze those peculiarities of the Meiji settlement which have, to a great extent, conditioned modern Japanese economy, political life and foreign policy, then to trace them from the end of feudalism to the consolidation of state power under the new constitution, at the end of the nineteenth century. Although several subsidiary subjects have been touched upon, the central problem throughout has been to explain the rapid creation of a centralized, absolute state after the Meiji Restoration (1868), and the growth of an industrial economy under conditions of state patronage and control.

This introduction makes a beginning, rather haphazardly, of relating to the present some of the generalizations drawn from an earlier age. Since this effort at application is scarcely more than indicated within these few pages, it becomes the reader's task to measure contemporary against Meiji Japan, dismissing what is irrelevant and ephemeral, searching out the more fundamental, far-reaching characteristics of Meiji government and gauging their effects upon the unfolding of Japanese policy during the past half-century. It is hoped that by constantly keeping the present in mind, the reader may enhance whatever of interest or of value he may find in this work.

Some of this historical essay upon the Meiji era may seem remote to the reader who is pondering the Japan of 1940. Yet much of Meiji Japan lingers on, even flourishes in contemporary Japan; the growth and ramifications of the bureaucracy and of the military caste; the pusillanimity of parties and Diet; state intervention in enterprise; the mushrooming of small-scale industries; the adaptation to Japanese needs of Western technology; the recurring crises in agriculture with the overcrowded village, the small-scale farm and a land-hungry peasantry; the low purchasing power of the home market; these are but some of the more obvious phenomena which have molded Japanese life. They are matters which cannot be appreciated

3

without some understanding of the Meiji period. As a background for this period in turn, the salient features of the preceding Tokugawa era are an essential, hence the second chapter presents the historical setting for the Restoration of 1868.

The Buddhist doctrine of karma illustrates the tiresome truism that whatever goes before, through the catena of cause and effect, necessarily shapes and conditions that which follows; and so the student is ever pushing back his study of history in search of the *primum mobile*. Yet one need not admit, as would full acceptance of the Buddhist doctrine, any ineluctable determinism in the affairs of men and states. The will of man striking obliquely at the flowing stream of historical development, its channel already partly fixed, can bend its course to this side or that, but cannot block it altogether. So it was in Japan; the design lay with the Meiji architects, but the material was largely ready to hand, a legacy of the preceding age.

In the case of Japan, there was no fore-ordained solution to the problem arising out of a decayed feudalism, but circumscribed as she was by her Tokugawa heritage, the alternatives or variations were fewer than in some of the older modern states. And yet this very limitation could be turned into advantage, as interpreted by the Meiji pioneers. They could warn the nation of the perils lying ahead, dispelling all illusion as to the possibility of any short-cut either to Utopia or Empire. Accordingly politics and diplomacy in their supple hands became an infinitely complex kind of *ju-jutsu*, the art of converting a weakness into strength or a fall into a fresh attack. They realized that a country emerging so tardily from a feudalism which had been allowed to consume and rot the body politic, would require time and care to recuperate under a new regime before it could challenge any of the dominant world powers, or even before it could risk a war with the tottering Ch'ing dynasty. This realization of Japan's limitations took the form of watchful waiting for the moment when the Great Powers should be severally embroiled, of retreating before the threat of joint action on the part of these powers, then of timing its blow to coincide with this moment of greatest confusion. Examples of this sequence of events will occur to the reader without need of recapitulation here; but to epitomize this characteristic of Japanese foreign policy one can do no better than to recall the striking words of Viscount Tani who declared in 1887:

Make our country secure by military preparations—encourage and protect the people at home, and then wait for the time of the confusion of Europe which must come eventually sooner or later, and although we have no immediate concern with it ourselves we must feel it, for such an event will agitate the nations of the Orient as well, and hence, although our country is not mixed up in the matter, so far as Europe is concerned, we may become the chief of the Orient.[1]

The postulates on which Japanese statesmen have acted during and since the Meiji period can be summarized in this fashion: first, Japan has been handicapped by her late entry on the stage of world politics and by her economic insufficiency; second, unity of purpose and action among the Great Powers can never be maintained for long. The conclusion to be drawn, as it was by Viscount Tani, is that Japan's opportunity comes at the moment of sharpest tension between the powers. Patience, good judgment, and the will to strike fast and hard at a moment's notice have continued to be the characteristics of Japanese foreign policy. In this way she has acquired with a comparatively small output of energy what other nations of greater economic strength have achieved only after long wars, setbacks and even defeats. The Japanese Empire was built in the course of thirty-five years or so; during that time Japan engaged in three victorious wars, 1894-5, 1904-5, and 1914-8. None of these exhausted Japan unduly, still less did her next great advance of 1931-3, by which Manchuria was pried loose from China with only desultory fighting. A weakness weighed and understood, together with a shrewd appraisal of the strength of potential enemies can reduce the risk of disaster almost to nothing. As a yardstick to measure the success of this policy one might mention the continual reverses and defeats suffered by the immense empire of Tsarist Russia during the nineteenth and early twentieth centuries, at a time when its small neighbor and rival was transforming itself from an impoverished feudal state into a naval and colonial power of the first rank.

But it is upon domestic politics and economics that the Meiji settlement has left the greatest imprint. The political compromise of merchants with feudal elements at the time of the Restoration, as described at some length in this study, has enabled the former feudal leaders and the feudal outlook to exercise far greater influence than in most other modern societies. Thus

---

[1] Quoted in Foster Rhea Dulles, *Forty Years of American Japanese Relations.* New York and London, 1937, pp. 13-4.

both during the Meiji era and even after it, business interests have been less obtrusive, have enjoyed less direct government responsibility than in such countries as France or the United States. An important by-product of this compromise was the creation of the bureaucracy which in its origins showed a marked feudal coloring. Although in normal times it is the obedient instrument of the government, nevertheless it enjoys a certain quasi-independent life of its own, generating an intense *esprit de corps.*

Historically, the bureaucracy came to enjoy its unique position partly through the nice equilibrium of those forces personified on the one hand by the reforming feudal clans and on the other by business interests, just after the Restoration. Soon it became entrenched and took over the administration of the strategic and state-controlled industries such as armaments and ship-building. Its higher members who were largely selected from former feudal and aristocratic classes could afford to despise the pettifogging career politicians; it has scarcely brooked any interference from such lowly quarters as the Diet or even from ministers who try to reform or ignore its corporate will. For instance, in very few countries would it be possible to witness a strike of the Foreign Office staff such as took place in Tokyo in the autumn of 1939, which compelled the Premier and Foreign Minister to adopt a very conciliatory, almost apologetic attitude. This is a passing but significant incident illustrating the inner cohesiveness and, as it was already expressed, the quasi-independent position enjoyed by the bureaucracy.

During the days of struggle for internal reconstruction, for security and international recognition, this body was an invaluable organ of administration. Whether it is so today would be a matter of personal opinion. That a certain vague resentment is felt toward it is evidenced by the phrase often applied to it ot the "extraterritorial government," implying certain privileges and immunities enjoyed with no equivalent responsibilities discharged.

One might also speculate on the importance of the bureaucracy in preventing the complete victory of fascism in Japan. It is becoming apparent that with each passing month the extreme fascist elements are as far from *full* control of the state machine and policy-making as on the eve of their sensational bid for power—and this is not to minimize their very considerable influence. In fact it appears at the time of writing as if they are being unobtrusively but none the less firmly dislodged from some of the strongholds of government. It would be rash to suggest that they are finally or even decisively beaten, but it seems as if Japanese business circles have profited from the experience of Germany, where complete Nazi control over state and foreign policy has eventually become a Juggernaut menacing some of the very interests and men who helped it to power. There is no indication that a Japanese Thyssen will have to abandon his country and his wealth; on the contrary it would not be impossible that some Japanese Goering may presently be on the retired instead of the active list. It is a safe assumption that this insulation against totalitarian extremism has been possible to no small extent through that ubiquitous anonymous body, the bureaucracy, acting often in conjunction with higher court circles. Behind this bureaucracy again stand the older more conservative financial houses, which after a period of political hibernation show signs again of taking a more active part in shaping both domestic and foreign policy.

Throughout this study, two aspects of the Restoration have been emphasized: first, the speed and manner of the transition from feudal to new Japan and, second, the social character of the leaders who accomplished it. The latter came from one wing of the feudal aristocracy (the anti-Tokugawa) and were backed by the great merchant houses of Osaka and Kyoto. The autocratic manner in which the transition was carried out permitted the leaders to apply the brakes promptly so as to stop short of a leveling democracy. To make a hazardous parallel, it were as if the French Revolution had terminated with the triumph of the Gironde and the Feuillants, with a reformed monarchy supported, in the first instance, by the more liberal aristocrats, such as Mirabeau, and even more typically Lafayette, together with such respectable burghers as Barnave and Roland. This comparison, however, distorts history since the strength of the French merchants with their monopolies, their overseas and colonial trade was far in advance of that of the Japanese in 1868, both materially and in their political ascendancy over the feudal aristocracy. Thus the Japanese moneyed class had to occupy a more modest place in government's councils than their French counterpart of pre-Jacobin days.

The destruction of Tokugawa feudalism *from above* made possible the curbing of any insurrectionary attempts by the people, particularly the peasantry and city poor, to extend the anti-feudal movement by action *from below*. Once the crumbling bastions of the Tokugawa rule had been stormed in the war for the Restoration (1867-8) and after the flank attacks upon the feudal immunities and privileges in the years following had been executed, the new Government set itself as firmly against any demand for further reform on the part of the lower orders as it did against attempts to restore the old regime. Such a policy required a powerful state-machine, a centralized government with a considerable constabulary or military force at its disposal. This need was the driving force in the enlightened absolutism characteristic of Meiji Government which cherished and extended those necessary political reforms following the overthrow of feudalism, initiated industrialization and created a modern army. This army served in the first place as a bulwark against the encroachments of Western powers, and, in the second place, as a last line defense against attempts at a restoration of the old regime, but more particularly it guarded against the newly awakened spirit of militant liberalism which, in those early years, threatened to extend and implement forcefully the incipient democratic trends. The personnel in this early army and within the police force and bureaucracy, consisted almost exclusively of ex-*samurai* or former feudal retainers, and hence was inspired (with rare exceptions) by a feeling of hostility toward all manifestations of liberalism.

Although the Meiji leaders borrowed heavily from the Occident in the industrial arts, in the banking system, in the military and educational systems, yet the very proximity to the feudal past and more especially the far-reaching compromise of feudal and merchant classes adumbrated here and traced in greater detail in the body of this study, have left deep marks of the old regime, especially in the spiritual realm. The ideal of feudal loyalty, the patriarchal system, the attitude toward women, the exaltation of the martial virtues, these have acquired in Japan all the garish luster of a tropical sunset. This metaphor is used to suggest that there is a waxing and a waning even in what often appears to be the inherent and inalienable spiritual or cultural tinting of a nation. In Japan there has been a time-lag between the adoption of a new mode of life and the full maturing of its cultural and psychological expression. As long as this lag persists, we have the fascinating picture of a nation whose sky is blackened by the smoke of great industrial centers yet whose fields and villages are peopled by millions with loyalties and emotions which can be quickened by the remembrance of the "Spirit of Old Japan." This spirit is not some inborn endowment; it springs from centuries of acquired training, tradition and habits of thought which two generations of a "modernization" that is far from being catholic in its extent cannot obliterate. For good or ill, as the industrial civilization of New Japan grows, germinates, and thrusts forth new branches and deeper roots, it will scarcely leave any space for the patriarchal and often genial traditions of its medieval past.

Some observers might regard this spiritual legacy of Old Japan as a gloomy specter which haunts and inhibits its present. But here again, the anomalous, the accidental and the outmoded have been turned to good purpose; a weakness, if you like to call it that, has been transformed into an advantage. Much of the stress and shock of industrial life, its ugly clashes of jostling interests, have been cushioned by the old habits of thought. Individualism has its virtues and rewards, but not in a peasant family whose tenuous bonds can often be maintained only on the pittance remitted by a daughter working in some textile mill. Or again, the old feudal sense of clannishness has been modified to embrace the whole nation so that it has served at moments of great national crisis to forge a spirit of national unity which all the tawdry theater of a Mussolini or a Hitler cannot so effectively evoke. Writing over twenty years ago, Veblen commented pithily upon this interval between the borrowing of Western industrialization and its full psychological acclimatization and termed it Japan's Opportunity.[2]

Turning at last from questions of Japan's foreign relations and polity as these were shaped in the Meiji days, we see in agriculture also the vestigial remains of feudal conditions; excessive

[2] One might call it Japan's opportunity—to make the best of both worlds while it can, the feudal and the capitalist. See Thorstein Veblen, *Essays in Our Changing Order*, New York, 1934, pp. 248-66.

rents (whether in kind or in money), atomization of land, the persistence of certain branches of domestic or *heimat* industry together with a primitive agricultural technique. These relics of a feudal past have a direct bearing upon such urgent social problems as the surplus stagnant population in the villages, the high proportion of female labor in industry, and the narrowness of the home market for the disposal of manufactured goods.

In the last analysis, agrarian relations have profoundly affected the form taken by the labor movement; they have also colored the prevailing psychology in an army composed largely of peasant conscripts. So vital is this peasant problem in the industrial as well as in the political and social development of Japan that a chapter has been devoted to agrarian relations and the Meiji settlement. Changes, of course, have taken place since the period described, but changes in degree rather than in kind. There have been quantitative modifications, not any radical rearrangements in the original pattern of tenant-landlord relations which have been preserved clearly enough, it is hoped, for the analysis in the following pages to be still applicable, *mutatis mutandis,* to contemporary Japan.

Some description of the typical Japanese landlord as he was 60 or 70 years ago should help in understanding first, the twofold nature of the early Liberal Party (the *Jiyuto*) compounded as it was of radicalism and conservatism, and second, its later evolution into the die-hard conservative *Seiyukai.* Accordingly, this work concludes with a chapter on parties and politics which follows quite logically the chapter on agrarian relations.

CHAPTER II

THE BACKGROUND OF THE MEIJI RESTORATION

The Decay of Feudalism

Among the most remarkable phenomena which marked the Meiji Restoration and subsequent years was the speed of the transition from a feudal into a modern industrial society. This rapidity was noted by contemporary journalists and travelers, who scarcely attempted any explanation. The question was virtually dismissed by translating it into the realm of the miraculous or was cited as an example of an apt pupil faithfully learning its lesson from its master—the West—a view as flattering to Westerners as it was unjust to the Japanese.

The comparative ease with which Japan burst the fetters of feudal economy can be explained, partially at least, as the result of the fortuitous conjunction of two processes, (1) the internal crisis of feudal society, (2) pressure from the Western nations. Since this time-factor of *speed* has left an indelible mark upon the social and political structure of Japan, it is important to examine the circumstances attendant upon the Meiji Restoration, in order to discover how these two forces of internal decay and external pressure coincided so as to shorten that period of travail—a period which in the case of China has been agonizingly prolonged.

Tokugawa feudalism dates from the early 17th century when Tokugawa Ieyasu established the hegemony of his family and its collaterals over a large part of Japan and exerted indirect control throughout the three great islands of Honshu, Kyushu and Shikoku. Ieyasu (1542-1616) set up the last in a series of Shogunates, or hereditary military dictatorships, whereby the greatest feudal family exercised political power while relegating the Emperor and court—with suitable euphemisms of veneration and obedience—to the obscurity of a cloistered life in Kyoto. The Shogunate (or *Bakufu*) was established as a seat of separate power by Minamoto no Yoritomo (1147-99) Political domination of the court by some great family like the Soga,

11

Fujiwara or Taira was nothing new in Japanese history, but the Shogunate implied a distinctly separate seat of government, with the Emperor and his court shorn of all actual power. Thus the Restoration meant the abolition of this dual system with Emperor as sovereign and the Shogun as ruler, and the return to the earlier system when the Emperor was both sovereign and ruler.[1]

This late feudalism represents one of the most conscious attempts in history to freeze society in a rigid hierarchical mold. Every social class, and every subdivision within it, had its own regulations covering all the minutiae of clothing, ceremony and behavior, which had to be strictly observed on pain of punishment. The criminal code, severe even by feudal standards, distinguished between *samurai* and commoner; in every conceivable way the Tokugawa administration emphasized the difference, the relative degree of superiority or inferiority of one class to another. Both in their foreign and their domestic policy, the Tokugawa rulers displayed a most sensitive regard for their own feudal philosophy of life in contrast to the needs and interests of the commercial classes of the country. Partly to avoid all danger of political control by the Europeans, either through trade or through the intrigues of Catholic missionaries

[1] Ieyasu was able to exercise a more widespread control than any of his predecessors in the Shogunate. In fact some historians such as Asakawa and Fukuda Tokuzo, have denied that a state so highly centralized as Tokugawa Japan could be described as feudal. Without entering into this problem, it is assumed here that a society in which political power derived exclusively from control over agricultural produce and the agricultural producer, regardless of the extent of sub-infeudation, might justly be called feudal.

In Japanese feudal society, where the revenue in rice and not the direct ownership of land determined power, there were necessarily great differences from European feudalism. Professor K. Asakawa has shown how the sharing of the profits from the land (*i.e., shiki*, literally "offices") rather than the subdivision of land characterized Japanese feudalism, see K. Asakawa, *Documents of Iriki*, Yale University Press, 1929, especially pp. 2-15. It seems convenient to adopt the terminology of the Japanese social historian, Professor Honjo, who speaks of early or *decentralized feudalism,* and late or *centralized feudalism,* a distinction which can justly be applied to European feudalism. (For this process from decentralized to centralized feudalism, see, for instance, Petit Dutaillis, *The Feudal Monarchy in France and England,* London, 1936.) But in Japan for all its centralization, the greatest single feudal magnate, the Tokugawa family, depended for its maintenance on the fruits of serf-labor as did all lesser lords or *daimyo*; hence even if Japan had been completely centralized by the Tokugawa (as France was for instance by Louis XI) it would still be feudal in a socio-economic sense. The importance of the centralization of Japan by the Tokugawa was that it made possible a quick transitional period from the *Bakufu* to the Meiji Government.

partly as a logical corollary to their own physiocratic theory of the relative value of trade and agriculture, the Tokugawa authorities expelled the Spaniards in 1624, and the Portuguese in 1638. After 1640, all foreigners and foreign trade were excluded from Japan except for a small trading station in Deshima (Nagasaki) where the Dutch and Chinese were kept under strict supervision and allowed limited trading rights. In 1637, the Shogunate forbade any Japanese to leave the country; to disobey their law and to return to Japan meant death. To enforce seclusion, the capacity of each ship was henceforth limited to 500 *koku* (*koku* = about 5 American bushels). Thus did the Tokugawa government attempt to seal Japan and prevent any breath of foreign thought from disturbing the feudal atmosphere.

At the apex of the hierarchical pyramid was the Tokugawa family with its three branches, the Owari, Kii, and Mito, administering a domain which covered almost a quarter of the country and included the great trade centers of Edo (the seat of government), Sakai (Osaka), Kyoto—where the Imperial court was situated—and Nagasaki. It derived its main source of revenue from the rice tribute which reached 8 million *koku* out of a total yield of 28 or 29 millions.[2] Mining and the grant of trade monopolies also were a profitable source of income. The remaining three-quarters of Japan was divided up among *daimyo* or feudal lords. Those who had sided with Ieyasu from the first, the *fudai daimyo* in hereditary vassalage to the Tokugawa, 176 in all, were favored by him and from their ranks alone high government appointments were made. Those *daimyo* who submitted only after the decisive battle of Sekigahara (1600), including the wealthiest lords such as Mori of Choshu, Shimazu

[2] Although the area of land under the Shogunate was not so great, it was scattered throughout 47 of the 68 provinces, and these holdings were so placed that they acted as buffers against the formation of a solid bloc of hostile fiefs. The figures given above for the revenue of the Tokugawa Shogunate are for the earlier period of its rule; they are taken from G. B. Sansom, *Japan: A Short Cultural History*, New York, 1936, p. 455. For the later period, according to Professor Tsuchiya's estimate, the total yield was well over 30 million *koku* of which 4.2 million went to the Shogun and 2.6 to his retainers. That is to say the Shogun still controlled a quarter of the rice yield of Japan. Tsuchiya Takao, "An Economic History of Japan," *Transactions of the Asiatic Society of Japan* (henceforth cited as TASJ), Second Series, Volume XV, Tokyo, December 1937, p. 223.

The *koku* differed according to locality and period, but as standardized later it is 4.96006 English bushels, or 5.11902 American bushels, or 1.80391 hectolitres. Honjo Eijiro, *The Social and Economic History of Japan*, Kyoto, 1935, (Appendix 2) p. 370.

of Satsuma, Date of Sendai, and Maeda of Kaga, were known as *tozama* or "outside" lords, 86 in number. The *tozama* were excluded from any share in governmental responsibility and in return were permitted to exercise a ·partial autonomy in clan affairs.

The *Bakufu* or Shogunal Government maintained itself by a skillful system of checks and balances; by the geographical distribution of hereditary vassals (*fudai daimyo*) among the outside lords (*tozama*): and by the *sankin-kotai* or hostage system perfected by the third Shogun Iemitsu in 1634, which required that all *daimyo* reside alternately in their domains and in Edo, leaving their wives and families behind them in the capital as hostages when they returned to their own fiefs. All intercourse between fiefs was frowned upon, and travel was discouraged by a strict passport system.[3] Espionage was organized on so vast a scale that it has left a heritage of anecdote and proverb, eloquent testimony of the deep mark which it stamped upon the people's consciousness.[4] Marriage alliances between *daimyo* families had first to be ratified by the *Bakufu;* castles or moats could not be built without the Shogunate's permission; when repairs were made, the architectural plans of these changes had to be forwarded to Edo. The *daimyo* were forbidden to have direct contact with the court in Kyoto; even the Emperor was kept under

[3] Not only were barriers built as a check on travelers but roads and bridges were deliberately allowed to fall into disrepair in order to diminish traffic. Passport officials were particularly on the alert for *de-onna iri-deppo* (literally "outward going women, inward going guns") indicating the attempt of the *daimyo* to smuggle his wife out of Edo and guns into his fief. Kuroita Katsumi, *Kokushi no Kenkyu* (Study of Our National History), Tokyo, revised edition (1937) Volume III, p. 386. Also Sansom, *op. cit.*, p. 437.

[4] Espionage was carried on under the supervision of *metsuke* or censors who reported on the activities of the *daimyo* and their vassals. The use of a secret political police was perhaps more highly developed under the *Bakufu* than in any other feudal society. One of the first economic and social historians of Japan, Fukuda, was so impressed with the dictatorial nature of the *Bakufu* that he characterized ·it as "die absolute Polizeistaat." Fukuda Tokuzo, *Die Gesellschaftliche und Wirtschaftliche Entwickelung in Japan*, Munchener Volkswirtschaftliche Studien. Stuttgart, 1900, pp. 116 *et seq.*

These political police were quite astonishingly similar to modern secret police in their thorough training, *e.g.*, careful cultivation of some remote dialect, in their ubiquity and in their unscrupulous but imaginative ingenuity as shown in the numerous ruses used to gather intimate information about the household of some *daimyo* suspected of malfeasance.

For an interesting account of the organization and method of the Tokugawa secret police see Fritz Stumpf, "Ninjutsu" in *Yamato Zeitschrift der Deutsch-Japanischen Arbeitsgemeinschaft*, Berlin, Numbers 4-5 (July-October), 1929, pp. 205-10.

a close if respectful surveillance, his activity and ceremonies rigorously circumscribed by *Bakufu* regulations.[5] Financial burdens were imposed on the *daimyo* to keep their treasuries empty; the *Bakufu* would ask some *daimyo* to undertake a large project that would strain his finances to the utmost.[6] Even under feudalism the adage "Pecunia nervus belli" held true. Using every device to weaken and divide the *daimyo,* the *Bakufu* still had good reason to fear the powerful *tozama* of the Southwest, the Shimazu of Satsuma, the Mori of Choshu, and the Nabeshima of Hizen who were too weak to withhold their submission to Ieyasu after Sekigahara, and yet too powerful for the Shogunate to risk a direct attack upon their semi-autonomy.

Most formidable of these was Satsuma in Southern Kyushu. Protected by its great distance from the centers of *Bakufu* power, surrounded by clans equally hostile to the Tokugawa, with one of the greatest revenues of feudal Japan and soldiers famed for their intense local patriotism and fierce fighting ability, this clan scarcely troubled to hide its resentment toward Tokugawa domination.[7] It was a pioneer in the use and manufacture of modern arms, and despite the ban on foreign commerce, Satsuma maintained trading relations with China, using the Ryukyu Islands as a base.[8] Enriched by foreign trade and al-

[5] Detailed accounts of the elaborate system of Tokugawa policy and administration of which a few salient features have been selected here, may be found in any standard history in Japanese or English. For the former a straightforward reliable authority is Kuroita, *op. cit.*, Volume III, especially pp. 382-96, for the policy toward the Imperial House toward *fudai daimyo* and *tozama*, and for the *sankin-kotai* system, pp. 397-408. For an English account see James Murdoch, *History of Japan*, London, 1903-26, Volume III, Chapter I, "The Social and Political Structure," pp. 1-61. See also Antoine Rous de la Mazelière, *Le Japon, Histoire et Civilisation*, Paris, 1907, Volume III, Chapter 1, "Le Gouvernement," pp. 212-40. Chapter II, "La Société sous les Tokugawa; Conditions Sociales et Economiques," pp. 241-304.

[6] An example of such public works undertaken at the orders of the *Bakufu* was the Kisogawa project (north of Nagoya) to which the distant Satsuma clan had to contribute in 1754 and which strained its finances seriously. See Ohara Kenji, *Saigo Takamori* (Life of Saigo Takamori), Tokyo, 1938, p. 16. The *sankin-kotai* system was the steadiest drain on the finances of a *daimyo*.

[7] The Japanese term *han* is translated as fief or clan, the latter perhaps more commonly used. But the word clan, it should be emphasized, carried no idea of a family unit such as conveyed by the Scotch clan or the old pre-feudal *uji* in Japan. In feudal Japan, clan simply means the territorial division over which a *daimyo* exercised political control and from which he drew his rice revenue.

[8] In 1609 Satsuma conquered a part of these islands and established an administrative center at Nawa, tacitly permitting the ruler of the islands to acknowledge Chinese suzerainty. (Kuroita, *op. cit.*, Volume III, p. 582.) The nature and extent of the contraband between Satsuma and the Ryukyu Islands is given by

most encircled by the sea, Satsuma looked more toward the sea-borne civilization from the South, than toward distant Edo.[9] With its accumulation of trading capital, its early efforts at introducing Western industry largely for military purposes,[10] and its hatred of the *Bakufu*, it was no historical accident that this clan, supported by three other southwestern clans, the Choshu, Hizen, and Tosa was the spearpoint in the attack upon the political hegemony of the Tokugawa.

Standing below the Shogun and the *daimyo* were the *samurai* who owed allegiance to their lord in return for the rice-stipends paid them. During the earlier period of decentralized feudalism, most *samurai* were cultivators of the soil who followed their lord in war and tilled their fields in time of peace. With the revolution in the military system—the use of firearms and the accompanying need for strong castle defenses—the *samurai* were gathered into castle-towns, leaving their fields to be farmed by the peasantry. This differentiation between *samurai* and farmer was accentuated by Hideyoshi, who conducted the sword-hunt of 1587, whereby he decreased the danger of popular revolt and also accentuated the class distinction between farmer and sword-bearing warrior.[11] Divorced from any productive function, the *samurai* now drew his rice stipend in return for fighting at his lord's command. But the long years of peace after the establishment of the Tokugawa Shogunate sapped the martial ardor of the *samurai* and rendered their existence superfluous, so that they became virtually a parasitic class. The *Bakufu*, which relied on the *samurai* for its support, did what it could to glorify

Takekoshi Yosaburo, *The Economic Aspects of the History of the Civilization of Japan*, New York, 1930, Volume III, pp. 225-6. The anomalous position of these islands was a source of irritation between Japan and China and caused the *Bakufu* much embarrassment when the English and French asked that the islands be opened to foreign trade, a request which Satsuma supported. Takekoshi, *op. cit.*, Volume III, pp. 277-8. See also Horie Yasuzo, *Nihon Shihonshugi no Seiritsu* (The Formation of Japanese Capitalism), Tokyo, 1938, p. 106, note 4.

[9] La Mazelière quoting Siebold's account of his visit with the retired lord of Satsuma, Shimazu Shigetaka, in 1826, shows the extent of Dutch influence in Satsuma. This *daimyo* displayed a considerable knowledge of the Dutch language and showed a keen curiosity about Western things. Boats had been built after Western design, forts were constructed and cannon manufactured. La Mazelière, *op. cit.*, Volume IV, pp. 114-5.

[10] *Infra*, pp. 117-9.

[11] The great religious and agrarian revolts of the Muromachi period (15th century) had impelled many lords to disarm their peasants, and Hideyoshi only enforced this policy on a national scale. See Sansom, *op. cit.*, pp. 422-3.

the warrior code and to favor the *samurai* above all classes, but when their position grew clearly more anomalous and as their rice-stipends were cut by impoverished *daimyo*,[12] the more restless spirits among them cast loose from their allegiance and became *ronin* (literally "wandering men," owing no fealty and professing no fixed occupation). Many *ronin* settled in cities where they studied Western languages and science, thus becoming the intellectual harbingers of the opening of Japan to the world, while the great mass of them, filled with hatred for the *Bakufu* government which shadowed their every step, became the most ardent champions of Restoration.[13]

The *Bakufu*, which depended upon the peasantry for its revenue and looked to its *samurai* for protection, affected a great contempt for the *chonin* or merchant class, placing them last in the social scale. They were regarded as an unproductive, shifty class which would stoop to any method to make money. The authorities hedged them about with numerous restrictions; their style of clothing, use of foot-gear, umbrellas, all these and a thousand other petty details were regulated by law. The government would not even allow a merchant to have a name which

[12] A study of the decay of the *samurai* class has been made by Martin Ramming, "Die Wirtschaftliche Lage der Samurai am Ende der Tokugawa Periode," *Mitteilungen der Deutschen Gesellschaft fur Natur-und Volkerkunde Ostasiens*, Band XXI, Teil A, Tokyo, 1928, 47 pp.
He bases his study on memorials presented by persons of little consequence in reply to the invitation of the Shogun for the expression of public opinion. The author considers these to be of greater historical value than those submitted by *daimyo* who were naturally prone to write only what was pleasing to the Shogun. Analyzing the various grades and incomes of *samurai*, Ramming concludes that the average annual income for a *samurai* of middle rank was 100 *koku*, roughly equivalent to the income of a rich peasant, while the average for all *samurai* was well under 35 *koku*, which put them on the same economic plane as a peasant. But financial difficulties often induced the *daimyo* to reduce the grant to his *samurai*. Ostensibly such a reduction was a loan to reorganize clan finances, but it usually became a permanent reduction in the *samurai's* income. Honda Rimei (early 19th century) wrote: "There is at present none left to pay his vassals full allowance, and the *samurai* hate their masters as their worst enemies."

[13] The *Bakufu* had good reason to fear the discontent and daring of these unattached warriors. As early as 1651 Yui Shosetsu, a *ronin*, together with a companion, Marubashi Chuya, attempted a *coup d'état* against the *Bakufu*, see Kuroita, *op. cit.*, Volume III, p. 431. The bands of *ronin* became so numerous by the end of the Tokugawa period that they terrorized whole towns and cities (especially Kyoto), see Hirao Michio, "Bakumatsu Ronin to Sono Hogo oyobi Tosei" (The *Ronin:* Their Livelihood and the Policy for Their Protection at the End of the *Bakufu*), in *Meiji Ishin Shi Kenkyu* (Researches into the History of the Meiji Restoration), edited by the Shigakkai (Historical Society), Tokyo, 1936 edition, pp. 528-9.

resembled a *daimyo* name, nor would it permit tradesmen to live in the *samurai* district.[14] In fact no feudal aristocracy could express greater distaste for money-making and money-makers than the Tokugawa moralists and legislators. There was even written into the Tokugawa administrative code the famous right of *kiri-sute-gomen*, that is the privilege of a *samurai* to cut down a commoner with impunity.[15] Despite the manifold social restraints put upon the Japanese merchant class, their increasing economic power stultified both sumptuary legislation and moral discourses upon the dangers of luxury. Although officially placed at the bottom of the social ladder, the merchant class was assuming a more important position in a feudal society where money economy was gradually supplanting a natural or rice economy. This process was made inevitable by the increased productivity of agriculture and manufacture which in turn stimulated the growth of trading centers and cities where the circulation medium was money. The rapid development of communications attendant upon the *sankin-kotai* system greatly facilitated commodity circulation. This development of cities and transport was an indication of the extension of the market, and together with this growth in the market went specialization in manufacture and commerce. The distinction between producer and distributor was drawn very sharply in the Tokugawa period, and with the *Bakufu's* tendency to issue administrative regulations governing the activity of each group in the community, the merchants formed a few big monopoly wholesale units (*tonya*), with rigid corporation stipulations and privileges for which they paid the government a charter fee, *unjo* (or "thank-money") and occasional taxes, such as *myoga-kin* and *goyokin* which were virtually forced loans.[16] One of the most important

[14] Takizawa Matsuyo, *The Penetration of Money Economy in Japan*, New York, 1927, p. 103.

[15] The "Hundred Articles" or *Hyakkajo* set forth the basic administrative custom of the Tokugawa house. Paragraph 45 in this code says, "Common people who behave unbecomingly to members of the military class, or who show want of respect to direct or indirect vassals may be cut down on the spot." J. H. Gubbins, "The Hundred Articles and the Tokugawa Government," in the *Transactions and Proceedings of the Japan Society*, London, Volume XVII, 1918-20, p. 156.

[16] There were ten such wholesale guilds known as the *Tokumi Donya*, see Takizawa, *op. cit.*, pp. 58-9. The merchant guilds of the Tokugawa period became more and more monopolistic so that the *Bakufu* government, on the advice of its Councilor Mizuno Tadakuni, abolished them in 1841. They continued in reorganized form again from 1851 until the Restoration. See Fukuda,

results of this rise of a merchant class was the growing dependence upon it of the *daimyo* and *samurai* classes. Receiving their income in rice, these feudal classes, who became more urbanized with the economic development noted above, found it necessary to convert their rice into money. To this end *samurai* (especially the *hatamoto,* the Shogun's retainers) entered into commercial relations with a class of rice brokers (*fudasashi*) while the *daimyo* usually maintained large warehouses in Osaka and Edo in charge of financial agents (*kuramoto*).[17] The social repercussions of the economic rise of this merchant capitalist class were far-reaching. Numerous contemporaries recorded how the wealthier merchants were adopted into *samurai* families and how impoverished warriors were glad to enter a merchant family either by marriage or by adoption. This fusion of the feudal classes with a few of the more powerful merchant families is a phenomenon of such importance in the social history of Japan that in a later section we shall discuss it in greater detail. Here it is sufficient to note that, slipping through the meshes of the feudal system, even occupying a leading position in the councils of many clans, there was a class of merchants and money-lenders who were nominally at the bottom of the social scale. Nevertheless, the Tokugawa ban on foreign trade, together with the pettifogging restrictions devised by feudal prejudice, served to retard the development of the Japanese merchant class, especially in its accumulation of capital, wherein it lagged far behind the great trading companies of 17th and 18th century Britain and Holland.[18] The economic activity of the *chonin* could not but

---

op. cit., pp. 157-8. The fullest description of the merchant guild system will be found in Takekoshi, *op. cit.,* Volume III, pp. 1-5 and on workmen's guilds, *ibid*, pp. 242-73. A Study of the *Kabu-Nakama* or Federation of Guilds has been made by Professor Koda Shigetomo and appears in English in TASJ, 2nd Series, Volume XIV, June 1937, "Materials on Japanese Social and Economic History," Tokugawa Japan (ed. by N. Skene Smith), pp. 78-116.

[17] For further details on the functions and power of these commercial agents of *daimyo.* and *samurai,* see Honjo, *op. cit.,* pp. 125-222, and also Takekoshi, *op. cit.,* Volume III, pp. 61-85 on the *fudasashi*; pp. 86-101 on the *kuramoto.*

[18] This forceful stunting of the growth of a merchant capitalist class is of considerable importance in the history of industrialization in Japan since it strengthened the trend toward State subsidy. (*Infra,* Chapter IV.) Had the policy of trade and colonization which existed prior to the Tokugawa been maintained, Japanese historical development must have been radically different. It is often forgotten that in the 15th and 16th centuries Japan was a great maritime nation with trade centers all along the Eastern seaboard of Asia, and with colonies of settlers as distant as Java and Siam. See Takekoshi, *op. cit.,* Volume I, Chapter XXXIV, "Japanese Expand Abroad," pp. 480-503. Tsuji

eat into the foundations of feudalism, thereby arousing the ill-concealed animosity of the *Bakufu* which was displayed for instance in the confiscation of the wealth of more ostentatious rice merchants such as the famous Yodoya Saburoyemon.[19] Although the merchant class as a whole was too deeply involved in the feudal system to struggle consciously for its overthrow, the restrictions of the tyrannous Tokugawa government alienated the support of large sections of the merchant class, and when an alternative government became possible at the time of the Restoration, which promised greater freedom in the economic sphere, this class wholeheartedly supported the political struggle against the old regime by generous contributions. But, as we shall see, they were content to play a subordinate part in the struggle.

The Atlas which supported this society of feudal lords, warriors and merchants was the peasantry. Small-scale agriculture was the economic basis of the Shogunate as well as of the daimiates. Thus the efforts of the feudal rulers were bent toward encouraging increased agricultural production. On the negative side, these efforts were expressed by prohibiting the peasant from leaving the countryside;[20] while as early as 1643, the *Bakufu* prohibited permanent alienation of land, thus indicating its desire to check the disappearance of the small inde-

---

Zennosuke, *Kaigai Kotsu Shiwa* (Lectures on the Intercourse Beyond the Seas), Tokyo, 1930, revised and enlarged edition, Chapter XXIV, "Toyotomi Hideyoshi no Nanyo Keiei" (Hideyoshi's Project for the South Seas), *i.e.*, Malaya, East Indies etc., pp. 410-49. Chapter XXXII, "Nanyo no Nihonjinmachi" (Japanese Settlements in the South Seas), *i.e.*, in Annam, Luzon and Siam, pp. 582-99. The most recent study on the subject of Japanese trade with the Asiatic continent before the Restoration is by Akiyama Kenzo, entitled *Ni-Shi Koshoshi no Kenkyu* (A Study in the History of Intercourse between Japan and China), Tokyo, 1939. The author draws on hitherto neglected sources, notably the Chinese *Ko Min Jitsu Roku* (The Authentic Record of the Ming Dynasty), the Korean *Ri-cho Jitsu Roku* (The Authentic Record of the Court of Li) and finally the *Rekidai Hoan* (a journal of Chinese traders in the Ryukyu Islands). This exhaustive work describes in great detail the early invisible maritime empire of Japan and the growth of a merchant capitalist class which, like its European counterpart, was enriching itself through overseas trade, and which was checked in its growth by Tokugawa policy. This study will replace earlier works on the subject to a very large extent.

[19] Takizawa, *op. cit.*, p. 103.

[20] By 1712 the decrease in the agricultural population began to alarm the authorities. Therefore the *Bakufu* made a census with the purpose of compelling all those who had migrated to the town to return to the country, Takizawa. *op. cit.*, p. 80.

pendent producer.[21] The same fear underlay the law against the partition of lands—unless the estate were larger than 1 *cho* (2.45 acres) and yielded at least 10 *koku*.[22] On the positive side, agricultural production was encouraged by precept, by improvements in agricultural technique and by administrative squeezing—in a word, by pressure both economic and political.[23] A well known saying characterized Tokugawa agrarian policy— "To impose taxes upon farmers to such an extent that they could neither live nor die." The Tokugawa policy has been neatly expressed in the words of Sir George Sansom to the effect that statesmen thought highly of agriculture but not of agriculturalists. The division of produce was traditionally in the ratio of "four to the prince and six to the people" (*shi-ko roku-min*), but it was not unusual to find even a higher proportion going to the lord, five-five or even seven to three. As the lord's need for money increased, he made heavier exactions upon the peasants, often even requiring part of his due in money. To the peasant who surrendered a large part of his produce in the form of tax, a good crop often meant a greater tribute while a poor crop reduced him to starvation. Further, with the penetration of money economy into the countryside the peasant could no longer obtain everything he needed merely by barter; for an intensive agricultural system such as the Japanese, the peasant had to buy manure and fertilizer as well as agricultural implements at rates which rose steadily as the standard of living rose generally throughout the country—that is for all classes except the peasant.[24] In many cases the peasant had to turn in desperation to the usurer for aid, offering his land as surety. Thus the golden opportunity of the usurer lay not in the prosperity of the peasant, but in his "Asiatic" wretchedness.[25] Failing to meet the usurer's terms, the peasant was forced to surrender his tenure of the land which still theoretically belonged to his lord; but the usurer now became legally the "cultivator," responsible for

[21] K. Asakawa, "Notes on Village Government in Japan after 1600," *Journal of the American Oriental Society*, Volume XXXI, pp. 258-9. Only in the Mito clan was there an exception to this law prohibiting sale of land, see Honjo, *op. cit.*, pp. 38-9.

[22] *Ibid.*, p. 39.

[23] For the development of agricultural production see Tsuchiya, *op. cit.*, pp. 153-7. On the intensification of feudal exactions, see Honjo, *op. cit.*, pp. 225-52.

[24] Sansom, *op. cit.*, p. 506, especially note to that page. Also Takizawa, *op. cit.*, p. 72.

[25] *Ibid.*, pp. 74-5.

paying the tribute and he increased the peasant's load in order to leave a net profit in his own hands.[26] Thus the invasion of money economy into the village made possible the concentration of land in fewer hands and increased tenancy. Despite the prohibition on the sale of land, various schemes were devised for its transfer or mortgage. Thus between the simple relations of ruler (feudal lord) and ruled (peasantry) another element—the usurer-landlord—had wedged itself. The usurer, who became a familiar figure in the Japanese village and has played an important part in social history right down to the present day, was often a wealthy peasant of an old family who had accumulated large estates, but the great majority of usurers were villagers who were at once peasant and merchant.[27] Hence in addition to the customary feudal overlord the peasant was now burdened by the exactions of a new landowning-usurer class which steadily grew in power until at the time of the Restoration its influence was a contributing factor in the land settlements.[28] Let us glance

[26] One of the most usual methods by which merchants and usurers became landowners was to reclaim waste-land under contract. See Matsuyoshi Sadao, "Tokugawa Jidai no Shinden Kaihatsu toku ni Osaka, Kawaguchi, no Keiei" (The Opening up of Reclaimed Land in the Tokugawa Period, especially the Plans for Kawaguchi, Osaka) in *Keizai Shi Kenkyu* (Studies in Economic History), Volume II, Number 7, pp. 129-56. Also a recent monograph by the same author *Shinden no Kenkyu* (A Study of Reclaimed Lands), Tokyo, 1936, especially pp. 131-65.

[27] Tanaka Kyugu (died 1729) in his *Minkan Seiyo* written in the first half of the 18th century, says, "You find here and there peasants of comfortable means, but they are rich not just from agriculture, but also from trading." This passage is taken from a treatise by the above author and appears in the collection *Nihon Keizai Taiten* (Cyclopaedia of Japanese Political Economy) compiled by Takimoto Seiichi, Tokyo, 1928, Volume V, pp. 103-4.

In the *Kanno-Saku* of Takemoto Tatsuhei we read, "While most people are suffering from poverty, some are quite well off. The reason for their wealth is not agriculture alone but also their trading in oil, sake, and other merchandise, together with the pawnshop business. Some do no trading but lend money and become wealthy on interest." *Ibid.*, Volume XXXII, p. 675.

[28] The following account is based on memorials presented to the daimiate of Mito and assembled by Fujita Yukoku from 1792-1807. It gives a clear example of how the intrusion of usurer between the peasant-lord relationship burdened the peasant still more. "Since the sale of land was prohibited, the needy peasants had secretly to solicit the rich to buy their land. The rich, who were in a more favorable position to bargain, would so word the terms of the deed as to escape the burden of taxation. For instance, if a peasant wished to sell seven out of the ten *tan* of his land, the buyer would pay him money for the seven *tan* but make him sign the deed as if he had sold only three *tan* and retained seven *tan*. As a result, the poor peasant was legally the owner of seven *tan* in spite of the fact that he had actually only three *tan*; consequently he was obliged to pay the taxes upon seven *tan*, while the buyer paid only upon three *tan* but reserved the produce from the seven *tan*." This account is taken from Takizawa, *op. cit.*, p. 75.

at some of the burdens on the peasant as listed by the famous Tokugawa Councillor, Matsudaira Sadanobu (1758-1829). (His account is somewhat abridged here.) "The exactions from the peasant eat up 50% to 70% of his produce. There are countless other taxes—such as a tax on the field, a tax on doors, a tax on windows, a tax on female children according to age, a tax on cloth, a tax on sake, a tax on hazel trees, a tax on beans, a tax on hemp . . . if the peasant added a room to his hut a tax was levied on it. . . . The nominal tax is a *koku* of rice and a *katori* of silk but actually it is increased threefold through bribery and extortion. At harvest time officials make inspection tours—and are lodged among local inhabitants. If entertained poorly, they either increase the amount of exactions or levy forced labor upon the household. Taxes are often collected some years in advance and the other forms of exaction and tyranny are countless."[29]

The *corvée*, like taxation, took protean forms, but none was more burdensome perhaps than the *sukego* or system of requisitioning horses and men for the courier or postal service; in a village which could not supply its quota of horses and men, commutation of services was required at an exorbitant rate.[30] This is merely one aspect of the bitter, grinding life of the peasant, whose condition in good times was wretched enough, but in lean years became brutish beyond description. Small wonder then that even the conservative peasant was driven to resist further feudal exactions. This resistance took two forms, passive and active. By passive, I mean the practice of infanticide or *mabiki* (literally "thinning") which became so widespread that it taxed the administrative ingenuity and Confucian ethic of Tokugawa legislators.[31] Another method of passive resistance

[29] This is a condensation of a few pages from Matsudaira's "Kokuhon Ron" in *Nihon Keizai Taiten*, (cited), Volume XIII, pp. 336-9.

[30] Honjo, *op. cit.*, pp. 211-2.

[31] There is a considerable literature on this aspect of the population problem in Japan. In English, the best reference perhaps is Honjo, *op. cit.*, pp. 177-85. There is also an article by the same author translated into English as an appendix to his *Tokugawa Bakufu no Beika Chosetsu* (An Examination into the Price of Rice during the Tokugawa Bakufu), Tokyo, 1924. The article is entitled "Tokugawa Jidai no Jinko" (Population During the Tokugawa Period); see especially pp. 36-40 in this appendix. More accessible to Western readers is an article by the same authority entitled, "The Population and its Problems in the Tokugawa Era" in the *Bulletin de l'Institut International de Statistique*, Tome XXV-2 ième Livraison, Tokyo, 1931, pp. 60-82. A convenient and reliable source in Japanese is the article in *Keizaigaku Jiten* (A Dictionary of Economic Science) entitled "Mabiki." Volume V, pp. 2438 *et seq.* Also the article "Nihon Jinko Shi" (History of Japanese Population), *ibid.*, Volume IV, pp. 2021 *et seq.*

was the flight of peasants to the cities, especially in famine years, a movement which the authorities tried in vain to check.[32] Active resistance of course means revolt—the final resort of peasants made desperate by conditions of life often below subsistence level. As the agrarian crisis became chronic, these revolts occurred with even greater frequence and violence, often embracing the peasantry of several districts.[33] Toward the end of the *Bakufu* period, these revolts became endemic and may be said to have weakened the strength of the feudal regime so dangerously that they made possible to a large extent the victory of the *political* movement directed against the *Bakufu*.

The decline of the independent producer and the rise of money economy aggravated the financial plight of the Shogunate and daimiates, and finally drove them into bankruptcy.[34] This same process impoverished the body of feudal retainers who often deserted their lords[35] and became, as we have seen, *ronin,* swashbucklers, brigands and adventurers, as well as devoted anti-*Bakufu* patriots and scholars looking beyond Japan for inspiration in their desire to re-fashion their country. The angry cries of these poverty stricken but proud retainers helped to swell the chorus of complaint against the rigid caste-system and showed the extent to which their loyalty to overlord, whether *daimyo* or Shogun, was undermined.[36] As this friction between the lower classes of retainers and the fief or Shogunal authorities became sharper, it finally had to take the form of a *political*

[32] Takizawa, *op. cit.,* pp. 80-1.
Honjo, *op. cit.,* pp. 236-7.
Tsuchiya, *op. cit.,* pp. 163-4.

[33] Many monographs and collections of source materials on the subject of these peasant revolts have been undertaken by such scholars as Ono Takeo, Kokusho Iwao, Kimura Seiji, Honjo Eijiro and others. Using both Japanese documents and the results of Japanese research an extensive survey of peasant revolts in the Tokugawa period has been made by Dr. Hugh Borton, "Peasant Uprisings in Japan," *TASJ,* second series, Volume XVI, May 1938.

[34] A study of the financial income of the *Bakufu* and its inadequacy to meet the strain caused by the fluctuations in the price of rice has been made by Sawada Sho, "Financial Difficulties of the Edo Bakufu," in *Kokushi Gaku,* Volume XXII (February 1935), pp. 1-20, and has been translated by Dr. Hugh Borton in the *Harvard Journal of Asiatic Studies,* November 1936, pp. 308-26. This article shows the effect which the debasing of currency and the rise in the price of commodities had upon *Bakufu* finances. The extent of bankruptcy among the *daimyo* is also indicated.

[35] The economic decline of this class is succinctly described by Tsuchiya, *op. cit.,* pp. 233-9.

[36] See the interesting passage from a contemporary record *Shohei Yawa,* quoted in Honjo, *op. cit.,* pp. 228-9.

struggle. These retainers who from being hereditary vassals were reduced to mere hirelings receiving dwindling rice-stipends, often cut off without any means of sustenance, had every reason to turn against the rigid clan system which thwarted their ambitions and jeopardized their social security. The corrosive of economic uncertainty destroyed the fabric of feudal loyalties and made it natural for *samurai* who were ejected from their time-honored status to search for some higher, more universal symbol worthy of devotion and sacrifice.[37] This body of lower retainers acted as the spear-point in the attack upon the *Bakufu* and supplied the most steadfast leaders in the Restoration, many of whom even in the years before the defeat of the *Bakufu* tilted against parochial obscurantism and political repression, striving to rouse Japan to national consciousness.[38] These lower *samurai* and *ronin* were to become most vocal when, spurred on by the threat of Western aggression, they linked the slogan *Son-no* (Revere the Emperor) to the cry *Jo-i* (Expel the Barbarian). While the *Son-no* slogan gave most conscious expression to the prevailing feeling of distrust of the *Bakufu*, *Jo-i* became the most effective slogan strategically, since it provided a legal cloak to the openly rebellious anti-*Bakufu* movement and at the same time inspired incidents which entangled the *Bakufu* with foreign powers.

Finally the political struggle against the *Bakufu* embraced a section of the aristocracy of the Imperial court, the *kuge*—a pre-feudal class distinct from the feudal aristocracy, the *daimyo*. This refined circle of aristocrats was at the zenith of political and cultural influence in the years of the Fujiwara domination and in that epoch its life and interests were minutely and sensitively recorded in the *Genji Monogatari* of Murasaki Shikibu and the *Makura no Soshi* of Sei Shonagon.[39] Under the Toku-

---

[37] The shift in the loyalty of the *samurai* from the clan to the Imperial court as the symbol in the anti-*Bakufu* struggle is described by Fujii Jintaro, "Meiji Ishin to Samurai Kaikyu" (The Meiji Restoration and the Samurai Class), in *Meiji Ishin Shi Kenkyu* (cited), p. 464.

[38] The role of these lower *samurai* may be compared to that of the English country gentry in the Tudor period who as justices of the peace worked so indefatigably to create the administrative bases for the new Tudor monarchy. On the lower *samurai* as leaders in the Restoration, see Ukita Kazatami and Counts Okuma and Itagaki, "History of Political Parties in Japan" in *Fifty Years of New Japan*, compiled by Okuma Shigenobu and translated from the Japanese *Kaikoku Gojunen Shi*, under the editorship of Marcus B. Huish, London, 1910, Volume I, p. 143.

[39] These works have been translated into elegant English by Arthur Waley.

gawa the *kuge* were reduced to penury and impotence,[40] but they preserved the memory of past days when skill in poetry or calligraphy brought greater glory than all the arts of war. In return the *Bakufu* and the military classes regarded with contempt the essentially humanistic civilian outlook of the *kuge*. Nevertheless the Shogunate, realizing that these courtiers might entertain resentment against it, took precautions to prevent any *daimyo* from establishing contact with them.[41] Some of the more active *kuge*—Iwakura, Sanjo, Tokudaiji—established a secret alliance with the most resolute anti-*Bakufu* elements, notably the Choshu clan. These few *kuge*, whose immunity from police-surveillance and whose position near to the Emperor's person gave them obvious importance, supplied a small core around which the dissident *daimyo* (*i.e.* of Satsuma, Choshu, Tosa and Hizen) built an anti-*Bakufu* league. The first conscious political movement against the Shogunate may be said to be this League or Union of Court and Military (*Kobu-Gattai*).[42] This League became most active when the *sankin-kotai* system was relaxed in 1862 and the *daimyo* could visit Kyoto without restraint.[43] However as the political struggle became sharper, the union was discarded, the lower *samurai* and *ronin* pressed forward as leaders in the Restoration movement, and the *daimyo*, bewildered by the rapid turn of events, and startled by the violent extremism of their lower retainers—especially in Choshu—allowed the reins of power to slip into the hands of ambitious councilors or *ronin*.[44]

[40] La Mazelière writes of their condition at the end of the *Bakufu*. "Les revenus des 143 familles de *kuge* s'élevaient seulement à 1,750,000 francs; la plus riche était Konoe, qui avait 70,000 livres de rentes; quelques *kuge* en étaient réduits à travailler pour vivre, peignant des cartes à jouer, faisant des parapluies en papier, taillant des cure-dents ou des bâtonnets à manger." La Mazelière, *op. cit.*, Volume IV, p. 196.

The famous *kuge* Iwakura Tomomi (1825-83) was so impoverished that, taking advantage of the privilege which the *kuge* enjoyed whereby the Shogun police could not enter their houses, he allowed a gambling resort to be kept within his premises, using its proceeds as his chief means of support. See Takekoshi, Yosaburo, *Prince Saionji*, Tokyo, 1933, p. 31.

[41] Murdoch, *op. cit.*, Volume III, p. 724. The *daimyo* and their agents established contact with the *kuge* through the medium of Buddhist temples such as the great Nishi Honganji in Kyoto which was traditionally very close to the Imperial court.

[42] Murdoch, *op. cit.*, Volume III, p. 725. The initiative in this union of *kuge* and *daimyo* is said to have been taken by Sanjo Saneyoshi and agents of the Tosa clan.

[43] Kuroita, *op. cit.*, Volume III, p. 541.

[44] The *daimyo*, with only a few exceptions such as Matsudaira Shungaku of

There is a certain irony in the fact that the continual emphasis which the feudal authorities of the *Bakufu* laid upon *loyalty* was turned against them when the slogan *Son-no* (Revere the Emperor) was taken up by their political enemies. It was a cry which was difficult for the *Bakufu* to meet—and in fact there could be no reply to it. The position of the Throne during the Tokugawa regime was not unlike that which prevailed under such preceding Shogunates as the Kamakura and Ashikaga. The theory by which the Shogun exercised actual power and by which the Emperor was relegated to the austere obscurity of the Kyoto palace was that the Emperor's person ought not to be contaminated by the cares of State; hence he delegated temporal power to his generalissimo—or *Sei-i-tai-shogun*, to give him his full title—but he still remained in theory the source of all power. Despite the existence of a rival dynasty in the fourteenth century, the rise and fall of various Shogunates and the continued seclusion of the Emperor, the magic power of the Throne was such as to evoke the most passionate feelings of loyalty which were never completely dissipated. A discussion of the long historical background of this deep-seated devotion to the Throne would take us too far afield; but it is important to realize that although the Shogunate wielded actual power, it never dared to challenge the final right to reign which was inalienably vested in the Throne. The sanction upon which the Shogunate rested was such that the Throne could in its own right intervene at any time in the affairs of State.

In practice, however, the Tokugawa Shogunate succeeded in surrounding the Throne with such an impenetrable hedge of ceremonial obstructions and in so removing the court from all possible contact with the outside world that the Throne could never be a controlling factor in the course of events. But during the two and a half centuries of Tokugawa rule there was maturing a political philosophy which exercised an ever-expanding

---

Echizen and Yamanouchi Yodo of Tosa, had virtually ceased to be the real policymakers of the clan. Just as in the whole realm so in the clan, dual government or government from behind the screen prevailed. The *daimyo* became virtually *rois fainéants* while able *samurai*, often of the lowest rank, became leaders in the clan, with revolutionary results. Maurice Courant quotes a contemporary Japanese pamphlet, describing the decadence of the *daimyo*: "Les *daimyo* ont été élevés dans le gynécée, traités en enfants délicats ils n'ont jamais soupçonée le froid ni la faim ni aucune des realités de l'existence; il en est de même de leur karo: *ainsi les affaires sont laissées à des inferieurs souvent indignes*" (italics mine E.H.N.). M. Courant, *Okubo*, Paris, 1904, p. 142.

sway over the minds of the lettered classes. In the Mito clan there grew up around the Maecenas of historical studies, Toku-gawa Mitsukuni (1628-1700), a school of historiographers under the influence of the Ming exile Shu-Shunsui or Chu Shun-shui (1600-82). This scholar was invited by Mitsukuni to assist him in composing a history of Japan, the *Dai Nihon Shi*, in which the central theme was loyalty to the Throne. Writers have perhaps exaggerated the immediate importance of this work since it was not printed until 1851, and then only in part; further it was written in a too severely classical style for the ordinary *samurai*.[45] But it was the first work of its kind and un-doubtedly acted as a stimulant for treatises expressing a similar view.[46] More potent propagandists were the advocates of Shinto revival, usually called the *Kokugakusha* or members of the Na-tionalist School. The greatest figure among them was Motoori Norinaga (1730-1801), who denounced the infatuation with everything Chinese which pervaded so much of Japanese letters, and glorified the purely indigenous culture. Motoori and his followers breathed into large numbers of their countrymen the spirit of devotion to the Imperial family and the exaltation of the Japanese genius. However it would be a mistake to believe that a narrow and exclusive nationalism blinded the leading thinkers of the day to the value of foreign learning. While the *Kokugakusha* tirelessly preached loyalty to the Throne with an implication diminishing the prestige of the *Bakufu*, some of the keenest minds among them saw no contradiction in turning toward Western science. Through the medium of Dutch not a few of them acquired a respectable knowledge of Western sci-

[45] Murdoch, *op. cit.*, Volume III, p. 665. Although not completed until 1905, part of this work covering the sections entitled "Chronicles of the Emperors" and "Biographies," in 100 volumes was presented to the Emperor in 1810 leaving 145 volumes still to appear. See Hugh Borton, "A Survey of Japanese Historiography," *American Historical Review*, Volume XLIII, Number 3, April 1938, p. 493.

[46] The impact of the works of Rai Sanyo (1780-1832), namely his *Nihon Seiki* and especially his *Nihongaishi* was far greater than that of the *Dai Nihon Shi*. Rai discussed only pre-Tokugawa history, but to achieve his end of attacking the existing regime, he criticized unsparingly the earlier Shogunates, particu-larly the Ashikaga, and exalted the Throne. Both the Tokugawa authorities and the reading public appreciated his partisanship, the former by censoring his books, the latter by reading them diligently. Only scholars favored by the Tokugawa, such as Hayashi Razan or the great Arai Hakuseki, were permitted to write of events after 1603, the date of the foundation of the Tokugawa *Bakufu*.

ence and ideas.[47] The most avid scholars of Dutch learning were often *ronin* or lower *samurai* who, thanks to their freedom from clan interference and duties, were able to give their whole time to study.[48] It was not an easy matter for these men to acquire a mastery of a foreign language. Almost every difficulty obstructed their path; lack of any means of self-support, scarcity of books, the prejudice of orthodox Confucian scholars, persecution at the hands of the authorities and even assassination by anti-foreign fanatics.[49] These enterprising spirits, men like Sakuma Shozan, Watanabe Kazan, Takano Choei, Yoshida Shoin, paid with their lives for their desire to acquire Western knowledge and apply it to Japanese conditions. Their successors who lived on into the Meiji period, were like them, poor *samurai* or *ronin*, who had felt to the full the repressive hand of the *Bakufu*, but who had nevertheless become acquainted with developments in the other parts of the world and were peculiarly fitted to play a leading part in the overthrow of the *Bakufu* and the establishment of the new regime.

Herein lies a fundamental difference between Japan at the end of the Tokugawa period and China during the Opium Wars.[50] In China, the ruling bureaucracy was civilian in out-

[47] The formal prohibition of reading and translating also European books except religious ones was removed by Yoshimune (Shogun from 1716 to 1744). Kuroita, *op. cit.*, Volume III, p. 474. For the extent of Western science and learning in Tokugawa Japan, see N. Yamasaki, *L'Action de la Civilisation Européenne sur la Vie Japonaise Avant l'Arrivée du Commodore Perry*, Paris, 1910. In a study devoted to pre-Meiji times it is natural that the Dutch influence should loom very large, especially after the closing of the country. For the renaissance of Dutch studies after the lifting of the prohibition against foreign learning, see *ibid.*, pp. 95-118.

A work of more recent research on the same subject is C. R. Boxer, *Jan Compagnie in Japan 1600-1817*. An essay in the Cultural and Scientific Influence Exercised by the Hollanders in Japan from the Seventeenth to Nineteenth Centuries, The Hague, 1936.

[48] Fujii Jintaro, "Meiji Ishin to Samurai Kaikyu" (cited), in *Meiji Ishin Shi Kenkyu*, p. 466.

[49] A vivid description of some of the dangers and obstacles in the path of a Japanese who wished to master Dutch studies is to be found in the *Autobiography of Fukuzawa Yukichi*, translated by E. Kiyooka, Tokyo, 1934. He shows the incurable conservatism and prejudices of the clan authorities (p. 45), the poverty of student life in Osaka and the laborious patience required to study a language before proper facilities were available, Chapter IV, "Student Ways at Ogata's School." He tells how he had to copy out for his own use the text of Doeff's lexicon, of which there was only one copy in his school, (pp. 87-8), also how he and his fellow-students copied a textbook on electricity (pp. 94-5).

[50] The difference in the attitude of Ch'ing China and pre-Restoration Japan toward learning from abroad is brought out by K. S. Latourette. *The Develop-*

look, recruited through the civil service examination system, chiefly from the gentry class. This scholar-bureaucracy had become the jealous guardian of Confucian orthodoxy, compliance with which was the pass-key into this bureaucracy. They ignored or despised all manifestations of Western culture which was, at least in the 19th century, displayed to China in its worst light as a mixture of commercial cupidity and military arrogance. The attitude of the Chinese literati was epitomized in the famous reply of the Emperor Ch'ien Lung to the British envoy Lord Macartney in 1793. "The stores of goods at the Celestial Court are plenteous and abundant; there is nothing but what is possessed, so that there is really no need for the produce of outer barbarians in order to balance supply and demand."[51]

Perhaps the comparison ought to be made not between China and Japan, but between both China of the Ch'ing dynasty and Tokugawa Japan on the one hand, and Meiji Japan on the other. Both the Ch'ing Dynasty and the *Bakufu* displayed a deep-seated prejudice against any new learning tainted with Western (read Christian) origin; they both set their faces sternly against any basic social change which would encroach upon the privileges of the ruling bureaucracy—civil in China, military in Japan. In Japan, however, the lower *samurai* with their military outlook, their sturdy nationalism and their successful leadership of the Meiji Restoration (1867-8), saved Japan from becoming a second China only by adapting to their own use the industrial technique and the necessary institutions which had given the Western nations their superior strength in dealing with "backward" nations. Unlike the *samurai*-bureaucrat whose loy-

---

ment of Japan, Fourth edition, New York, 1938, p. 90. See also the suggestive remarks comparing the two countries by G. F. Hudson, *The Far East in World Politics*, Oxford, 1937, Chapter III, especially pp. 36-49.

A summary of the different policies adopted in regard to industrialization by Meiji Japan and contemporary China has been made by J. E. Orchard, "Contrasts in the Progress of Industrialization in China and Japan," *Political Science Quarterly*, Columbia University, New York, March 1937, p. 18 *et seq.*

[51] "From the Emperor of China to King George the Third—From the Tung-Hwa Luh or Published Court Records of the Now Reigning Manchu Dynasty," translated by E. H. Parker in the *Nineteenth Century*, London, Volume XL, July 1896, p. 49. "Trade, it is true has' grown . . . but as yet it is far from what our predecessors looked for; and the reason is not that the Chinese Government actively opposed foreign commerce, but that the Chinese people did not require it. Chinese have the best food in the world, rice; the best drink, tea; and the best clothing, cotton, silk and fur. Possessing these staples, . . . they do not need to buy a penny's worth elsewhere. . . ." Sir Robert Hart. *These from The Land of Sinim.* London, 1901, pp. 60-1.

alty to the *Bakufu* regime had become estranged and whose ambitions were obstructed by the Tokugawa caste-system, his Chinese administrative counterpart, the Confucian literatus, was so committed to the *ancien régime* and its institutions that he shrank from undertaking any far-reaching reforms. The mandarinate did its best no doubt to patch up and repair the cumbrous administrative structure until, caught in its collapse, the bureaucracy perished with it beneath the ruins. But this social upheaval and the subsequent reconstruction came almost three-quarters of a century later than in Japan. It was too late for China to break the shackles of the unequal-treaty system which were now firmly riveted upon her; too late also to throw off the burdens of her own social decay, aggravated as it was by this very foreign domination. Superficially at least the difference between Japanese and Chinese historical evolution lies in the fact that the breakdown of feudalism in Japan released latent social forces which were guided by the *samurai*—who, with *chonin* support, and carried along on the crest of agrarian revolt, were able to destroy the Shogunate and set up a new regime before national independence was irreparably weakened. In China the interventionist forces of the Western Powers and the undivided loyalty of the ruling bureaucracy succeeded in suppressing signs of revolt and attempts at social reform so that national independence and national regeneration had to be postponed for generations to come.[52]

It is easy to see how the acceptance of Western learning and science would spell the end of the monopoly of learning and office enjoyed by the Confucian bureaucracy. Christianity, the natural sciences, even the military sciences were all repugnant to it. It is clear from the fiasco of the Hundred Days of Reform in 1898 that the mandarinate was incapable of undertaking reforms—that China could only be modernized, that is

[52] On the role of foreign intervention in the Taiping Rebellion one of the few Western authorities on the subject writes: "Foreign intervention was not responsible for the failure of the rebellion . . . but it put backbone into a resistance which though daily becoming more overwhelming was still far from bringing the rebellion to a speedy conclusion." G. E. Taylor, "The Taiping Rebellion. Its Economic Background and Social Theory" in the *Chinese Social and Political Science Review*, Vol. XV, No. 4. January 1933. Peiping. pp. 612-13. "The Manchu Government of which an English diplomat has said that its corruption was only limited by its weakness, owed its new lease of life in no small measure to foreign support." *Ibid.*, p. 614.

to say *industrialized,* by an uncompromising political revolution which first and foremost would have to sweep away the self-sufficient, conservative mandarinate. In Japan there was no similar dominant class or caste with a vested interest in maintaining Confucian or even Shintoist learning. In Japan, the class from which administrators and councilors were drawn was the *bushi* or warrior class. This governing class had often learned from the foreigner whether Chinese, Korean, Portuguese, Dutch; now when they were given a practical illustration of the superiority of Western military science, they hastened to adopt it not only in order to protect national independence, but to maintain their own prestige in a society which glorified the military virtues. Hence, so far from threatening the social hierarchy in Japan as it did in China, the adoption of Western learning and science, especially its military aspects, was a matter of vital importance to the military leaders of pre-Restoration Japan, both *Bakufu* and clan.[53]

[53] One of the most original of Chinese social historians, Kuo Mo-jo, in a recent series of essays has touched upon this fascinating problem of the divergent paths taken by China and Japan. He lists the following reasons why Manchu China failed in modernization: (1) China was a very large country, rich in various products, not very densely populated. From ancient times the people's livelihood under the old mode of production was sufficient for their maintenance, so they felt no urgent need for a new mode of production. It followed that the science and culture pertaining to the new mode of production could not easily penetrate into this self-sufficient civilization. This accounts for the indifference displayed in former times to the knowledge and science of the West. (2) The frontier peoples of China, in Malaya, Annam, Burma, Korea, Mongolia, had an extremely low standard of living; accordingly their requirements were few and could not act as a stimulant upon China's productive forces. (3) The burden of a rich and ancient culture has always weighed heavily on China. Pre-capitalist culture lasted many epochs, at least thirty centuries, and the Chinese became drugged or spellbound by the rich store of their cultural tradition—narcissists, indifferent to all around them except their own cultural excellence. (4) Under the Ming Dynasty Chinese culture entered into close contacts with European. If it had been given a chance to grow and bear fruit, it might have evolved into something of value in terms of modernization and national defense. But in the same period China received a setback in the form of the Manchu invasion. The Manchu Dynasty used exclusively the traditional Chinese culture to rule and administer China, maintaining the examination system for almost 260 years during which time the best talents of China were buried in the composition of "eight-legged" essays (the key to passing the civil service examination). Those who rebelled against this crushing examination system (and Kuo gives some examples of them) were restricted to turning back to the study of antiquity, in such branches of learning as phonetics, morphology, etymology, which have weighed heavily on sinology to this day. The contributions of the best minds of the time could be only interpretations and classifications of ancient Chinese cultural life, they could not advance a step beyond ancient scholarship. Thus

As the Tokugawa regime passed the two-century mark in its history, it was faced with problems of the gravest nature. Natural calamities such as earthquakes, flood, famine and fire ravaged the country throughout its later years. Agrarian conditions were so wretched that a poor crop inevitably brought famine in its wake. The year 1833 was memorable for the calamities which befell the country. Years of famine followed one after the other, and it is recorded that in 1837 hundreds of corpses were left unburied in the streets of Nagoya.[54] Chronic agrarian distress bred peasant revolts which toward the end of this epoch grew in number and violence.[55] Rice riots or *uchi-kowashi* broke out in the great cities from time to time, and a most ominous symptom—these riots were often led by *ronin* or even petty officials. The most notable example of this trend was the ill-fated Osaka rising of 1837, associated with the name of Oshio Heihachiro.[56] A scholar and minor police official, Oshio was so

China stagnated and lost 300 years of development, thanks to the obscurantism of the Manchu policy.

Japan, on the other hand succeeded in modernization for the following parallel reasons: (1) its territory was small, arable land was scarce, and a sense of crowding had turned the Japanese mind outward, making them impatient of living at the stage reached under the old mode of production. (2) Chinese demand for Japanese goods acted as a vigorous stimulant for Japanese machine production and industrialization. (3) Although the Japanese have their own civilization and have received a great cultural debt from China, in the last analysis their cultural burden was not so oppressive as China's, so they could advance uner.cumbered by the weight of an ancient civilization. (4) In the period of change and reform in Japan there happened to be the Meiji Emperor who was a most unusual ruler, supported by able and intelligent ministers like Saigo, Okubo, Kido and Ito. At that time the Japanese leaders welcomed European culture enthusiastically and treated with disdain their own traditional culture, especially its Confucian coloring. See Kuo Mo-jo, *Mo-Jo Chin Chu* (in Chinese) (Recent Writings of Kuo Mo-jo), Shanghai, 1937, essay entitled "Chung-Jih Chih Wen-Hua Te Chiao-Lui" (Crosscurrents of Sino-Japanese Culture), pp. 141-61, especially pp. 149-53.

[54] Borton, *op. cit.*, p. 88.

[55] *Ibid.*, pp. 120-1.

[56] Oshio Heihachiro was deeply influenced by the Oyomei philosophy—a branch of Confucian teaching stemming from Wang Yang-ming (1472-1528). It was less authoritarian in its emphasis than the Chu Hsi school, officially recognized and supported by the Tokugawa government which accordingly suppressed the Oyomei influence with its more individualistic and democratic outlook.

For a fuller account of the Oshio Heihachiro affair, see Takizawa, *op. cit.*, p. 107; Takekoshi, *op. cit.*, Volume III, pp. 175-6 and 223; Murdoch, *op. cit.*, Volume III, pp. 453-6; and Sansom, *op. cit.*, p. 499 and 515. For Oshio's manifesto see Honjo, *op. cit.*, 210.

For a fuller account in Japanese see Kuroita, *op. cit.*, Volume III, pp. 510 *et seq.* One of the fullest accounts in Japanese appears in *Osaka-Shi Shi* (History of the City of Osaka) , compiled by the Osaka-shi Sanji Kai, Osaka, 1913, Volume II, pp. 496-508.

moved by the incompetence of the authorities in the face of desperate poverty that he drew up a manifesto justifying his action and instigated an uprising of the poor. Although this coup was smothered through treachery, it caused such a sensation in the country that other revolts of city poor or peasants led by *ronin* claiming "to be disciples of Oshio" and wishing to "strike down the robbers of the country" broke out in distant parts of the country.[57] The collapse of centralized authority made the suppression of such revolts exceedingly difficult and encouraged bolder spirits to challenge the authority of the *Bakufu*. Highwaymen infested the roads and since the Shogunate dared not interfere with them, wealthy citizens recruited their own bodyguards.[58] A large number of people now dared to denounce the exclusion policy of the *Bakufu*, urged the opening of the country to Western trade, and stimulated the desire for foreign learning. The great merchants, restricted by feudal regulations against foreign trade and annoyed by the resort of the bankrupt *Bakufu* to *goyokin* or forced loans, looked about them for support in their inherent desire to widen the national market and to find better opportunities for investment than was afforded by land-holding and usury. They saw their political allies in the great *tozama* of Satsuma, Choshu, Tosa and Hizen, who were cautiously drawing together for a concerted attack upon the *Bakufu*. Both the basic producing class, the peasantry, and the most politically active class, the *ronin* and lower *samurai* who often were able to draw their superiors along with them, thus directly menaced the Tokugawa regime. The *Bakufu* tried desperately to fend off its enemies by appeals to Confucian morality in an age when money power was becoming more important, by trying to tighten the links of the caste-system at a time when the acid of social and economic distress was rotting these bonds. But it had become abundantly clear to the Tokugawa administrators that it was futile to exorcise social calamities by invoking Confucian ethics; among the more farsighted leaders of the government doubts began to grow as to the wisdom of maintaining rigid exclusion.[59] Pursued by bankruptcy and revolt, the *Bakufu* now found itself face to face with the

[57] Borton, *op. cit.*, p. 95.

[58] Takekoshi, *op. cit.*, Volume III, p. 175.

[59] For example, men like Mizuno Tadakuni and Matsudaira Shungaku. For the former, see Murdoch, *op. cit.*, Volume III, p. 528-30, for the latter see W. E. Griffis, *The Mikado; Institution and Person*, Princeton, 1915, p. 67 *et seq.*

threat of invasion from abroad. This foreign menace, occurring just at the period of greatest confusion in the feudal regime, at the time of rising revolt and of greatest political discontent, proved to be the decisive factor in demonstrating once and for all the incompetence of *Bakufu* rule. The Shogunate blundered repeatedly over this question and exposed the country to the danger of foreign conquest, making it clear to all men of discernment and to many of its own supporters that it had forfeited the right to rule.

The Forcing of the Closed Door

We have seen how the various groups in feudal Japan were gradually turning against a regime which was felt to be responsible for the chaos and distress. Now we must note how this threat from abroad, coinciding with the process of decay and revolt, was utilized by the foes of the *Bakufu* as a lever to overturn it. Geography was an ally of exclusionist Japan. Of all Asiatic countries it was farthest removed from the reach of the great European naval powers. It was protected from the land power of the Romanov Empire by the vast half-explored steppes of Siberia, while before the development of California and the building of the Panama Railway, the United States, the power which was destined finally to open Japan was even further from eastern Asia than was Europe. Nevertheless it was clear to both the Western traders and Japanese statesmen that Japan, by relying on this accident of geography, could not forever avoid the day when some power would wait outside the closed gates, demanding an answer to the imperious command that Japan either be opened to world trade and intercourse or suffer the fate of India or China. Long before the arrival of Biddle and Perry, the rulers of Japan had good reason to be alarmed at the interest their country aroused in the minds of European navigators and empire-builders.

Russia, after extending her power to the shores of the Pacific, was to be a most constant specter troubling the sleep of feudal Japan. At the end of the 18th century the *Bakufu* felt concern at the southward gaze of Russia as she moved down into Saghalien and threatened the island of Yezo (modern Hokkaido).[60] The Russians made persistent attempts to open Japan

---

[60] The *Bakufu* took some haphazard steps toward meeting this menace by fortifying the Chiba peninsula and strengthening the defenses of Yezo through colonization. See Tsuji Zennosuke, *Kaigai Kotsu Shi Wa* (cited), p. 768.

Some of the more alert thinkers of the day attempted to goad the government

partially at least, and the trips of Laxman (1792), Rezanov and Krusenstern (1804), and Captain Golovnin (1811), although unsuccessful, served to keep Japanese eyes focused upon the intentions of their Northern neighbor. Russian attention was diverted elsewhere as friction between Russia and Britain became acute over the Afghan question[61] and when Russia became involved in the Crimean War (1854-6), abandoning perforce many ambitious plans for colonization and trade in the Far East. Repulsed in her ambition for the control of the Bosphorus, Russia again turned her gaze eastward and reappeared as a menace to Japanese security.[62] In 1859 Court Muravieff of Amur fame sailed with a fleet to Shinagawa and demanded that La Perouse Strait be fixed as the boundary between the Russian and Japanese empires.[63] The high point of Russian aggression was reached in 1861 when Captain Birileff seized the strategic island of Tsushima. Britain, who had her own plans intervened, and in an age which knew not the meaning of that sesame "*appeasement*," compelled Russia to renounce all claims to the island; but on the minds of the Japanese a lasting impression had been made which in succeeding years deepened into hostility and distrust.[64]

into a more conscious realization of the danger. One of them, Hayashi Shihei (1754-93), in his *Kaikoku Heidan* and *Sangoku Tsuran*, exalted the Emperor and obliquely criticized the Shogunate for its neglect of this menace. He was arrested by the *Bakufu* in 1791 for "stirring up discontent and unrest" in the former of these two books. Tsuji, *op. cit.*, p. 769. Hayashi's *Sangoku Tsuran*, a description of Korea, Yezo and the Ryukyu Islands, was translated into French by the savant Klaproth early in the 19th century. While on a trip through Siberia in 1805 he received the MS from a Japanese living in Irkutsk whose name he gives as Sin Sou and who had taken the Russian name of Nicolas Koloyghin. See the preface to J. Klaproth, *San Kokf Tsou Ran to Setsu. Ou aperçu des trois royaumes*, Paris, 1832.

For an account of Russian penetration into Saghalien and the Kuriles see W. G. Aston, "Russian Descents into Saghalin and Itorup," *TASJ*, Volume I, Part 1, pp. 78-86.

[61] The effect of the Afghan question on Russian as well as English foreign policy especially in Asia is discussed in a monograph by William Habberton, *Anglo-Russian Relations Concerning Afghanistan 1837-1907*. Illinois Studies in the Social Sciences, Volume XXI, Number 4, Urbana, Illinois, 1937.

[62] Gregory Bienstock, *The Struggle for the Pacific*, London, 1937, p. 137.

[63] Count Taneomi Soyeshima, "Japan's Foreign Relations," Chapter IV, in *Fifty Years of New Japan*, Volume I, p. 99.

[64] Russian ambitions were rewarded in 1875, when Japan surrendered all title to Saghalien in return for the Kurile Islands. See Shimada Saburo, "Japan's Introduction to the Comity of Nations," Chapter III, in *Fifty Years of New Japan*, Volume I, p. 86.

More decisive than the rather clumsy moves of the Romanov dynasty was the part played by England and France, and finally by the United States. In the eastward advance of the great European powers, India was the first halting-place, China the second, and Japan, that Ultima Thule of Gulliver and Marco Polo—the third and final stage. Thus it was first India, then China which absorbed the territorial and trading ambitions of England until well into the middle of the 19th century. But the spray from the rapid advance of the East India Company into China waters between 1808 and 1825 splashed Japan's shores and startled out of its somnolence even the self-complacent *Bakufu* government. One of the first attempts of the British to test the defenses of isolation in Japan was made in 1808 when the H.M.S. *Phaeton* forcibly entered the port of Nagasaki causing considerable uproar among Japanese officials and the resident Dutch.[65] A suitable opportunity for the British to replace the Dutch as the sole European traders in Japan presented itself when Holland was incorporated in Napoleonic France, which was of course at war with Britain. After Java had been taken over by the British, that imaginative empire-builder Sir Stamford Raffles urged that the English East India Company not only replace the Dutch at Nagasaki but undertake more ambitious commercial and colonial projects in Japan than any other power had hitherto conceived.[66] Two British ships, the *Charlotte* and the *Maria*, sailed to Nagasaki in 1813 perhaps to make a survey of the possibilities of replacing the Dutch. However Raffles' project was thwarted by the astute Dutch factor Hendrick Doeff who, by refusing to comply with the former's demand to surrender Dutch trading rights to the British, succeeded in keeping Deshima the only place in the world where the Dutch flag was flying in the year 1813.[67] These incidents, together with the armed clash in 1824 between foraging English sailors and local inhabitants on Takara-shima in Kagoshima Gulf, so alarmed the *Bakufu* that it promulgated in April 1825 the famous *Uchi-harai rei*, the order to attack and drive off any

[65] M. Paske Smith, *Western Barbarians in Japan and Formosa in Tokugawa Days, 1603-1868*, Kobe, 1930, p. 130.

[66] *Report on Japan to the Secret Committee of the English East India Company 1812-1816* by Sir Stamford Raffles, edited by M. Paske Smith, Kobe, 1929. See especially pp. 178-83 and pp. 210-11.

[67] C. Muto in *A Short History of Anglo-Japanese Relations*, Tokyo, 1936, using Doeff's *Reminiscences*, tells how the English were balked in their plans both at the time of the *Phaeton* incident (pp. 63-4) and later in 1813 (pp. 65-7).

foreign ship which violated Japanese isolation.[68] The *Bakufu* now encouraged violent anti-foreign agitation. Later this was to become a source of embarrassment when, caught between Western insistence that Japan open its doors and the popular demand to expel the barbarian, the *Bakufu* after much vacillation finally referred the question of treaty-signing to the court in Kyoto and thus seriously damaged its political prestige. However, the failure of the farsighted Raffles to interest the East India Company in Japan was really an indication that the full force of British mercantile ambitions was now trained not upon the remote islands of Japan but rather upon China, the empire of fabled wealth. The seizure of Singapore in 1819 and the growing trade with China especially in opium signified that the next outpost of British commercial interests would be somewhere on the Chinese coast. In order to break down the barriers to trade, the British fought and defeated the Manchu dynasty and fastened upon China the first of the unequal treaties, the Treaty of Nanking (1842). British traders were far too busy exploiting in prospect if not yet in fact this rich market to be greatly concerned about the rocky islands lying to the North East. But the fate of China made a lasting impression on the best minds in Japan whose writings despite censorship and suppression sounded a clarion call for national defense and even the adoption of Western industry and military science.[69] Fearful

[68] Murdoch, *op. cit.*, Volume III, p. 528.
   Kuroita, *op. cit.*, Volume III, pp. 521-2.
   [69] The effect of China's defeat on political thinkers in contemporary Japan has been analyzed in an interesting essay by Professor Tsuchiya Takao, "Bakumastsu Shishi no Mita Shina Mondai" (The Problem of China as seen by Loyalists at the end of the *Bakufu*) in *Kaizo*, July 1938. pp. 154-67. Some of their arguments are amazingly shrewd and show a sound grasp of the international situation. For instance Aizawa Hakumin (1782-1863) in his *Shinron* maintained that Russia was the chief menace and would pursue one of two lines of approach in its expansion: if China were strong, Russia would encroach upon Japan by way of Saghalien and Yezo and then use Japan as a base from which to attack China; if China were weak, Russia would penetrate into North China and thence invade Japan. Sato Shin-en (1769-1850) in his *Kondo Hisaku* emphasized that a weakened China exposed Japan to a similar fate. He pointed out that although China was hostile to Western learning, it had been careless in permitting European economic power to gain a foothold. To him Britain appeared as the chief menace, and he proposed that Japan seize part of China as a bulwark against further British advance eastward. Sakuma Shozan (1811-64), the teacher of Yoshida Shoin, also urged vigilance against England, and warned against allowing it to gain a commercial hold upon Japan. Kusaka Genzui (1840-64), a pupil of Yoshida Shoin, in his *Hensui Ryaku Shi Biko* made a detailed study based on information supplied by the

lest a rigid maintenance of the *Uchi-harai rei* should in the end call down upon itself the fate of China, the *Bakufu* adopted a more conciliatory policy and issued in 1842 the regulation permitting foreign ships to be fueled and victualed in specified ports.[70] Through this change in policy, the *Bakufu* not only earned the enmity of the vociferous anti-foreign party which had been gaining in momentum, but ignited feuds and rivalries which had been smoldering for decades. The anti-foreign party which was made up of thinkers who wished to adopt Western methods to defeat Western ambitions now turned its battery upon the *Bakufu* for yielding to foreign pressure. That the anti-foreign slogan "Expel the barbarian" was a maneuver to turn the flank of Tokugawa reaction was seen as soon as the anti-*Bakufu* party assumed power after the Restoration (1868), when the more naïve adherents of this xenophobia were ruthlessly punished for attacks upon foreigners.

As befitted the most advanced capitalist nation in the world, Britain had been setting the pace in breaking down trade barriers in Eastern Asia. Its great shipping rival the United States, which had been running a close second to Britain in tonnage carried in her ships,[71] now began to show a keen interest in gaining definite treaty rights guaranteeing its shipping interests in the Far East. Commodore Perry wrote before his expedition to Japan: "When we look at the possessions on the east of our great maritime rival, England, and of the constant and rapid increase of their fortified ports, we should be admonished of the necessity of prompt measures on our part. . . . Fortunately the Japanese and many other islands of the Pacific are still left untouched by this unconscionable government (*i.e.*, Britain); and some of them lay in the route of a great commerce which is destined to

---

Dutch concerning the English campaign in China. These and other writers discussed by Professor Tsuchiya were highly critical of the Shogun's neglect of military defenses and urged that Japan master Western military technique so as to be spared the humiliation suffered by China. These men and their pupils were the spiritual fathers of the Meiji Restoration.

[70] Kuroita, *op. cit.*, Volume III, pp. 522-3. The *Bakufu* Councilor Mizuno Tadakuni was so impressed by the exaggerated account of British naval strength given by one of the leading spirits of the day Takano Choei (1804-50) in his *Yume-Monogatari*—that he adopted a more conciliatory attitude to foreign shipping interests. Murdoch, *op. cit.*, Volume III, p. 529.

[71] American shipping with its famous "Clippers" was pressing the British hard in the tonnage handled in the first part of the nineteenth century. Cf. H. B. Morse, *The Trade and Administration of China*, London, 1920, third edition, p. 312.

become of great importance to the United States. No time should be lost in adopting active measures to secure a sufficient number of ports of refuge."[72] American Far Eastern Policy already showed its peculiar characteristic: namely the pressure of the future on the present, and the resulting desire to guard the former by providing for it in the present.[73] In this concern to look for harbors and commercial footholds in the western Pacific, Perry and others had plans to take Formosa and the Ryukyu and Bonin Islands.[74] While France, Britain and Russia were engrossed in the Turkish question leading up to the Crimean War of 1854-6, and while Britain and France were most active in maintaining the newly established unequal treaty system in China, the United States after opening Japan in 1853-4 pressed its demands on the *Bakufu* and was finally rewarded in 1858, when Townsend Harris negotiated the first *commercial* treaty between Japan and a Western power. By yielding to foreign pressure, and so assuming regular diplomatic relations with the outside world, the *Bakufu* aggravated the anti-foreign feeling in the country; but above all by allowing foreign merchandise to enter Japan, it accelerated the economic disintegration of the country. The foreign trade of Japan now took a sudden leap: in 1863, Japanese exports, mostly raw materials, were estimated at 4,751,631 yen; in 1865, the figure was 6,058,718 yen while imports for the same period were 4,366,840 yen and 5,950,231 yen respectively.[75] Since the tariff for both imports and exports was limited by treaty provision, manufactured goods began to flood the country; the fantastic ratio of gold to silver prevailing in Japan—1:6 or 1:5 whereas the world ratio was 1:15—led to a serious outflow of gold[76] which disrupted

[72] Quoted in Tyler Dennett, *Americans in Eastern Asia,* New York, 1922, p. 273.

[73] Anatole Kantorovich, *Amerika v Bor'be za Kitai* (America in the Struggle for China), Moscow, 1935, p. 31.

[74] Dennett, *op. cit.,* pp. 272-4. The most ambitious plan for establishing an American protectorate over Formosa was devised by the pioneer American missionary, Dr. Peter Parker. A full discussion of this project and the reason for its collapse is to be found in Dennett, *op. cit.,* pp. 284-91. Commander John Kelly had taken formal possession of the Coffin group of the Bonin Islands in 1853, and not until 1873 did the U.S.A. disclaim all rights to them. *Ibid.,* p. 432.

[75] This is the lowest of three estimates of the value of exports made by Japanese scholars. For these figures see Tsuchiya, *An Economic History of Japan,* pp. 241-2.

[76] "By careful assay at the British mint it was subsequently found that silver coins in the currency of Japan bore the relations of hardly five to one with

Japanese economy but yielded tremendous profits to foreign traders. In 1860 the *Bakufu* began to debase the coinage, reducing the gold content of coins by over 85%;[77] the consequent inflation heightened economic distress by precipitating a steep rise in commodity prices.[78] This rise together with the violent fluctuations in the price of rice had a disastrous effect upon the Shogunate, the *daimyo* and their dependents, the *samurai*, whose income in rice was fixed but when translated into money actually shrank in meeting the rise in commodity prices. The precarious finances of the Shogunate had now to bear the burden of extraordinary expenditures on the construction of forts, iron foundries, or indemnities for attacks on foreigners, and on the despatch of envoys abroad—expenses which could not be met by any other device than by increasing the exaction on the agrarian population and by extracting forced loans (*goyokin*) from the merchants.[79] The fresh exactions which the Shogunate and the

---

gold, and were overvalued therefore to the extent of two-thirds above the original proportion (viz. fifteen and a half to one) which silver bullion bears to gold in the general market of the world." Sir Rutherford Alcock, *The Capital of the Tycoon: A Narrative of a Three Years Residence in Japan*, Two Volumes, London, 1863, Volume II, pp. 411.

On the great outflow of gold from Japan, see Takekoshi, *op. cit.*, Volume III, p. 333.

[77] *Ibid.*, III, p. 336. Sawada, *op. cit.*, p. 325, gives the date as 1859.

[78] Some indication of the erratic leaps in the price of Higo rice (Higo rice was the standard) can be gathered from the following table. Prices are given in silver *momme* (60 silver *momme* = 1 gold *ryo*, and at the Restoration one *ryo* = one yen).

1854	84.8 *momme*	1861	142.5 *momme*
1855	77.1	1862	172.0
1856	82.4	1863	100.5
1857	106.3	1864	325.5
1858	131.5	1865	513.0
1859	120.4	1866	1300.0
1860	203.0	1867	590.0

Abstracted from tables appended to Honjo Eijiro, *Tokugawa Bakufu no Beika Chosetsu* (Regulation of the Price of Rice During the Tokugawa *Bakufu*), Tokyo, 1924, pp. 414-15.

The prices of other agricultural products also rose sharply. In the interval between 1860 and 1867 the unit price of barley rose from 90 *momme* to 290, soy beans from 164 *momme* to 797.52, vegetable oil from 560 to 2,418, and salt from 2.19 to 21.00. Tsuchiya Takao, "Bakumatsu Doran no Keizaiteki Bunseki" (As Economic Analysis of the Unrest at the End of the *Bakufu*) in *Chuokoron*, October 1932, Volume XLVII, Number 11, p. 83.

[79] So desperate was the financial plight of the Shogunate that it had to mortgage to France the iron-foundry at Yokosuka and to default on payments for arms to France and also on a debt to the United States incurred in buying the warship *Stonewall*. For these and other details on the financial condition of the Shogunate and daimiates, see Tsuchiya, *op. cit.*, pp. 249-54.

daimyo made of the peasantry stirred up still more desperate agrarian revolts, while the swollen army of *ronin*, impoverished peasants, vagrants, and beggars poured into the cities to add to the general state of chaos.[80] The economic distress of the lower *samurai*, sharpened by the meteoric rise in prices, threw them into a truly wretched state of penury, deepened their hatred of the *Bakufu* and its foreign policy, and induced them to fasten the responsibility for their troubles on foreign barbarians and their trading operations.[81] Assassinations of leading *Bakufu*

[80] Professor Kokusho Iwao's tables, given as an appendix to his study on peasant revolts, show a marked increase in such revolts after 1860.

Year	Number of Revolts
1844–1851	14
1853–1859	16
1860–1867	39

Kokusho Iwao, *Hyakusho Ikki no Kenkyu* (A Study of Peasant Revolts), Tokyo, 1928, pp. 443-6. These figures are given in tables appearing on p. 262 as well. A more recent study by one of Kokusho's pupils based on newly discovered source material gives a much greater number of revolts for this period.

Year	Number of Revolts
1844–1851	31
1852–1859	40
1860–1867	86

Numazaki Hidenosuke, *Hyakusho Ikki Chosa Hokokusho* (Reports and Investigations of Peasant Revolts) (in mimeograph), Kyoto, 1935, Chart IV, (no pagination).

[81] The impact of the sudden importation of cheap manufactured goods upon the disintegrating feudal economy of Japan was revolutionary in its effect. Cheap cotton fabrics and yarns drove the domestic articles off the market, compelling the "Verlag" (quasi household) type of manufacturer, to adopt machine production while thousands of handicraft rural producers were ruined. Many of the latter were of *samurai* or peasant families, whose women folk engaged in spinning as a part-time means of sustenance. This, together with the effect of foreign imports in forcing up prices, gave a very plain economic motive for the bitter anti-foreign feeling of the declassed *samurai, ronin* etc. *Ronin* riots and outrages were thus partly stimulated by the revolutionary effects of foreign trade. The late Viscount Shibusawa Eiichi in his *Life of Prince Keiki* (Tokugawa) wrote, "The price of goods rose rapidly and the blow fell heaviest on those with fixed salaries. Accordingly they said to themselves, "These barbarians bring useless luxuries to our country, deprive us of our daily necessaries, impoverish the people, and have ambitions to annex Japan in the near future. It is the Shogun who sowed the seeds of this calamity." Quoted in Tsuchiya, *op. cit.*, p. 252. For a discussion of the economic background of *ronin* and anti-foreign activity, see Kada Tetsuji, *Ishin Igo no Shakai Keizai Shiso Gairon* (An Outline of Social and Economic Thought After the Restoration), Tokyo, 1934, see especially the chapter "Bakumatsu no Joiteki Keizai Ron" (Economic Discussion of Anti-Foreignism at the End of the *Bakufu*), pp. 1-30.

But perhaps the best short study of this problem is Professor Tsuchiya's

officials became frequent, beginning in 1860 with Ii Naosuke, *Kamon-no-kami,* the government advocate of opening Japan; terror was also directed against merchants who attempted to profit excessively by usury or by speculating on price fluctuations.[82]

Before going on to discuss the Restoration settlement, it might be pertinent to ask why Japan did not become a colony, or at least a country of impaired sovereignty such as contemporary China. The danger of Japan becoming subject to some one or more of the Western Powers was very real. Internal social and economic decay had reached so advanced a stage that it is pardonable to be puzzled as to how Japan avoided the fate of China. England and France were pushing their colonial stakes farther eastward. Fortunately for Japan their attention was absorbed by the far richer prize of China which they were busily engaged in "pacifying" for several decades after 1840. Britain in particular was watching and finally intervened in the great Taiping Rebellion, which broke out in 1850 and which was to last for some fifteen years. The period of 1860-5, the eve of the Meiji Restoration, was the most critical for Japan. The *Bakufu* was in full retreat before its political rivals; economic distress was

---

article, "Bakumatsu Doran no Keizaiteki Bunseki," in *Chuo Koron,* October 1932, pp. 75-91.

[82] A contemporary document depicts the *ronin* in Kyoto. "*Ronin* of all clans kept increasing more and more in number; among those who came into the city were both impoverished and debt-ridden *ronin;* but not only was there nobody who sued a single one of them (for recovery of debt) but they handed over to the *ronin* anything which the latter fancied." Quoted by Hirao in "Bakumatsu Ronin to sono Hogo oyobi Tosei" in *Meiji Ishin Shi Kenkyu,* p. 530.

Miss Utley gives an interpretation of the role of the *ronin* and the lower *samurai* which is difficult to accept. "By the middle of the nineteenth century there were so many of these *ronin,* and the poverty of the majority of the *Samurai* was so great, that as a class the lesser *Samurai* and the *ronin* were ripe for revolution; not a revolution for emancipation from feudalism, but rather a counter-revolution to re-establish the power of the feudal military aristocracy to which they belonged." In a footnote to the same page she writes, "From the account of the Revolution in La Mazalière's (sic) book (Volume IV), it is clear that the *ronin* were attacking the merchant usurer class, *e.g.,* the killing of merchants in Kyoto and Osaka, and the forcible reduction of rice prices." Freda Utley. *Japan's Feet of Clay,* New York, 1937, p. 221. Leaving aside the question of "revolution" and "counter-revolution," it seems quite clear that what these *ronin* and *samurai* accomplished regardless of their desires and personal ambitions was the Meiji Restoration which represents an anti-feudal movement inasmuch as it broke through feudal particularism and opened the way for a new State and all that it implied, the creation of a national market a revolution in property relation—in short a modern capitalist society.

most acute after the accumulative misery of chronic agrarian crisis; and finally the fabric of a rotten feudalism was rent to shreds by the intrusion of Western trade and thought.[83]

The France of Napoleon III had shown a desire to acquire territory and glory. In 1859, after emerging empty-handed from the Crimean War, Napoleon III backed Sardinia in a war against Austria, winning as his reward Savoy and Nice. This grotesque caricature of the great Napoleon was now to meet with one of the most shattering fiascos of his career in his Mexican adventure of 1862-7. (The American Civil War, added inducement for French intervention in Mexico, was incidentally a guarantee that no successor to the persistent Perry would trouble the rulers of Japan for some years to come.) By the time Napoleon had extricated himself from his Mexican adventure, the helmeted figure of Bismarck cast an ominous shadow over the Third Empire, deterring even the feckless Napoleon from sending his troops to the ends of the world. Nevertheless France, weakened as she was, turned her attention once more to the Far East to gain what she could by intrigue if not by conquest. Léon Roches, the French minister to Japan, trained in the hard school of colonial administration in Algeria, was a resourceful diplomat typical of the days before cable-diplomacy. His sojourn in Japan was marked by the closest relations with the *Bakufu* and a corresponding hostility to the anti-*Bakufu* clan-coalition, while Choshu and Satsuma drew closer to Britain. This friendship may seem strange if we recall the Namamugi Affair of 1862, when the Englishman Richardson was murdered by Satsuma retainers, in retaliation for which the British bombarded Kagoshima the following year. It seems as if this practical object lesson demonstrating the superiority of European armaments had the unexpected effect of convincing the Satsuma men, most war-like and arrogant of all feudal Japan, that friendship not hostility should be shown to people who were able to teach them something valuable in their own special field.[84] The same magical effect of bombardment was manifested in the case of Choshu when Shimonoseki was shelled by an international squadron in 1863. Whatever the complexity of motive behind the *volte-face* executed by these leading anti-foreign clans, one

[83] For the early influence of Western political thought in Japan see Chapter III. note 101 and Chapter VI. note 38. *infra.*

[84] See Shoda Magoya, "Ishin no Taigyo to Sasshu Han" (The Great Task of Meiji Restoration and the Satsuma Clan), in *Meiji Ishin Shi Kenkyu,* pp. 621-2.

cannot but respect the realism and equanimity which this action attests.[85] Thus France placed its hopes on the *Bakufu*, and Britain, represented in the person of Sir Harry Parkes, favored the "outside" clans. It is often not realized by Western observers how far France was committed to the support of the *Bakufu*; for instance, she helped build and finance the Yokosuka Iron works and offered military aid and advice when the *Bakufu* attempted to subjugate Choshu in 1864 and again in the following year.[86] Some historians go so far as to say that the *Bakufu* concluded a secret treaty with France through its envoy Tokugawa Akitake, dispatched to France in 1867 ostensibly to represent the *Bakufu* at the opening ceremony of the International Exposition in Paris.[87] If the French entertained any hopes of obtaining concessions for their services to the *Bakufu* cause, these were completely dashed by the turn of events in 1867-8 when the *Bakufu* was overthrown. To his credit the last Shogun, Tokugawa Yoshinobu (or Keiki), did not sink to the level of an

[85] A paragraph from a contemporary record of the shelling of Kagoshima written by a Satsuma retainer illustrates this new friendship for Britain. "The friendship which had sprung out of the Namamugi Affair continued to grow; mutual trade flourished through Nagasaki and a college called Kaiseijo was established in Kagoshima in 1864, where the mysteries of occidental science and learning were taught." Quoted in Muto, *op. cit.*, p. 73. See also Griffis, *op. cit.*, p. 108.

It would hardly be natural to expect the firm, even harsh methods employed by the Great Powers (especially Britain, represented by Sir Harry Parkes, a man of great parts but not celebrated for his patience or restraint) not to have left a legacy of bitterness lasting into the Meiji period. Thus overtones of the Satsuma and Choshu anti-foreign feeling still lingered on after the Restoration. The reasons for this slow dying xenophobia, illustrated by various incidents, are advanced in an article by Professor Oka Yoshitake, "Ishin-go ni okeru Joiteki Fucho no Zanson" (Survivals of the Anti-Foreign Trend after the Meiji Restoration), Part 2, in *Kokka Gakkai Zassi* (The Journal of the Association of Political and Social Science), Volume LIII, Number 5, Tokyo, May 1939, pp. 652-88.

[86] Details of the Anglo-Satsuma alliance and French support of the *Bakufu* together with a document in which Léon Roches offered the *Bakufu* military advice are to be found in Watanabe Ikujiro, *Nihon Kinsei Gaiko Shi* (Diplomatic History of Modern Japan), Tokyo, 1938, pp. 6-18. The document in question is quoted on pp. 9-10.

For Léon Roches' services not only to the *Bakufu* but indirectly to Japan see Honjo Eijiro, "Léon Roches and the Administrative Reforms in the Closing Years of the Tokugawa Regime," *KUER*, Volume X, Number I (1935), pp. 35 *et seq.*

Further details on the aid which France gave the *Bakufu* and the bitter resentment which this aroused in Choshu can be found in the original Japanese of Takekoshi Yosaburo's *Nihon Keizai Shi*, 12 volumes—the three-volume English translation is very much abridged—Tokyo, 1935, Volume X, especially pp. 343-7.

[87] Watanabe, *op. cit.*, pp. 7-8.
Tsuchiya, *op. cit.*, p. 253.

agent of a foreign power in order to maintain a precarious and shadowy position as a puppet ruler.[88] Whatever the motive of Britain in the benevolent attitude she had shown to the victorious "outside" clans, she did not attempt to press her claims after the overthrow of the *Bakufu*. Doubtless her reward lay partly in the defeat of the colonial aims of Napoleon III and his envoy.

The peculiar complexity of the international situation from 1850 right through to the end of the American Civil War and the outbreak of the Franco-Prussian War, and the stalemate resulting from the Anglo-French intrigues in Japan as outlined above—but most important of all, the absorption of Britain in China—gave Japan a vitally necessary breathing-space in which to shake off the restricting fetters of feudalism which had caused the country to rot economically and to be exposed to the dangers of commercial and military domination from abroad. It is not too much to say that after allowing for the fortuitous balance of international forces (especially the Mexican fiasco as a retarding factor on French Far Eastern ambitions), it was the sprawling prostrate body of China which acted as a shield for Japan against the mercantile and colonial greed of the European Powers. In comparison to the attractions and profits of the Chinese market, Japan had very little to offer either as a market for foreign manufacture or as a granary of raw materials for Western industry. Furthermore it presented considerable difficulties to any attempt at conquest. Taking advantage of this valuable breathing space, the Meiji leaders were able to destroy the feudal government of intrigue and dissension, setting up in its place a national, centralized government and opening Japan to the invigorating air of Western science and invention; and finally, through the foresight of this brilliant group of statesmen, the new regime laid the foundations for a strong independent nation thereby making invasion from abroad too dangerous or too uncertain an undertaking. The modern observer of the Far East is apt to forget that in the middle of the 19th century Japan was as weak as contemporary Burma or Siam, facing the most powerful nations of the West without allies, without a fleet or a modern army, with no monies in its treasury, its industry still handicraft, its trade negligible, its poverty profound, its ruler, the *shogun*—as distinct from the sovereign—a figure no longer commanding respect or obedi-

[88] Kuroita, *op. cit.*, Volume III, p. 575.

ence; a country moreover torn by revolts, factionalism and civil war. This was the Japan which the Meiji Government inherited. Time was short, resources scanty, and it is a cause for amazement that its leaders accomplished so much rather than a cause for blame because they had to leave so much undone in the way of democratic and liberal reform. Judged by the standards of a liberal democrat, much was left undone, but the exigencies of the historical situation, that is to say, the fact that Japan had to create in a generation what other nations had spent centuries to accomplish—meant that Japan had not the time to afford such luxuries as liberal institutions. Japan skipped from feudalism into capitalism omitting the *laissez-faire* stage and its political counterpart, Victorian liberalism. Thus speed was a determining element in the *form* which modern Japanese government and society assumed. The *speed* with which Japan had simultaneously to establish a modern state, to build an up-to-date defense force in order to ward off the dangers of invasion (which the favorable balance of world forces and the barrier of China could not forever postpone), to create an industry on which to base this armed force, to fashion an educational system suitable to an industrial modernized nation, dictated that these important changes be accomplished by a group of autocratic bureaucrats rather than by the mass of the people working through democratic organs of representation. These military bureaucrats were so far in advance of the rest of their countrymen that they had to drag a complaining, half-awakened nation of merchants and peasants after them. The autocratic or paternalistic way seemed to the Meiji leaders the only possible method if Japan was not to sink into the ranks of a colonial country.

It would perhaps be an exaggeration to interpret the efforts of the Western powers to open up Japan as a deliberate attempt to take advantage of a weak and distracted nation in order to set up a colony. This possibility, always present in the case of wealthy but weak countries like China, never reached the stage of invasion in Tokugawa Japan, but the spectacle of continued stagnation and military weakness would in time have made this possibility a certainty. The role of foreign commerce in Japan was revolutionary. But the impact of Western commerce upon the feudal structure of Japan was the final thrust required for its overthrow—or, to change the figure of speech, it was the catalyst which hastened the social transformation from feudal to modern capitalist Japan. The foreign barbarians were the unwitting allies of the fanatic chauvinists whose swords were quick to cut down an official of the Tokugawa government, an advocate of foreign learning, or a hated barbarian. Thus a motley band of *samurai, daimyo, ronin,* merchants, and peasants—*samurai* who despised both merchants and foreigners, yet all unknowing fought for closer relations with both; *daimyo* who thought only of replacing Tokugawa domination with a regime under their own clan; *ronin* who attacked foreigners or who risked their lives to study Western languages and thought; merchants who financed the revolution; peasants who protested against tyranny of local officials or the increase in taxes and cared nothing for national politics—all this heterogeneous mass, unified by the magnetic power of the Throne, refulgent once more after centuries of obscurity, gathered together to overthrow the tottering *Bakufu* regime. At the head of the new Government was a young monarch, the Emperor Meiji, impressionable and a fine judge of character, who, unlike his conservative predecessor the fashion of a modern state which could command respect men of the day; like them he was anxious to remold Japan in the Emperor Komei, was surrounded by the most imaginative in the world.

CHAPTER III

THE RESTORATION

The overthrow of the *Bakufu* was accomplished through the union of anti-Tokugawa forces, led by the lower *samurai* and *ronin*, particularly of the great western clans, Satsuma, Choshu, Tosa and Hizen, together with a few of the *kuge*, backed by the money-bags of the merchant princes of Osaka and Kyoto. The leadership in this epoch-making change was in the hands of the lower *samurai*, who gradually superseded the upper ranks of *samurai* and feudal lords as the political spokesmen of the day. Hence the Restoration from a narrow political view represents not only a shift from *Bakufu* to Imperial centralized control, but a shift in the governmental center of gravity from upper to lower *samurai*. They supplied the ablest men of the day—Kido Takayoshi, Okubo Toshimichi, Saigo Takamori, Omura Masujiro, Ito Hirobumi, Inouye Kaoru, and a host of lesser men—while clan leaders like Shimazu Hisamitsu of Satsuma, Mori Motonori of Choshu, Yamanouchi Yodo of Tosa gradually dropped out of the picture. However, these *samurai* and *ronin* could not have overthrown the *Bakufu* only by the sharpness of their swords or the daring of their resolve. Less dramatic than the political and military exploits of the *samurai*, but more far-reaching in accomplishing both the overthrow of the *Bakufu* and the stabilization of the new regime, was the financial support of the great *chonin*, especially of Osaka, where it is said 70 per cent of Japan's wealth was concentrated. According to Professor Honjo, the decisive battles in the war for the Restoration, Toba, Fushimi, Edo and Aizu, were fought and won with funds supplied by the *chonin*.[1] The official record of the House of Mitsui says, "The loans required for the military operations of the Imperial forces were largely furnished by the House of Mitsui."[2]

[1] Honjo, *op. cit.*, p. 193.
[2] *House of Mitsui, A Record of Three Centuries*, Tokyo, 1937, p. 15. When the capital was moved from Kyoto to Tokyo, Mitsui Tokuaki (1837-94) accompanied the Emperor to Tokyo as the government treasurer.

49

What is even more important, the new regime, inheriting the bankruptcy of the *Bakufu,* could not have extricated itself from its financial plight and begun the gigantic task of reconstruction but for the contributions and loans (*goyokin*) of such great merchants as the Mitsui, Konoike, Iwasaki, Ono, and Shimada.[3] For instance, in the first few days of its existence, on December 26th, 1867, the new government through its *Kinkoku-suitosho* or Revenue Office issued an urgent plea to the Mitsui-*gumi* (Mitsui Company) asking for financial donations.[4] Thus Mitsui, one of the great merchant princes in the feudal period, banker to the Tokugawa and later to the Imperial House, became right from the beginning one of the financial pillars of the new government.[5] The Meiji Restoration then was the outcome of this coalition of merchant class with lower *samurai* who, as *yonin* or chamberlain in a *daimyo* household, were the actual leaders in clan affairs. This alliance of one section of the feudal ruling class with the merchants was the culmination of the tendency in feudal Japan for the leading merchants to seek political protection from the feudal authorities in return for financial favors. Thus the political settlement of the Meiji, and especially "the abolition of feudalism" in 1871, that turning point in Japanese history which has left an indelible mark on the structure of the modern Japanese state, can only be understood by an examination of this feudal-merchant alliance, which if we are to gain the proper perspective will take us back once more to the Tokugawa period.

Historical Background of the Feudal-Merchant Coalition

In studying Japanese social history, it becomes apparent that one must dismiss all preconceptions based on a "class-struggle"

[3] "The Importance of Goyokin or Forced Loans in the Meiji Restoration" (Chapter XII), Honjo, *op. cit.,* pp. 323-47.

[4] The text of this plea is to be found in Honjo, *op. cit.,* p. 325. This document is quoted in full and its significance commented upon in Kada Tetsuji, *Ishin Igo no Shakai Keizai Shiso Gairon* (An Outline of Social and Economic Thought Since the Restoration), Tokyo, 1934, pp. 10-11.

[5] From the year 1707 onwards the Mitsui were appointed court bankers, helping to meet the expenses of funerals, weddings, new buildings, etc. See the *House of Mitsui,* p. 7. In 1823 they issued silver notes for the Lord of Kii, in 1867 for the Shogunate; in 1868 and in 1871 they issued currency notes for the Meiji Government. *Ibid.,* pp. 7-8. This Japanese counterpart to the House of Fugger was able to maintain its financial supremacy throughout the Tokugawa period and to consolidate it in the Meiji period, and has been extending its sphere of operations since that time.

interpretation as sometimes applied to the French or English revolutions. In the case of these countries, the great merchant bourgeoisie is depicted as waging a political struggle against the feudal aristocracy, against the final stronghold of feudal power, Church and Crown, and eventually winning a clear-cut victory in France, and a partial victory in England. In Japan, however, for all the animosity which rankled in the heart of a bankrupt lord indebted to a purse-proud creditor in Osaka, the interests of the feudal ruling class and the big merchants became so closely intertwined that whatever hurt one necessarily injured the other. The haughty *daimyo* had to pocket his pride if he wished to remain solvent. Should a *daimyo* adopt extreme measures, refuse to honor his debts, or threaten his creditor in order to obtain their cancellation, he soon found that whenever he applied elsewhere for credit he met with a polite but firm refusal. The *chonin*, by such a display of solidarity, protected their interests as a whole.[6] Since the big merchants lived off the interest on loans to *daimyo* and *samurai*, the utter ruin of the latter would inevitably entail the ruin of the former.[7] Here again we must note the comparative weakness of the Japanese merchant who lacked such opportunities for the accumulation of capital through trade and plunder as were enjoyed by his counterpart in 16-17th century Europe. Tokugawa exclusion

[6] One method by which *chonin* used to ostracize financially any *daimyo* or *samurai* who behaved badly was to plant a paper flag in front of the recalcitrant debtor's house. Honjo, *op. cit.*, p. 261. One quotation will help to illustrate this relationship. "Samurai were fired with anger (at the indignity of being hard pressed by merchants), but they forebore the insolence of merchants *and were even ready to give up bushido in their attempt to court the goodwill of the commoners for the sake of their lord* (who had to borrow from the commoners)." *Ibid.*, p. 260 (Italics mine E.H.N.).

The basic importance of the peculiar relations between *daimyo* and *samurai* on the one hand and *chonin* (merchants) on the other is clearly established in an article by Horie Yasuzo, "An Outline of the Rise of Modern Capitalism in Japan," *KUER*, July 1930, Volume XI, Number 1, especially pp. 99-100.

[7] This statement needs qualifications inasmuch as the *chonin* profited more from the *financial embarrassment* of *samurai* and *daimyo* resulting from the need for cash in exchange for rice, than from their prosperity. But fundamentally their interests were parallel in that they both looked to the peasant as the provider of the rice tribute. Thus the *daimyo's* attempt to meet his growing debts and pecuniary needs by increasing exactions from the peasantry was made not only in his own interest, but also for the *chonin* who obsequiously awaited the payment of his debts. The Japanese economist Takahashi Kamekichi goes so far as to say that for the *chonin*, especially the big *chonin*, to have destroyed the feudal system would have been tantamount to committing suicide. Takahashi Kamekichi, "Keizai Shijo ni okeru Meiji Ishin" (The Meiji Restoration in Relation to Economic History), in *Meiji Ishin Shi Kenkyu*, p. 129.

and the poverty of a peasantry still living so close to a natural self-sufficient economy—money economy had of course begun to seep into the countryside, but only slowly—prevented the *chonin* from developing an internal market of any great extent. As already shown, the *samurai* of the castle-towns and the *daimyo*, who together with their retainers were compelled by the *sankin-kotai* system to spend half their time in Edo, became the chief customers of the *chonin*. Quite logically then, the *chonin* felt that their own prosperity was closely tied to that of the warrior and noble classes, their customers and debtors. For this reason the *chonin* never dreamed of making a frontal attack on feudalism as a system, although they were prepared to finance a *political* movement against the *Bakufu* in concert with rival feudal elements.[8]

Since investment in foreign trade or in the development of manufacture was blocked by Tokugawa policy, the merchants, especially the smaller ones, often invested money realized from trade or usury in land. One method referred to in the previous chapter was to reclaim waste-land under contract, where the usual practice was to recruit tenant-farmers by offering them tenancy (*ei-kosaku*) for a period over twenty years.[9] Another type of tenancy was *shichiji-kosaku*, tenancy of mortgaged land which was usually held in pawn by a money-lender.[10] There were of course other types of tenancy whereby the feudal prohibition of annexation of land was circumvented; but what is important for our purpose is the fact that out of the decay of pure feudal relations there was growing up a new class of landlord which was finding it profitable to maintain modified feudal relations in the sphere of agriculture and which had accordingly more in common with the feudal class of *daimyo* than with the peas-

[8] This whole question seems so important that I shall quote the words of a Japanese social historian in this connection. "The reason why this nascent class of *chonin* did not even think of overthrowing the *bushi* (warrior) class was that the latter were their customers; and if they ruined their customers, if only for a brief period, the shock to their own economic power would have been disastrous. For this reason the *samurai* were able to maintain their position right up to the Restoration, long after they had lost their real power in the country." Takigawa Masajiro, *Nihon Shakai Shi* (A Social History of Japan), Tokyo, 1935, pp. 246-7.

[9] Ono Takeo, *Ei-kosaku Ron* (Discussion of Permanent Tenancy), Tokyo, 1927, p. 87.

[10] *La Restauration de l'Ere de Meiji et sa Repercussion sur les Milieux agricoles japonais, 1867-1930*, by Ikemoto Kisao, Paris, 1931, pp. 279-80.

antry.[11] It is easy to believe that the feudal authorities felt repugnance at the growing economic power of this new landlord class; and we are given an indication of this in the following passage from a contemporary record, the *Kanno Wakumon*, which well illustrates both the extent of this new landlordism and the alarm it caused in official circles. "If we speak of the evil of the concentration (of land) we see the rich with their excessive wealth swallowing up the share of the poor; the rich become richer, while the poor become still poorer. Fertile lands are entirely swallowed up by the rich, and the many calamities of the people finally become the calamities of the state. . . . Who does not know that the population is decreasing and wasteland increasing? It appears that there are those who cannot pay their taxes; consequently the number of tax-collectors is reduced, and there is nothing for it but to levy *goyokin* (forced loans). The source of all this is the concentration (of land)."[12]

[11] The relation between this class of new landlord, "Shinjinushi," and the feudal lords is the subject of controversy among Japanese social historians. One school represented by Hattori Korefusa maintains that this new landlord class co-operated with the lord in exploiting the peasant, and hence was accepted as part of the ruling feudal hierarchy. Opposing this view Professor Tsuchiya Takao doubts the existence of a union between feudal lords and the new landlord class and he attempts to prove that this intrusion of merchant and usurious capital was a threat to their own feudal interests, and consequently the clan authorities sometimes confiscated the estates of these upstart landlords (for instance, in Tsushima, Tsu, Saga, and Kaga) or strictly prohibited land-grabbing (as in Obi and Sendai). Tsuchiya Takao, *Nihon Shihonshugi Shi Ronshu* (Collection of Essays on the History of Japanese Capitalism), Tokyo, 1937. See the chapter entitled "Shinjinushi Ron no Saikento" (A Further Criticism on the Subject of the New Landlord), pp. 3-26. The above reference to confiscation of landed estates and prohibition of accumulation of land come from p. 9. The crux of the controversy between Tsuchiya and Hattori is whether this new landlord class was purely capitalist in nature and hence regarded as inimical to feudal interests (Tsuchiya), or semi-feudal, that is sharing power with the ruling feudal lords (Hattori). If an amateur may be permitted an opinion in a field where experts disagree, it seems possible that Hattori overlooks the effect of usury in acting as a solvent on feudal relations and in this way hastening the decay and dissolution of feudalism. (See also Chap. II, notes 26 and 28, and note 13 to this chapter.)

This rise of a new landlord class during the close of the Tokugawa period is also described by Ono Takeo in *Ishin Noson Shakai Shiron* (An Historical Treatise on Agricultural Society at the Restoration), Tokyo, 1932, chapter entitled "Jinushi no Suii" (Transition of the Landlords), pp. 285-9. Also another work by the same author *Noson Shakai Shi Ronko* (Discussions on the History of Agricultural Society), Tokyo, 1935, chapter entitled "Kinsei Jinushi no Hattatsu" (Development of the Modern Landlord), pp. 113-35.

[12] This passage is quoted from Professor Tsuchiya's essay, "Shinjinushi Ron no Saikento," p. 9, and is found in the original in *Nihon Keizai Taiten*, Volume XXXII, pp. 219-20.

While making full allowance for the jealousy which an aristocratic feudal class would exhibit when confronted with the
necessity of sharing with traders and usurers the fruits of its
hitherto exclusive right to extract tribute from the peasantry, it
is natural that in the face of a peasantry attempting whether by
revolt or flight to cast off some of its burden, this same aristocratic class would stand shoulder to shoulder with the despised
but economically powerful merchant and usurer class. Looking
at this alliance of new landlords and feudal authorities from the
point of view of the peasantry, we see that the latter revolted
against the financial exactions both of the feudal authorities and
of the new landlord class.[13] As the Tokugawa period advanced,
these two groups, the old feudal rulers and new landlords, drew
closer together making possible, as we shall see, a most significant compromise on the land question after the Restoration.

Of significance for our analysis is the fact that the *daimyo*
themselves had to look to the great money-lenders of Osaka for
financial aid. It often happened that the exchequer of a clan
would fall into the hands of a wealthy *chonin* who advanced
money to the needy *daimyo* at a high rate of interest with the
latter's rice income as security. The finances of the Sendai clan,
for instance, were controlled by an Osaka merchant, Masuya
Heiemon, who was described by a writer of the period, Kaiho
Seiryo (1816), as "having taken unto himself the management
of the household finance of the Lord of Sendai."[14] The record
entitled *Chonin Kokenroku*, written at the end of the 17th century by Mitsui Takafusa, a scion of the great Mitsui family,
tells how a great number of *daimyo* became indebted to fifty
of the wealthiest merchants of Japan.[15] Notwithstanding the
inbred contempt which a warrior caste poured upon a money-
grubbing merchant class, the economic power of the latter
blunted the edge of this contempt, made the mocking laugh-

---

[13] Tenancy disputes which are the expression of peasant antagonism toward
this new landlordism were one of the most frequent forms of Tokugawa
peasant revolt. See Borton, *op. cit.*, pp. 30-3; Honjo, *op. cit.*, pp. 52-5, especially
an illuminating passage quoted from the *Minkan Seiyo, ibid.*, p. 53.

[14] *Ibid.*, p. 259. In the *Keizai-Roku* of Dazai Shundai (1680-1747) we read:
"Present-day *daimyo*, both big and small, bow before wealthy commoners in
order to borrow money from them and depend on the merchants of Edo, Kyoto,
etc., for their continued living." Quoted in Honjo, *op. cit.*, p. 257.

[15] Among the *daimyo* debtors listed in this record were the lords of Kaga,
Hiroshima, Satsuma, Sendai, Higo, Tottori, Nambu, Owari, Kii, Tsuyama,
Choshu, Tosa, Saga, Yonezawa, Fukuoka, *ibid.*, p. 285.

ter of the bankrupt *daimyo* sound strangely hollow, and even called forth respect and fear.[16] As Ogawa Kendo wrote in his *Chirizuka-dan*, "Although in form the *samurai* govern and the commoners obey, in reality it seems to be an age when the commoners hold sway."[17] The recognition of the economic power of the *chonin* was the first step in accepting the most prosperous merchants into the ruling caste through adoption into *samurai* families. The warrior, when reduced to desperate straits, was now glad to take cover from the storm of economic distress by entering a *chonin* family either through marriage or adoption.[18] Many socially ambitious *chonin*, too impatient to negotiate a normal adoption or marriage, found it possible to buy their way into the warrior class by purchasing nominal adoption from needy *hatamoto* or *samurai* at standardized rates.[19] The sale of *samurai* rank became so scandalous that Yoshimune (1677-1757) tried to prohibit it, but with no lasting success.[20] The social importance of the *chonin* can be estimated by a survey of the Genroku period (1688-1702) with its love of luxury, sophisticated novels, elaborate drama, its pictures and books—the *ukiyo-e* and *ukiyo-soshi* which describe *demi-mondaine* life in Kyoto and Edo and the habits of the common people.[21] This *chonin* culture had an irresistible attraction for the *samurai* so that for all the prating of Confucian moralists about the "corruption of this modern age and the need to return

[16] Gamo Kumpei (1768-1813), a champion of the Imperial cause and an advocate of internal reform and coastal defense, is reported to have said: "The anger of the wealthy merchants of Osaka strikes terror into the hearts of the daimyo." Honjo, *op. cit.*, p. 201. See also Sansom, *op. cit.*, p. 512.

[17] Honjo, *op. cit.*, p. 199.

[18] *Ibid.*, pp. 202-4.

[19] Inouye Saburoemon in 1853 reported on the rates for adoption of commoners into the *samurai* class. "Fifty *ryo* for every hundred *koku* of an annual revenue of rice for the adoption of a son, while a *samurai* is in his normal position; seventy *ryo* and a hundred *ryo* for the adoption of a son in urgency." *Ibid.*, p. 206. This statement indicates the futility of Yoshimune's ban on such adoption. See note 20 *infra*.

[20] Yoshimune prohibited the sale of *samurai* rank. Kuroita, *op. cit.*, Volume III, p. 482.

[21] Sir George Sansom (*op. cit.*, p. 465) describes Genroku culture as follows: "It may be taken for granted that by the year 1700 the townspeople had reached a high stage of affluence and culture; and, though the *samurai* might pretend that the *chonin* were people of base origin, disreputable occupation and low tastes, the *chonin* had very definite and very strict ideas of their own as to a good book, a good play, a good picture, and it should not be forgotten, as to good behavior."

to simpler manners," it molded their habits and tastes.[22] The literature of that period bears convincing witness to the fusion of the *samurai* and *chonin* class, particularly the upper layer of the *chonin*—a fusion, moreover, which permitted the *chonin* to take a leading part in clan politics and administration as well as in purely financial matters.[23] This gradual infiltration of *chonin* elements into key positions within the feudal hierarchy became very important toward the end of the *Bakufu* in assuring co-operation between the big merchants of Osaka and the leading anti-Tokugawa clans. Ito Hirobumi, for instance, one of the great Meiji statesmen, was descended from a family of plebeian origin which had achieved *samurai* rank in the Choshu clan. Other examples of this amalgamation of feudal rulers with merchant capitalists can easily be found.[24]

The Clan Monopoly System and Its Effects Upon Feudal-Merchant Relations

A less obvious but more deep-rooted economic attachment between *chonin* and *daimyo* was created by the system of clan monopoly in trade and manufacture. Each fief or *han* promoted the manufacture of staple products for export to other *han*, while at the same time, impelled by the underlying motive of mercantilism, the desire to accumulate specie, it tried its utmost to keep out the imports from the other *han*. The right of each clan to issue its own notes created such monetary chaos in the

[22] "This new class of *chonin* was not only at the top of the scale financially, but they were open-minded; they discovered new horizons of intellectual interest; they attempted to be the intellectual leaders of the nation, both in scholarship and the arts." Takigawa, *op. cit.*, p. 246.

[23] So affected were clan affairs by financial or mercenary considerations that the *Buke-Hatto* (a series of laws promulgated by the Tokugawa house regulating the military class) in a stipulation issued in 1710 says, "It is contemporary custom to regard the amount of property as more important than blood relationship in fixing one's heir." Honjo, *op. cit.*, p. 204.

[24] For instance, the account by Kobayashi Shojiro in his *Bakumatsu Shi* (History of the End of the Bakufu): "Some of those who purchased the positions of such low-grade *samurai* as *yoriki* or *kachi* rose to the position of *hatamoto*, through their own endeavours, especially towards the end of the Tokugawa regime. An example may be found in the case of Kusu-Sado-no-kami-Sukeaki, one of the very powerful *samurai* during the time when Mizuno-Tadakuni held the office of *roju;* Sado-no-kami was first in the province of Shinano, but through the purchase of the position of *samurai*, he rose to fame and power, eventually occupying the office of *kanjo-bugyo*. His son Suketoshi was also known as Sado-no-kami and was appointed to a high office in the city of Osaka." Honjo, *op. cit.*, pp. 205-6.

country that it seriously hampered the merchants in buying or selling transactions outside the clan.[25] To surmount this obstacle, the merchants had to seek the cooperation of the clan government which in almost all cases maintained in Osaka and other centers *kurayashiki* (warehouses) managed by the clan-agents, the *kurayakunin*, and their subordinates, the *kuramoto*, who disposed of clan produce at a commission. As the market gradually expanded along with increased agricultural productivity and better communications, local economy was swept into the main reaches of national economy, and Osaka became the chief entrepôt for the basic national produce, rice, as well as the clearing house for the monopoly products of clans. The agents who marketed these products were the *tonya*, the guild of wholesale merchants organized in the highly monopolistic *Tokumi-Donya*.[26] Such was the system through which merchants in Osaka and more especially the local merchants under clan control carried out their business.

Although each *han* issued its own notes, it could not exclude the *Bakufu* notes against which in fact its own were guaranteed. As most leading commodities were sold in Osaka in exchange for various notes, the Osaka market price became the standard for the local market. Each *han*, in its desire to accumulate specie by increasing exports and decreasing imports, had to force its way into the Osaka market in pursuit of this aim. Thus clan isolation, at least in economic matters, became impossible. The upshot of this was that feudal lords to whom local merchants looked for charters of trade monopoly had in turn to seek con-

[25] On the monetary confusion at the end of the Shogunate, see André Andréadès, *Les Finances de l'émpire japonais et leur évolution*, Paris, 1932, pp. 23-4.

[26] For Osaka as the center of Japanese trade in the late Tokugawa period, see the monograph by Kanno Wataro, *Osaka Keizaishi Kenkyu* (A Study in the Economic History of Osaka), Tokyo, 1935, especially Chapter One. The author quotes a contemporary record which says, "Of recent times, the gold and silver of the realm has increased, and since over half of it is in Osaka, that city is considered to be one of the greatest in wealth and affluence in the empire. The lords of east and west all come to Osaka to raise funds by borrowing money. The rice and cereals of the north, west and central provinces are all gathered together in Osaka, and furthermore red-headed people (Europeans) cross over from China with medicine, sugar, etc., which are first sold in Osaka, whence they are distributed for sale throughout the various provinces. For this reason much gold and silver is collected in Osaka." This quotation is taken from *Yume no Shiro*, written by Yamgata Banto, in 1802, and appears on page 10 of the study cited above.

nections with the big merchants and rice-brokers in the central market areas, especially in Osaka.[27] In this way the clan monopoly system and the national trade monopoly drove the merchant class (both local and in Osaka) and the *han* authorities into each other's arms.[28] That this embrace was not of choice, that it produced much discontent can easily be imagined. But necessity, arising from the manifold peculiarities of Tokugawa society, dictated it; despite strain and stress, temporary or local rupture, this union persisted until the Restoration, when after an interregnum of confusion and testing, it received the lasting seal of legality and social respectability.[29]

Introduction of Capitalism into the Clans

The *daimyo*, who as a class were becoming more hopelessly sunk in the morass of debt and whose revenues were steadily shrinking and expenditures rapidly mounting, found that one method of retrieving their financial position was to become monopoly traders, even small scale industrial entrepreneurs. Dazai Shundai (1680-1747) had noticed even in the middle of the 18th century that most of the *han* were in desperate financial straits, but that those which had adopted the monopoly system

[27] Takekoshi, *op. cit.*, Volume III, pp. 65, 86-92, 96.

[28] This summary of clan monopoly is based on a most lucid study of the subject by Professor Horie Yasuzo, *Waga Kuni Kinsei no Sembai Seido* (The Monopoly System in Our Country in Present Times), Tokyo, 1935. See especially pp. 7-15. In the Appendix (pp. 269-76) Professor Horie gives in tabular form the various fiefs, their rice-revenues, the staple commodity which each *han* sought to monopolize, the form of the monopoly, the market for the staple products and the duration of the monopoly.

[29] Professor Allen describes this tendency as follows: "Under the feudal regime banking in the modern sense scarcely existed. In those days each *daimyo's* territory was practically an independent economic unit; society was organized on a military rather than on a commercial basis, and industry was conducted on a small scale and for a limited market. Such conditions required no elaborate financial organization. From early times, however, there had existed certain merchant families who conducted banking operations of a kind, and money could be sent from one place to another through their branch establishments in the principal centre of population. The feudal lords used to appoint these merchants as their financial agents to collect their revenues, which were paid in rice, and to sell them in the few commercial centres, such as Osaka. . . . Many of the leading modern banks in Japan, such as the Mitsui and Konoike, are directly descended from those old merchant bankers. It is worth noticing, also, that at Osaka there was a form of guild, known as Zeni-za, which lent money to the *daimyo* on the security of their crops, and that the various clans kept representatives in the city to deal with the guild." G. C. Allen, *Modern Japan and its Problems*, New York, 1927, pp. 148-9.

were comparatively secure.[30] The monopoly system existed early in the Tokugawa period but it had been strengthened later. The *sambutsu-kaisho*, the official organ of monopoly and staple industry, was first created to encourage production, but later it became a convenient instrument by which to control the provincial or local market in a monopolistic manner.[31]

We can see the successful development of monopoly manufacture in the case of Satsuma and examples of it in the production and marketing by the clan in the wax monopoly of Tottori, Uwajima, and Yamaguchi, pottery in Yonezawa, iron in Matsue, paper in Tsuwano, Uwajima, Yamaguchi, Hamada, etc.[32] Most famous were the porcelain industry of Owari, the manufacture of crepe fabrics in Nakahama, paper in Tosa, lacquer and faience in Kaga, silk-weaving in Kozuke and Shimotsuke—all of which were developed under the patronage and for the profit of the clan lord.[33] Mining was undertaken by some feudal lords, notably in the south where, as early as the Kyoho era (1716-35), the Miike coal mine was opened and exploited to the profit of the Tachibana, *daimyo* of Chikuzen.[34] Thus under the political protection of feudal lords and through the financial support (but not control) of merchant capital there

---

[30] Honjo, Eijiro, "A Survey of Economic Thought in the Closing Days of the Tokugawa Period," in *KUER*, Volume XIII, Number 2 (October 1938), p. 26.

[31] Honjo, *Economic and Social History of Japan*, pp. 133-4, and Takekoshi, *op. cit.*, Volume II, pp. 141-7.

[32] The wax monopoly in Tottori, Uwajima and Yamaguchi is described in three separate chapters devoted to each of the three clans in Professor Horie's monograph: Tottori, pp. 165-74. Uwajima, pp. 175-89. Yamaguchi, pp. 190-216. For the other monopolies see the tables referred to above in note 28.

[33] Fukuda, *op. cit.*, p. 158. Other industries organized on the domestic system, such as silk-reeling, and spinning, were often begun under clan protection. See Tsuchiya, *Economic History of Japan*, p. 180. The author gives instances of the manufacture by the clan of iron, cannon, glass, etc., in the late Tokugawa period. *Ibid.*, p. 182. These of course were undertaken for military purposes rather than for profit, a motive which was strongly felt in the development of heavy industry in the early Meiji period.

[34] Professor Tsuchiya, describes this and many other examples of primitive mining carried out by Tokugawa and clan governments, *op. cit.*, p. 174.

Laurence Oliphant in his record *A Narrative of the Earl of Elgin's Mission to China and Japan in the Years 1857-1858-1859*, New York, 1860, mentions a coal mine at "Wakumoto" (p. 337) in Hizen which was very well worked. He was told by a Dutch resident that the mines of the Prince of Satsuma brought in an annual revenue of 200 chests of silver. He also reports the existence of glass factories and a cannon foundry where 800 workmen were employed. *Ibid.*, p. 338. For mining in Satsuma, a clan which had gone a considerable way toward industrial development for military purposes, see Takekoshi, *op. cit.*, Volume III, p. 293.

was emerging in the late Tokugawa period, still on a limited scale, a system of industrial production not of the handicraft or guild type, but rather capitalist.[35] One must not, however, exaggerate the extent to which feudal lords turned to trade monopoly and manufacture as a means of increasing revenue. Only in the clans where the authorities had assimilated the merchant or capitalist spirit and in the richest clans where the counsel of *chonin* advisers prevailed,[36] did this policy become dominant, whereas in most clans the lords sought more obvious methods of postponing financial ruin by commuting the rice tribute into money and at the same time increasing it by various pretenses,[37] and above all by "borrowing" from their own *samurai* by the simple method of cutting their stipends.[38] This had the effect of driving the peasantry to more stubborn revolt, of straining the loyalty of *samurai* to their lords—in a word, it helped to sap both the economic and political bases of feudalism.

[35] A summary of citations in Western material relevant to this question of the "feudal starting-point of Japanese capitalism" will be found in an article by K. A. Wittfogel, "The Foundations and Stages of Chinese Economic History," in *Zeitschrift fur Sozialforschung*, Paris, Volume IV, Part I, (January 1935), note 1, p. 58.

[36] Typical of advanced thinkers of the day was Honda Rimei (1744-1821), who wrote a treatise the *Seiiki Monogatari* (Tales of Western Lands), in which he showed that the power and wealth of Western nations depended fundamentally on foreign trade, shipping and above all manufacture, a view radically at variance with the current Confucian doctrines. He advised Japan to adopt a similar line of development as well as to expand its territories by the acquisition of the surrounding islands as far north as Alaska, and as far south as Malaya. This work appears in the *Nihon Keizai Taiten*, Volume 20, pp. 211-86.

The views of Sakuma Shozan (1811-64) also display a remarkable grasp of Western thought and history. He advised his clan (Matsushiro) and the Shogunate to adopt Western technique, especially for military purposes. He was imprisoned for his pains and finally assassinated by a xenophobic *ronin* in Kyoto. Among his disciples was the well-known patriot Yoshida Shoin. For the influence of Sakuma Shozan on Yoshida Shoin, see Horace E. Coleman's translation of Tokutomi Iichiro's "Life of Shoin Yoshida," in *TASJ*, Volume XLV, Part One, September 1917, especially pp. 149-55.

[37] For the tendency of the *daimyo* to relieve their own distress by increasing the tribute from the peasantry, see Takizawa, *op. cit.*, pp. 92-3.

[38] In order to cut down their expenses, the *daimyo* often withheld a portion of the rice stipends of their *samurai*. This was known as the *hanchi* system (literally "one-half the stipend"). Although regarded as a loan from their *samurai*, it was merely a euphemism for a reduction in stipend since it was never repaid. Dazai Shundai wrote in his *Keizairoku Shui:* "Of recent times, the *daimyo* both small and great are suffering because of their poverty. They are borrowing from *samurai* the sum amounts (sic) anywhere between one-tenth and six-tenths of the *samurai's* grant of rice." Honjo, *op. cit.*, p. 216. See also Chapter II, note 12.

To understand the Restoration, one must realize that the continual degradation of the warrior class, the conversion of loyal *samurai* into indigent embittered *ronin*, was a major factor in shifting the loyalty of this class from the clan or Shogunate to those forces working for the overthrow of the *Bakufu*.[39]

The Feudal-Merchant Alliance and the Meiji Restoration

We see then a twofold and mutually interrelated process accompanying the decay of feudal society: (1) the *chonin* by their economic power gain admission to the warrior class through adoption or purchase, and from that vantage point some of them become the most clear-sighted pilots who as *yonin* (or chamberlains) steer the anti-*Bakufu* forces through the troubled waters at the end of the Tokugawa period; and (2) the feudal rulers (both *Bakufu* and clan), always on the brink of bankruptcy and anxious to increase their income, chiefly for military purposes, adopt capitalist methods of production and to a considerable degree they become tinged with the capitalist outlook.[40] *Samurai* frequently sought shelter in *chonin* families and were among the first organizers of industry in post-Restoration Japan. Already, before the Restoration one notes a blurring and breaking down of the old class lines, the uneven fusion of one wing of the feudal ruling class, the anti-*Bakufu* leaders, with the more powerful merchants, and the absorption of *chonin* into high official positions as symbolized by their newly assumed badge of authority, the *samurai's* two swords. This was a portent even in Tokugawa times of that union of the "yen and the sword" which has characterized not only Meiji but contemporary Japan. This amalgamation of classes at the end of the *Bakufu* period clearly foreshadowed the breakdown of the rigid caste-hierarchy so elaborately erected by the Tokugawa administrators, yet it would be an exaggeration to say that this fusion was consciously anti-feudal. It was most assuredly anti-*Bakufu* and it represented a concerted political movement directed against the Tokugawa hegemony, but it probably did not imply any conscious desire to uproot the feudal system. On the contrary it was to a great extent a movement designed to shake off the dead hand of conservatism and lethargy so char-

[39] Fujii Jintaro, "Meiji Ishin to Samurai Kaikyu" (The Meiji Restoration and the Samurai Class) in *Meiji Ishin Shi Kenkyu*, p. 462.

[40] This intermingling of classes is well described by Sansom, *op. cit.*, pp. 512-13.

acteristic of later Tokugawa rule, and to accomplish the vitally necessary reforms without precipitating any cataclysmic changes in the social structure. Thus one might say that the Meiji Restoration does not connote so much a complete reversal of pre-Restoration policy in trade, industry and diplomacy as a thorough house-cleaning which permitted the more rapid and effective working-out of tendencies already visible in the closing decades of the Tokugawa era.[41] The rubbish cluttering up the house was the ornate but fusty feudal trappings of the Tokugawa caste system which had to be thrown away, and in the process of renovation the windows were thrown wide open, allowing the air of Western science and culture to blow in and revivify the atmosphere of age-old exclusion. The revolutionary aspect of the late *Bakufu* period was typified by the incessant *jacquerie* which might be said to have been the *motive* power behind the anti-feudal movement. True, it lacked consciousness of its goal but it so shook the foundations of the old structure that, combined with the threat from abroad and the political activity of lower *samurai* and *ronin*, these revolts of ever widening extent underlined the crying need for a new regime capable of winning the loyalty of all classes and of solving the chronic agrarian problem, if society was not to descend into worse decay and anarchy. The lower *samurai*—often *chonin* in the position of *samurai*—were the most conscious leaders in the movement to overthrow the *Bakufu*, and they, together with the younger *kuge*, were the most consistent champions of Restoration.

Origin of the Modern Bureaucrat in the Movement for Clan Reform: Example of Choshu

It now becomes germane to an analysis of the Meiji Restoration to illustrate the political aspect of this fusion of *chonin* with one section of the feudal ruling class in which the leadership of the lower *samurai* can be most clearly seen. Those *samurai* who were not blinded by caste-prejudice were often the most active spirits in steering clan policy toward mercantilism. This en-

[41] It is wrong to think of the spirit of pre-Restoration Japan as being wholly unsympathetic to the development of trade and industry. Under the force of circumstances, the *Bakufu* as well as clans adopted, often reluctantly, many reforms so that with the advice of foreigners like Léon Roches the *Bakufu* made considerable progress toward laying the foundation for military industries, shipping, foreign trade, etc. See Honjo, *op. cit.*, Chapter XI, "The New Economic Policy in the Closing Days of the Shogunate," pp. 292-322.

tailed a monopoly over trade with a view to the accumulation of specie in order to begin manufacturing, especially of armaments—in a word, to shift the economic basis of the daimiate to merchant capitalism.[42] The clan bureaucrats, whether of pure *samurai* or *chonin* origin, virtually took over clan affairs, and by serious economic rather than moral methods attempted to increase the depleted clan treasury and to raise money for the struggle against the *Bakufu*. The most advanced among this group went so far as to promote the adoption of Western military science, meeting of course the blind opposition of clan authorities steeped in the old, time-honored military usage. We can understand the unique position held by the bureaucracy and the military clique in modern Japan if we examine this trend in Choshu, the clan most adamant in its hostility to the *Bakufu* and one of the highest in the councils of the Meiji Government.

[42] This is clearly brought out in a lengthy quotation from the *Keizai Roku* of Dazai Shundai which appears in Honjo, *op. cit.*, pp. 132-3. It is sufficiently important to merit reproduction here in part. "All high *samurai* and *daimyo* nowadays use money in all transactions, just as merchants do, and so they are bent on possessing themselves of as much gold and silver as they can. They seem to regard the possession of money as the most essential need of the day. The shortest way to get money is to engage in commercial transactions. In some *han* it has been a long-established practice to find the wherewithal to pay the expenses of their *han* by means of such transactions, thereby making up for the smallness of their fiefs. The *daimyo* of Tsushima, for instance, is master of a small province, and his fief produces only a little over 20,000 *koku* of rice. He is, however, rich, and is even better-off than a lord with a fief of 200,000 *koku*, because he purchases Korean ginseng and other goods at low prices and sells them at high prices. The *daimyo* of Matsumae has a small fief of 7,000 *koku*, but through the sale of the products of his own fief and of articles produced in Ezo (Hokkaido), he is richer than a *daimyo* with say, a fief of 50,000 *koku*. Again, the *daimyo* of Tsuwano, despite his small fief of 40,000 *koku*, has wealth comparable to that of a lord of a fief producing 150,000 *koku* of rice, because much profit accrues to him from the manufacture and sale of pasteboard. The *daimyo* of Hamada follows the example set by the *daimyo* of Tsuwano and encourages the manufacture of pasteboard in his own fief. This makes him as rich as a lord with a fief of more than 100,000 *koku*, though his fief produces only 50,000 *koku* of rice. Satsuma is, of course, a big *han*, but its incomparable wealth is due to its monopolistic sale of goods imported from Ryukyu. Chinese goods also are imported into Satsuma through Ryukyu, and then sold widely in this country. Since the *daimyo* of Tsushima, Matsumae and Satsuma have a monopoly of the importation of foreign goods and sell them to other *daimyo*, they are much richer than other *daimyo* of similar dimensions. As for the *daimyo* of Tsuwano and Hamada, they are rich because of their sale of the products of their respective fiefs. The *daimyo* of Shingu has a fief of only 30,000 *koku*, but as he sells the land and marine products of Kumano, his wealth is to be compared with that of a lord of a fief of 100,000 *koku*."

Admirably situated in respect to trade and foreign inter-course, Choshu was one of the most "advanced" of the various anti-*Bakufu* clans in its policy and administration. The nominal leaders of the clan at the end of the *Bakufu*, were the two Mori, Motonori (1839-96) and his adoptive father Yoshichika (died 1871). They were driven into temporary retirement as expiation for the riotous turbulence of Choshu men in Kyoto which reached its climax in the bloody *émeute* in the summer of 1863. On this occasion, Choshu *ronin* and *samurai* had tried to seize the person of the Emperor to extricate him, as they would say, from the clutches of traitors, the Tokugawa politicians. Without going into the complexities of clan politics, suffice it to say that the clan was split into two factions—the party of the Vulgar View (*Zokuronto*) which was conservative, and the party of the Enlightened View (*Kaimeito*) which was radical. After first experiencing defeat, the latter party finally emerged victorious from this clan feud and annihilated the leaders of the conservative party. It then immediately acted as the *de facto* leader of the clan, determined its policy toward Shogunate and Court, and re-organized the military system against the punitive expedition which the Shogun was preparing to launch in 1864. Just prior to that however, Choshu, which had been the most vocal in its demand to expel the barbarian, suffered a severe bombardment at Shimonoseki from the combined fleets of England, France, Holland and America. This proved a turning-point in Choshu policy and even in Japanese history. The party in power, the party of the Enlightened View, quickly made its peace with the foreign powers toward which they bore no grudge for such a rough lesson in *realpolitik*, and now concentrated all their resources in opposing the *Bakufu*.[43]

At this critical juncture a young *samurai* came to the fore in clan affairs, Takasugi Shinsaku (1839-67), probably the out-

[43] Despite the presence of strong anti-foreign feeling in Choshu, the party in power (the Enlightened View Party) was represented by radical, younger *samurai* amongst whom were Ito Shunsuke (later Prince Ito Hirobumi) and Inouye Kaoru, who had both just returned from Europe and were staunch advocates of friendly relations with the Western nations. Henceforth, that is after the bombardment of Shimonoseki, the Choshu leaders dropped their program of expulsion of the foreigner and like Satsuma became attentive students of Western science and learning. See *supra*, Chap. II, note 85. For details on Choshu and its struggle against the *Bakufu*, see Takekoshi, *op. cit.*, Volume III, pp. 355-64, and also Watanabe Yosuke, "Ishin no Henkaku to Choshu Han" (The Revolution of the Restoration and the Choshu Clan), in *Meiji Ishin Shi Kenkyu*, pp. 625-83.

standing Japanese military genius of his day.[44] Although he died prematurely from consumption on the eve of the Restoration, those closely associated with him were among the great names of the Meiji era: Omura Masujiro (1869) and Hirozawa Sanetomi (1871), both ministers in the Meiji Government who were assassinated, Shinagawa Yajiro, Kido Takayoshi (1878), Ito Hirobumi, Inouye Kaoru, Yamada Akiyoshi and Yamagata Kyosuke (later Prince Yamagata Aritomo).

Takasugi brilliantly outmaneuvered the Shogun's forces, and in the campaigns of 1864-65, punctured what little remained of the *Bakufu's* prestige. His instrument in this was the *Kiheitai* (literally, shock or surprise troops), a band of volunteer soldiers recruited and trained by Takasugi and his lieutenants. The revolutionary element in this *Kiheitai* lay in the fact that many of the rank and file and lower officers were drawn from the nonmilitary classes, well-to-do peasants, small townsmen, and of course *ronin* of all shades. The historian La Mazelière writes of Takasugi and his *Kiheitai,* "Mais aussitôt une révolte éclate dans le Nagato, son chef est Takasugi Shinsaku—*du parti des idées élevées,* qui depuis quelques années a formé des troupes d'irréguliers avec des samurai, des rônin et même des gens du peuple; ces troupes, qui touchent une solde, sont habillées, armées et exercées à l'européenne." (Italics in original.)[45]

By routing the feudal levies of the Shogun, the *Kiheitai* first demonstrated that the *samurai* was not the only man of fighting caliber in Japan, a concept which cut at the root of preceding history and tradition. In this sense the *Kiheitai* was the precursor of general conscription enacted in 1873.[46] Secondly, the *Kiheitai*

[44] Many of these young Choshu *samurai* had been pupils of Yoshida Shoin (1831-60), who was in the tradition of Choshu radicalism stemming from Murata Seifu. This radicalism was mixed with a certain conservatism, often an intense chauvinism and expansionist outlook together with unusually advanced views on foreign intercourse, and economic and above all military reform. This same mixture of radical and conservative has survived in the spiritual descendants of Yoshida, particularly among the "younger officers" in the Japanese army, but today many other mutually conflicting elements have mingled with the original comparatively simple amalgam. For a study of Yoshida Shoin's life and thought, see Heinrich Dumoulin, "Yoshida Shoin (1830-1859). Ein Beitrag zum Verstandnis der Geistigen Quellen der Meijierneuerung," in *Monumenta Nipponica,* Tokyo, July 1938, Volume I, Number 2, pp. 58-85. See also Horace E. Coleman, *op. cit., TASJ* Volume XLV (September 1917) Part One, pp. 119-88.

[45] La Mazelière, *op. cit.,* Volume IV, p. 308.

[46] Omura Masujiro, one of the close associates of Takasugi, was the vice-minister of war in the Meiji Government and a strong champion of general conscription modeled on the French system. He was assassinated by an out-

gave scope to men of talent from the ranks of commoners, whether merchant or rich peasant, enlisting their loyalty and above all their financial support so necessary for the purchase of modern weapons.[47] The *Kiheitai* also produced the first example of the modern Japanese military bureaucrat. The effectiveness of the military reforms instituted by the Choshu *Kiheitai*, makes it easier to understand the function and history of the military bureaucracy in Japan. This Choshu plebeian army, composed of poor *samurai, ronin,* peasants and townsmen backed by good burgher gold, led by a young *samurai* from the lower strata of the warrior class, presents a microcosmic replica of the similar social intertwining and interrelationship which characterized government and society in Meiji Japan. In fact we might say that the struggle which went on within Choshu on the eve of the Restoration—the struggle of the Enlightened View Party against the Vulgar View Party—was a rehearsal *in parvis* of that nation-wide struggle fought out at the time of the Restoration, between the emergent forces of Westernization and modernization on the one hand and of conservatism and isolation on the other. The victory of the Enlightened View Party in Choshu was an earnest of the triumph of those same forces on the national stage in 1867-68 and the years following.[48]

raged *samurai* on account of his views. Yamagata Aritomo was a comrade-in-arms of both Takasugi and Omura who finally carried out the original plan of his two teachers. For the influence of Omura on Yamagata, see Ogawa Gotaro, *The Conscription System in Japan,* New York, 1921, pp. 7-8.

[47] Some merchants of considerable wealth were active supporters of the *Kiheitai,* and later when Choshu took a commanding position in the Meiji Government, they were drawn very closely into Government circles. There is an account of these relations in a book rather too journalistic to be accepted as authoritative but full of picturesque details and anecdotes: Shiravanagi Shuko, *Nihon Fugo Hassei Gaku* (A Study of the Origin of Japanese Plutocrats), Tokyo, 1931. The close relations of a certain merchant Nomura Michizo (also known by his trade name, Yamashiroya Wasuke) with Yamagata (later Prince Yamagata) is told on pp. 18-23. Another wealthy Osaka merchant, Fujita Danzaburo, whose father came from Choshu and set himself up in the *sake*-brewing business, entered Takasugi's private military school, became a close friend of his teacher and a generous financial supporter of his *Kiheitai. Ibid.,* pp. 23-7.

[48] Takasugi did not live to see the Restoration, but one of his closest associates Omura Masujiro (see *supra,* note 46) was vice-minister of war in the Meiji Government. Omura, who was fourteen or fifteen years older than Takasugi, studied under the Western scholar Obata Koan, who taught him Dutch. Although Omura was of higher rank in the clan than Takasugi, the younger *samurai* far outshone his senior both in popularity and intellectual brilliance. While resident in Edo, Takasugi mastered the science of artillery and grasped the full import of Western military theory, becoming an unrivaled strategist

The great clans which joined together for the overthrow of the *Bakufu* were precisely those which were marked by the greatest development in commerce and staple industries as organized under the clan monopoly system where Western capital was most deeply implanted. Of these clans, Satsuma, Choshu, Tosa and Hizen were most conspicuous for their economic strength based upon the new mercantilist policy described above. Staple industries included handicrafts, sugar-refining, tobacco and rice monopoly. In Satsuma there were a comparatively profitable mining industry, textile mills and trade monopoly.[49] In Tosa, where *ryogaeya* or money changers abounded, money economy had penetrated deeply into the feudal interstices;[50] moreover it was famous for its production of paper and for such diversified agrarian products as indigo, the wax tree (*rhus succedanea* or *haze*, Japanese) as well as for its rigid trade monopoly.[51] Choshu, situated astride the straits of Shimonoseki through which all marine transport between Korea, China and Osaka had to pass, was able by means of trade and transport monopoly to accumulate considerable wealth. The Saga clan in Hizen was the center of the Arita porcelain industry,[52] and also one of the pioneers in the manufacture of guns under Dutch instruction (1842) and also in the use of the reverberatory furnace (1850).[53]

---

on the field of batttle. The spectacular success of his *Kiheitai* made possible to a large extent the great prestige of Choshu in the new government, and hence it thrust upward to high office such men as Yamagata, Omura, Hirozawa, Inouye, Ito and Maebara Issei, see Shirayanagi, *op. cit.*, pp. 22-3.

Those interested in reading more about the *Kiheitai* might consult Takekoshi, *op. cit.*, Volume III, pp. 364-70; also Murdoch, *op. cit.*, Volume III, pp. 748-50; and *Kinse Shiriaku, A History of Japan From the First Visit of Commodore Perry in 1853, to the Capture of Hakodate*, by Shozan Yashi (pseudonym?), translated by Ernest Satow, Yokohama, 1873, pp. 58-60; J. H. Gubbins, *Progress of Japan 1853-1871*, Oxford 1911, pp. 161-5. A documentary study of the *Kiheitai* in four volumes, edited by the Nihon Shi Seki Kyokai has been compiled from the diaries and letters of prominent men in the *Kiheitai*. It is entitled *Kiheitai Nikki* (Kiheitai Diaries), Tokyo, 1918. The history of the origin of the *Kiheitai* is to be found in Volume I, Part Two, pp. 79 *et seq*.

[49] Satsuma also was a pioneer in shipbuilding. In 1815 the lord of Satsuma built secretly (because the *Bakufu* ban against the building of sea-going vessels was still enforced) two or three ships in foreign style. S. Mogi and H. Vere Redman, *The Problem of the Far East*, London, 1935, p. 44.

[50] R. B. Grinnan, "Feudal Land Tenure in Tosa," in *TASJ*, Volume XX, Part One, p. 247.

[51] See also, Horie Yasuzo, *Waga Kuni Kinsei no Sembai Seido*, pp. 24, 54 and 275.

[52] *Ibid.*, p. 11.

[53] Sansom sums up this trend of clan policy. "Deeply involved in debt, the

In these clans the *Kinno* or Loyalist party, the clearest expression of anti-*Bakufu* feeling, had been making steady headway until it finally dominated clan policy. This political trend was accompanied by a radical reform in clan organization, roughly on the model of Choshu, carried out by the younger *samurai* and clan *goyonin* (financial assistants and advisers) who became the clan bureaucrats, able, disinterested, domineering, devoted to the Imperial House and with a deep-dyed military psychology. This clan reform which signalized the defeat of the old clan leadership, traditionalist and parochial to the core, drawing together the other clans of a similar tendency, represented the first stage in the process of centralization which was one of the greatest accomplishments of the Meiji Government.

In the economic sphere these reforms, while rescuing the clan finances from bankruptcy, strengthened rather than weakened the monopoly system, and so placed heavier burdens on the peasantry and artisan class.[54] These clan reforms, so far from

---

daimyo looked round for means of making or saving money. A few encouraged industries in their fiefs, such as cotton-spinning and the production of special kinds of silk textiles, and gradually it became clear to many members of the military class that they could get out of the grip of the merchants only by following the merchants' example." *Op. cit.*, p. 512. So marked was this tendency toward clan monopoly that it was quite obvious to an observant foreign visitor. S. Wells Williams, one of the pioneer missionaries to China who accompanied Perry to Japan as an interpreter, wrote, "The proportion of rich men is probably small, and wealth generally belongs to the *class of noblemen, or monopolists, by whom the industry of the masses is either compelled or formed for their benefit.*" (Italics mine E.H.N.) Richard Hildreth, *Japan As It Was And Is*, Boston, 1855, note by S. W. Williams in the Appendix, "Products of Japan," p. 561.

On the military aspect of early industrialization Orchard writes: "At first the new industries attracted the great feudal lords because of their promise in strengthening the defenses of the country." John E. Orchard, *Japan's Economic Position*, New York, 1930, p. 92.

[54] We can deduce this fact from data given us showing the increase or decrease in the taxation by prefectures during the transitional period 1868-73, that is before the revision of the land tax as compared to after the revision. Since the method and rate of taxation was left virtually untouched during this transition period, it is safe to assume that wherever the tax was high in this period it would be correspondingly high in the last years of the Shogunate. The table in question gives the prefecture, the number of fiefs formerly contained in the prefecture, a general summary of tax conditions in these prefectures under the old system and the absolute increase or decrease in the land tax after tax revision. When we examine those prefectures in which the great "outside" clans were contained, we note the following: In Yamaguchi (six clans formerly comprising Choshu) the tax was very harsh under the old system and decreased by 118,970 yen after revision. In Kochi (formerly the territory of the Tosa clan) although the tax was more uniformly distributed, it was very heavy and decreased

tending to emancipate the peasantry and in this way create an internal market for manufactured goods, kept prices up by the monopoly system and by the practice of commuting rice tribute into money, as well as by levying fresh extortions which aggravated agrarian distress. Thus it is no mere coincidence that the peasant revolts were most bitter and prolonged in the domain of these rich anti-*Bakufu* clans where merchant capital was strong and where factory industry was beginning to take root on a limited scale.[55] To suppress such revolts the *daimyo* had to call on the *samurai* who, accordingly, for all their growing economic distress felt closer to the governing class than to the rebellious peasantry. This *samurai* psychology is apparent also in the turmoil of the early Meiji.[56] It would be wrong to believe that the increase in the fortunes of a few leading *daimyo* by reason of the shift from the earlier agrarian to a mercantile policy turned them either into modern entrepreneurs or their peasants into independent farmers. But this trend illustrates two remarkable phenomena: first, the stunting of the growth of a capitalist class and its consequent dependence on a section of the feudal ruling class, and second, the social transformation from a feudal to a capitalist economy carried out with the minimum of social change in agrarian relations. These clan reforms were accomplished, not through the momentum of popular revolt nor by the participation of the people's deputies in the clan govern-

---

by 390,879 yen. In Kagoshima (comprising seven Satsuma clans) although various conditions existed in the taxation system, the rate here also was high and the tax decreased by 283,093 yen. These comparisons become all the more striking when we learn from the same table that in most prefectures the Meiji land tax (including the local tax) after its revision in 1873 did not mean a decrease as compared to the old system which prevailed under the Tokugawa and lasted until 1873. The above data was taken from a table in Azuma Tosaku, *Meiji Zenki Nosei Shi no Sho-Mondai* (Various Problems in the History of Agrarian Policy in the First Half of the Meiji Era), Tokyo, 1936, pp. 57-60. For the whole problem of taxation after the Restoration, see Chapter V, *infra*.

[55] Peasant revolts and town riots *(uchi-kowashi)* aimed at the clan monopoly system are frequently referred to in studies on uprisings in the Tokugawa period. See Borton, *op. cit.*, pp. 25-6. Revolts broke out in Kyushu in 1811-12 against "officials who worked together with local merchants for mutual aggrandizement." *Ibid.*, p. 19. Among the most common demands made by revolting peasants was the abolition of the monopoly system. *Ibid.*, pp. 71-2, 75-6, 179 and *passim*.

[56] For many generations the peasant felt resentment against the *samurai* who were often called upon to chastise them. Thus the cry, "Down with the Samurai," was not uncommon in time of peasant revolt. See Sansom, *op. cit.*, p. 510, and Honjo, *op. cit.*, p. 51.

ment, but by a handful of military bureaucrats whose political inheritance was autocratic or paternalistic and whose insight taught them the need both for sweeping military and economic changes in the face of the foreign menace and for an absolutist centralized government as the only instrument able to undertake these tasks swiftly and decisively in the face of continued social unrest. The logic of their position dictated to them the creed of "a firm hand at the helm" or in other words an enlightened absolutism. Hence from the first, even during the transitional years, Japan experienced no liberal era. The only magnetic force capable of holding together the centrifugal atoms of feudalism was the Throne, and the only agents in a position to perform the gigantic task of reconstruction were the clan bureaucrats of the four great "outside" clans, men such as Kido Takayoshi (sometimes known as Katsura Kogoro), Inouye Kaoru, Maebara Issei and Hirozawa Saneomi, all of Choshu; Okubo Toshimichi, Saigo Takamori, Kuroda Kiyotaka and Terajima Munemori of Satsuma; Itagaki Taisuke, Goto Shojiro and Sasaki Takayuki of Tosa; Okuma Shigenobu, Eto Shimpei and Oki Takato of Hizen—together with a few *kuge*, notably Iwakura Tomomi and Sanjo Saneyoshi. Here we have returned to the postulate whence we set forth at the beginning of the chapter, that the political leadership in the Meiji revolution was in the hands of the lower *samurai* but that the economic propulsion behind it was the growing money power of the big merchants, such as the Mitsui, Sumitomo, Konoike, Ono and Yasuda.[57]

The Agrarian Movement in the Early Meiji Period (1868-1877)

But, the reader asks, where do the peasantry, the bulk of the population, fit into this picture? Although the Meiji Restoration represents an epoch-making change from feudalism into modern capitalism, it would be an historical misunderstanding to expect the appearance of a full-grown industrialized society on the morrow of this successful political revolution which first and foremost removed the chief obstacle to the sprouting of the seeds of capitalism already germinating within feudalism. In a country so tardily awakened from its isolation and feudal sluggishness,

[57] For this combination in the Meiji Restoration of *samurai* leadership and *chonin* financial support, see the article by Horie Yasuzo, "An Outline of the Rise of Modern Capitalism in Japan," in *KUER*, July 1930, Vol. XI, No. 1, pp. 99-101. See also Kada Tetsuji, *op. cit.*, pp. 10-12.

where nature had been niggardly in resources and where capital accumulation was meager, after the establishment of a centralized state a long transitional period was required for the initiation of industry under government auspices, for the setting up of military defenses based on this industry, for tariff revision and above all for the liquidation of such social problems as *samurai* unemployment and peasant discontent. This political revolution cleared away the feudal underbrush and laid the foundation for a modern industrial society. It was not, however, the victorious outcome of a social revolt of city *sans-culottes* and land-hungry peasants, as in France, but a settlement arrived at by one wing of the feudal class, the great *tozama* with their *samurai* and *goyonin* as spokesmen, and allied to the wealthiest city merchants. This is not to minimize the effect of peasant revolt in loosening the shackles of Tokugawa feudalism, but unlike France these revolts did not succeed in cutting through those bonds, and so the peasant was left relatively unaffected on the immediate morrow of the Restoration. The position of the various groups in the Restoration has been admirably summed up by a Japanese writer on agrarian conditions. "Vu les conditions de l'économie sociale des villages et des agriculteurs à l'époque précédant la révolution de Meiji, les guerriers de condition inférieure participèrent à la révolution en tant que réalisateurs puis à l'arrière les bourgeois y contribuèrent en tant que soutien financier, mais *les paysans qui formaient la majorité de la population entière se tenaient en dehors du domaine de la révolution*" (Italics in original).[58]

The peasantry, bewildered by the rapid succession of dramatic events leading up to the Restoration, enjoyed no substantial benefit from the new regime. In fact they behaved even more riotously than before, possibly because in some instances vague hopes had been raised by the overthrow of the old regime, hopes that their burden of tribute and debt would be lightened. Promises had been held out by the new Government that all state land (except temple lands) would be divided up among the peasants.[59] But they soon discovered that their burden of rice

---

[58] Ikemoto, *op. cit.*, p. 209.

[59] Such was the import of a decree issued by the *Dajokan* (Council of State) in 1868. The text of the decree is quoted by Owatari Junji, "Kokuyu Rin no Mondai" (The Problem of State Forests) in *Kaizo*, January 1936, second section, p. 52.

tribute was not to be lessened,[60] nor was there any question of their receiving allotments from state lands. Disappointed in their expectation of release from the yoke of the old regime, suspicious of the purposes and innovations of the new, the peasantry renewed those revolts which had been characteristic of the last decade. Agrarian revolts reached a crescendo of violence and frequency in the year 1873, after which they decreased until by 1877-8 they became small and inconsequential riots. Thus the year 1877 forms a convenient dividing line in analyzing the significance of peasant revolts in the early Meiji era. Professor Kokusho Iwao makes a striking comparison between the intensity of agrarian unrest in the early Meiji and in the Tokugawa period. He gives the number of revolts in the 265 years of Tokugawa rule as somewhat under 600, while the number for the first decade of the Meiji era (1868-78) is well over 190.[61] The most arresting feature of these early Meiji uprisings is that they were precipitated by two contradictory forces—one revolutionary, that is to say anti-feudal, aimed at the final eradication of feudal privilege over the land and those who worked it, and the other reactionary, in the sense that many of these risings arose from the instinctive opposition of a conservative-minded peasantry toward the innovations of the new government.[62]

[60] Kokusho Iwao, "Meiji Shonen Hyakusho Ikki" (Peasant Revolts at the Beginning of the Meiji Era) in *Meiji Ishin Keizai Shi Kenkyu* (A Study of the Economic History of the Meiji Restoration), edited by Honjo Eijiro, Tokyo, 1930, p. 717.

[61] Kokusho, *op. cit.*, p. 707.

[62] In a standard history of the Meiji period by Professors Fujii Jintaro and Moriya Hidesuke, *Meiji Jidai* (The Meiji Period) which forms the twelfth volume in the series *Sogo Nihon Shi Taikei* (A Synthesis of Japanese History) Tokyo, 1934, p. 524, it is categorically stated that none of these uprisings had any revolutionary significance, and by revolutionary is meant intended overthrow of government. Obviously it is futile to attempt to fathom the actual political motives of the participants except where these were recorded in the shape of demands or slogans. Probably we are safe in saying that these angry peasants visualized no political goal, but their efforts to reduce the feudal tribute, partially effective in realizing the tax reforms of 1873-7, were certainly one aspect of a people's revolt against feudal burdens. These revolts aiming at the overthrow of the government and the substitution in its place of one resembling in all but name the Tokugawa *Bakufu*, would by the same token be counter-revolutionary. The uprisings in La Vendée are the best European example of this type of revolt. But Professor Kokusho seems to differ from Professors Fujii and Moriya in his evaluation of these revolts when he states that certain of the *samurai* (not the peasants), finding themselves out of place in their new social environment, dreamt of a return to a society where the warrior class would be the élite. (Kokusho, *op. cit.*, pp. 712-3.) The efforts of

Indeed at first glance, many of these revolts appear to be merely demonstrations of resentment against the many aspects of modernization. Tumult and rioting only too often greeted decrees announcing the reform of the calendar, the abolition of the queue, the legalization of Christianity, the emancipation of the *Eta* (outcasts), vaccination, the establishment of government schools, conscription, the land survey, numbering of houses and the like. Peasants frequently were excited by wild rumors that the numbering of houses was a preliminary measure to the abduction of their wives and daughters; that the phrase "blood-taxes" in the conscription decree of 1873 was to be taken literally, so that in joining the army their blood would be drawn and shipped abroad to make dye for scarlet blankets; that the telephone and telegraph lines would be used to transmit the blood; that the children herded into the new schools would also have their blood extracted.[63] But if we look closer we notice that while these old wives' tales and naïve misunderstandings of the healthy attempt of the government to modernize the nation acted as the *spark* which ignited the uprisings, somehow the *flames* always spread to the quarter of the richest usurer, the land-grabbing village headman, the tyrannous official of the former feudal lord. When the new calendar was introduced, consequent indignation could easily arise from the not unjustifiable fear that money-lenders would take advantage of the reform to juggle accounts to their own advantage.[64] The feeling against the school system arose possibly because government schools might necessitate an increase in the local tax. Conscription meant less hands to help on the farm, and although it flattered the peasant to be told he was fit to bear arms, it also insulted the *samurai* who, as we have seen were often in a position to set themselves at the head of a peasant uprising

some *samurai* to harness the peasant revolt to serve their own ambitions, which if successful would have checked the progress of the new regime, might justly be termed counter-revolutionary or at least reactionary. We see a more positive indication of the *samurai* attempts to set themselves at the head of the peasant movement and thus to achieve their own purposes in Yoshikawa Hidezo, "Meiji Seifu no Shizoku Jusan" (Meiji Government's policy of Providing Employment for the *Samurai*) in *Meiji Ishin Keizai Shi Kenkyu*, p. 580.

See also Griffis, *op. cit.*, pp. 182-3.

[63] Kokusho, *op. cit.*, pp. 709-10, 719-20.

[64] For revolts provoked by the calendar reform, see Ikemoto, *op. cit.*, p. 223, and Fujii Jintaro, *Nihon Kempo Seitei Shi* (History of the Establishment of the Japanese Constitution), Tokyo, 1929, p. 180.

in order to direct its course against the government which dared to infringe upon their exclusive military prerogative. The objection to the land survey is even more obvious, when we learn that of its total expense of 40,000,000 yen, 35,000,000 yen was paid by the proprietors.[65] The reform whereby local lords yielded political power in their clans and were supplanted by governors appointed by the central government, was, like other reforms, received with mixed feelings by the peasantry. If the local lord had a reputation for benevolence, the peasants strenuously objected to his withdrawal in favor of an unknown appointee;[66] but in those fiefs where the lord was odious to the population, his final departure was a signal for an outburst of joy and relief and even for an assault upon his castle.[67] Other outbreaks such as those directed against the abolition of the outcast *Eta*, against toleration of Christianity and against vaccination, are clearly manifestations of prejudice which centuries of superstition, medieval bigotry and Buddhist indoctrination had burned into the consciousness of the people.[68]

According to Professor Kokusho, the fundamental underlying cause of peasant revolt in this period must be distinguished from the casual or accidental, both of which are so closely intermingled.[69] Even such a cursory survey of agrarian unrest before

[65] La Mazelière, *op. cit.*, Volume V, p. 118.

[66] Kokusho, *op. cit.*, p. 718 and p. 724, note 6.

[67] A vivid eye-witness account by W. E. Griffis, is quoted in Mazelière, *op. cit.*, Volume V, pp. 98-100. On the pretext of wishing to reinstate the prefectural governor in Bingo, the farmers began an uprising there in 1871, "wrecking the houses of the *shoya* (headman) and wealthy people." Borton, *op. cit.*, p. 127.

In Okayama prefecture the peasants demanded the re-instatement of the former prince (that is *daimyo*) and the reduction of taxes. Gregory Wilenkin, *The Political and Economic Organization of Modern Japan*, Tokyo, 1908, p. 14. It is significant of these peasant revolts that whatever the immediate cause for discontent, whether the removal of a benevolent lord, the emancipation of the *Eta*, the disestablishment of Buddhism, the law for general conscription, the establishment of government schools, always coupled with these widely varied complaints was the monotonous refrain "Reduce our taxes."

[68] Many priests of the more devout sects like Jodo and Shinshu were opposed to the anti-clerical policy of the new regime. The *samurai* of the Aizu clan (a Tokugawa clan which was one of the most harshly treated after the Restoration) spread the news among the peasants that the new government was strongly anti-Buddhist. Thus they made the question of Buddhism a major political issue, attempting in this way to rouse the countryside against the government for a restoration of the old regime. The greatest religious revolt broke out in Echizen in 1873; bad crops or some natural calamity were easily explained as a just punishment for the irreligious policy of the new government. Kokusho, *op. cit.*, pp. 721-2.

[69] Kokusho, *op. cit.*, p. 708.

1877 shows us of what a strange mixture of reaction and revolution, of superstition and shrewd estimate of class interest it was compounded. Though its weight was in the main thrown against the usurer, the rice-broker, the village headman or the harsh official representing the lord, in short against all personifications of feudal oppression, it had undeniably the other darker side, that feudal side which many *samurai*, chagrined at their failure to receive patronage or official position from the government and dreaming of a return to the old warrior-dominated society, were able to exploit in their own campaign against the government, thanks to their knowledge of peasant psychology.[70] What is common to the peasant movement of these ten years was a stubborn antagonism to rent, usury and exorbitant taxation. The basis for the intrusion of anti-feudal revolts from the pre-Restoration into the post-Restoration period can be summed up in this way; the burden of feudal dues and taxation, even after the surrender of the clan land-registers to the Government in 1869, was still maintained if not actually increased, with the result that peasant protest was intensified until the tax reduction in 1877, when the agrarian movement took another path.[71] As far as the peasant was concerned then, the Meiji Government, although holding out hopes of improvement, actually left him untouched for several years

[70] It must not be assumed that all *samurai* were just waiting to overthrow the new regime. The great majority and the most active of them were loyal adherents of the new government and did the best they could to secure positions for their less fortunate clansmen. Although Professor Kokusho tells us that the *samurai* tried consciously to direct the peasant movement against the government, he states that such a peasant-*samurai* alliance was bound to fail because the interests of these two classes did not run parallel to each other. Kokusho, *op. cit.*, pp. 712-3. Actually, a rebellion of disgruntled *samurai* against the government broke out in Saga in 1874, under Eto Shimpei, and in 1875 in Choshu under Maebara Issei, culminating in the great Satsuma Revolt of 1877 under Saigo Takamori, all of them purely reactionary movements and supported almost exclusively by *samurai*. Thus we see that the *samurai* were far from being a homogeneous class; some of them, relatively few in number, became the actual leaders in the new government, others went into trade and finance, where a few succeeded, others found employment as petty officials in the government apparatus, others became police constables, army officers, while a great number became part of the new professional class of teachers, lawyers, publicists, intellectuals. Still another large section of this class became impoverished farmers, artisans and even laborers.

[71] The question of the land tax will be treated below in Chapter V, and the agrarian movement after 1877 in Chapter VI. Reasons for the delay in the enforcement of the tax are given by G. H. Gubbins, *The Making of Modern Japan*, London, 1922, pp. 101-4.

after the Restoration. In fact we might say that whereas under feudalism peasant dues to the lord though high were traditional and thus subject to some flexibility (for in bad years a lord might not collect his full quota of the land revenue), in the early years of the Meiji the extremely high rate of exaction which existed under late feudalism—that is about 60 to 70 per cent of the produce—was legalized, standardized on a national scale, and strictly enforced regardless of all circumstances.[72] That the new government did not advance beyond legalizing and unifying the old feudal rice tribute is shown by the executive decree on taxation issued in the first year of its rule by the *Dajokan* (August 1868): "It is necessary to follow the old tribute laws of the various clans."[73] (This was true of course only in the transitional period lasting until 1873, when the land tax was revised.) Some social historians go so far as to say that after the Restoration the cultivator's net share of the produce actually decreased as compared to the Tokugawa period.[74] Attacks against usurers

[72] This legal enforcement of the high rate of feudal tribute gave rise to the fiercest peasant riots in the early Meiji era. One of the most striking examples of this is to be found in Takasaki, the fief of Lord Matsudaira (in modern Gumma prefecture). In this fief the extraordinary high rate of eight parts to the lord and two to the people prevailed for some twenty years before the Meiji Restoration. This rate was legalized and enforced by the Meiji Government as a result of which a series of peasant uprisings broke out in and around Takasaki in August 1869. Tsuchiya Takao and Ono Michiyo, *Meiji Shonen Nomin Sojo Roku* (Chronicle of Peasant Uprisings in the Early Years of the Meiji Era), Tokyo, 1931, pp. 42-3.

Similar movements for the reduction of feudal rice-tax broke out in Hyogo in November 1870 (*ibid.*, p. 309); Oita in 1871 (p. 576); Mie in the same year (p. 271); and one of the greatest of all such revolts, in Akita prefecture in 1872 (p. 93).

[73] Quoted in Hirano Yoshitaro, *Nihon Shihonshugi Shakai no Kiko* (The Mechanism of Japanese Capitalist Society), Tokyo, 1934, p. 274. See also Ono, *Ishin Noson Shakai Shiron*, pp. 25-30, especially p. 26.

[74] This is illustrated by the following table (Hirano, *op. cit.*, p. 28):

Share of Produce	Under the Tokugawa	At the Time of Tax Reform 1873	At the Time of Tax Reduction 1876
State...............	37 (37)	34	30
Landlord...........	28 (20)	34	38
Tenant.............	35 (43)	32	32
	100	100	100

Of course under the Tokugawa the share of the State means the feudal lords share. The author bases his estimate of the division during feudalism upon Ono Takeo's analysis, *Tokugawa Jidai no Noka Keizai* (The Economy of Agrarian Households in the Tokugawa Period), p. 83. The alternate figures in the first column in parentheses are based on a study of rent and tax-tribute in the late Tokugawa era covering six provinces, by Kobayashi Heizaemon, "Tokugawa

and rich merchants with landed interests were also another aspect of the same anti-feudal tendency, but this naked class animosity was often cloaked under a religious or superstitious garb.[75]

The wealthier anti-*Bakufu* clans were able to reorganize their economy and finances by tightening monopoly control and by introducing some small-scale industries. We have seen how these same clans had to squeeze the peasantry harder than before and how consequently agrarian unrest became more wide-spread in those clans than in the more backward clans which were closer to a "natural" economy.[76] Just as in the case of clan reforms, the Meiji Restoration was carried out *from above* by a body of keen-witted *samurai* who as an enlightened bureaucracy carried through these changes largely on the material foundation of the land tax as the following table shows.[77]

SOURCES OF JAPANESE GOVERNMENT REVENUE

(Five Year Standard)
in percentages

Year	Land Tax	Business Tax	Consumption (excise)	Inheritance Tax	Customs	Miscel- laneous	Total
1875–9...	80.5	3.1	7.9	—	4.3	4.2	100
1880–4...	65.6	4.4	21.8	—	4.4	3.8	100
1885–9...	69.4	3.8	20.2	0.7	5.2	1.4	100*

* Calculation not the author's.

Jidai ni okeru Nomin no Sozei to Kosaku-ryo Gaku" (Tax and Tenant Rent of the Peasants in the Tokugawa Period) in *Nogyo Keizai Kenkyu* (Study of Agrarian Economics), Volume IV, Number 3.

Another table illustrating the same division in the early Meiji while substantiating the proportions given in the above table further shows the gain made by the landlords in their share of agricultural produce on a national scale as the Meiji era advanced.

Share of Produce	1873 (Year of Land Tax Revision)	1874–6 Average	1877 (Year Afer Land Tax Reducion)	1878–83 Average
State..................	34%	13%	18%	10%
Landlords.............	34%	55%	50%	58%
Tenants..............	32%	32%	32%	32%

From Tsuchiya Takao and Okazaki Saburo, *Nihon Shihonshugi Hattatsu Shi Gaisetsu* (Outline History of the Development of Japanese Capitalism), Tokyo, 1937, p. 68.

[75] Thus in the religious riots in Fukui, 1873, the populace took advantage of the disturbed conditions to burn the records of the title deeds of the land and to sack the houses of usurers and wealthy merchants. Tsuchiya and Ono, *Meiji Shonen Sojo Roku*, p. 243. These are the same riots referred to in note 68 supra.

[76] See *supra*, note 55.

[77] Figures from *Meiji Taisho Noson Keizai no Hensen* (Changes in Agricultural Economy in the Meiji and Taisho Periods) compiled and edited by Takahashi Kamekichi, Yamada Hideyo and Nakahashi Motokane. Tokyo, 1926, p. 151.

Thus especially in the transitional years of the Meiji era the peasant was not only left unemancipated from some of the most typical restrictions of feudalism but also he had additionally to shoulder much of the expense of the new regime. When we realize that Japan was still largely an agricultural country and that the government treasury was so depleted that it depended very greatly on loans from wealthy merchants at the outset, it is quite natural to expect that this government would look to the land tax, now centralized and unified, for its chief source of revenue. Here again the hand of the past lay heavy on the present. The nature of Tokugawa rule with its fetters upon merchant capital had so restricted the accumulation of capital that the new regime was compelled to rely upon the agricultural class for its basic source of revenue in meeting the task of modernization. In contrast to this, accumulation was realized in other countries such as England and France through foreign trade and the returns yielded by the early colonies.[78] For this reason the agricultural classes of these countries were to a certain extent free from those burdens which they had to shoulder in Japan.[79] Aside from the pivotal question of the feudal tax, the village population was still crushed by usurious debts, and in the years before a modern police force was organized, they were still governed through the *gonin-gumi*, five-man groups which formed the basic administrative unit of the villages, an oppressive system of collective responsibility designed to facilitate policing, debt and tax collection and carried out under the eye

[78] Honda Rimei (or Toshiaki), one of the first Japanese thinkers in the Tokugawa period to realize the need for abandoning exclusion and engaging in foreign trade, saw with amazing clarity the cost of exclusion in terms of the pressure upon agriculture. Without any knowledge of Western political economy, this thinker advanced these very arguments so frequently repeated by European mercantilists. Honda wrote toward the end of the eighteenth century, "As Japan is a sea-girt country, it should be the first care of the Ruler to develop shipping and trade. Through sending her ships to all countries, Japan should import such goods as are useful at home, as well as gold, silver, and copper to replenish her resources. The country will grow weaker and weaker if it remains contented with the policy of supplying its needs exclusively with its own products. *The weaker the country, the heavier will become the burden on the farmers, with the natural result that the farming population will become increasingly impoverished* (author's italics). Quoted in Honjo Eijiro, "Japan's Overseas Trade in the Closing Days of the Tokugawa Shogunate." *KUER*, April 1939, Volume XIV. Number 2, p. 4. See also *infra*, Chapter IV, note 11.

[79] One of the clearest statements and statistical proofs of this fact is found in an article by Horie in *KUER* and already referred to. *Outline of the Rise of Modern Capitalism in Japan*, especially p. 105. Also see Tsuchiya and Okazaki, *op. cit.*, p. 49.

of the village headman.[80] Some of the more stringent measures appertaining to the relation of landlords to tenants under feudalism still persisted. Among the more conspicuous examples, for instance, were the *kama-dome, tachi-gekari, tori kata no kinshi*—various terms to designate the right of the landlord to prohibit a defaulting tenant from harvesting his crop which would be reaped and gleaned for the landlord by laborers hired by him for the occasion—and the *kosaku kabu no toriage*, the right of the landlord to terminate tenancy, a privilege opening the way to rack-renting.[81]

The peasantry accordingly had to bear a double burden in the first transitional period, the burden of the old system which the government could not yet afford to destroy, and the burden of the new centralized regime which was being built upon the ground floor of the old. It was the pressure of this double burden which called forth such vigorous peasant protest in the first years after the Restoration. With this in mind we can understand better the reason for the contradictory nature of these peasant revolts, and perhaps get some inkling of the peculiarity of the agrarian question in modern Japan. Although the reduction in the land tax in 1876 and the strengthening of the central state machinery calmed the storms of those early years, the fact that the Japanese peasant passed from the old to the new regime under the unique circumstances just described, without experiencing a "1789," has left an indelible mark upon him. The Janus head of the peasant movement is clearly disclosed in the years 1868-76, and though partially obscured since that time, still presents that same double aspect—the revolutionary and reactionary. When foreign journalists use that vague term "radical" to describe the "anti-capitalist" ideology of Japanese soldiers recruited from the countryside, the reader is not quite sure whether

[80] Ono Takeo, *Nihon Sonraku Shi Gairon* (Outline History of the Japanese Village Community), Tokyo, 1936, p. 373. The official designations were changes, but the function often remained the same. For instance, the old names for village headman, *shoya, nanushi, toshiyori*, were abolished in favor of *kocho* (chief magistrate or headman) and *fuku-kocho* (deputy magistrate or vice-head man) as established in May 1872. But as of old, these headmen continued to be the richest merchant, peasant or usurer in the neighborhood, using their official position not always for unselfish ends. See Iwasaki Uichi, *Working Forces in Japanese Politics* (1867-1920), New York, 1921, p. 101. For the change in village administration see W. W. McLaren, "Japanese Government Documents" (henceforth cited as *JGD*), *TASJ*, Volume XLII, Part One, 1914, p. 255. See also Ono, *Ishin Noson Shakai Shiron*, pp. 155-7.

[81] Hirano, *op. cit.*, p. 277.

this means a tendency toward the left or right. (Most writers mean, of course, toward the right, that is fascism.) With the perpetuation of small-scale agriculture, high rents and a landlordism which has not completely lost its feudal coloring, the Japanese peasant has never known the intoxication of such heady doctrines as liberty, equality, fraternity, and so is very susceptible to appeals characterized by paternalism and exclusive racism which would not move the French peasant so easily. But also, as compared to the small independent and essentially conservative French peasant who has had his 1789, the Japanese peasant with his land hunger and his impatience of high rents and rack-renting can display a violence when provoked which would startle his French counterpart. For a parallel one would have to look to the Spanish peasantry of the late 19th century where firings of churches and attacks on grandees' villas, expressive of a landless peasantry's hatred of absentee landlordism, were combined with a rather literal acceptance of Christian doctrines and a child-like belief in the protection of miracle-working saints.

The Lower Samurai as Leaders of the Meiji Restoration

Implicit throughout this and the preceding chapter has been the historical role of the lower *samurai* as the leaders in the Restoration, with the big merchants of Osaka and Kyoto as its financiers. It is now necessary to examine the complex nature of this *samurai* leadership.

We have seen how the lower retainers of the great anti-*Bakufu* clans took virtual control of the clan, reformed its government, changed the course of its economic policy and worked together with the *samurai* of other clans for the Restoration. After the Restoration, while not occupying the highest post in the new government they nevertheless controlled its policy as fully as when they were serving their *fainéant* lords in their clans as chamberlains or councilors. In this connection we can do no better than to quote the words of one of the shrewdest commentators on Meiji history. "As a result of this traditional duality of control it came about that when the Emperor was elevated to the position of a ruling sovereign he could not himself assume his proper role, nor was there in the immediate circle of his Court anyone with sufficient ability to act in his stead. The nominal heads of the clans were in no better plight in this respect. The majority of them were feeble in body as well as mind, while the vigorous minority were devoid of nearly every statesmanlike quality. Shimazu, the lord of Satsuma, was so sunk in conservatism and so overweening in his pride that nothing could be expected of him and the great Saigo, though nominally his henchman, was in reality the leader of the clan. Hence the only men qualified to guide the new government were the *samurai*, and it was these men who exercised the authority, though they did not fill the highest offices in the government."[82]

However, it would be a mistake to imagine that of the vast army of *samurai*, any more than a small fraction secured positions in the new government as officials or administrators. Out of a total population estimated at 34.3 million in 1870, the ordinary *samurai* or *sotsu* (a term later abolished when these lower class *samurai* became *heimin* or commoners and the remainder were absorbed into the *shizoku* or military class) numbered 408,823 households embracing 1,892,449 persons,[83] that is between 5 and 6 per cent of the total population. It might be interesting to compare the ratio between the feudal gentry and population of France at the time of the Revolution. The total number of those belonging to what the historian called *les privilégiés*, including nobility and clergy, was about 270,000; in the twenty-five to thirty thousand households in the nobility proper there were 140,000 persons, and in the clergy 130,000. This number (270,000) out of a total population of roughly 26 million[84] represented between 0.5 and 0.6 per cent of the total population, and be it noted that in this comparison we have included the French clergy among *les privilégiés* and excluded the Japanese Buddhist clergy. The Japanese clergy, excluding acolytes and nuns, numbered 16,092 Shinto priests and 75,563 Buddhist priests, in 1884.[85] These figures will help to give us a

[82] McLaren, Introduction, *JGD*, p. xxix.

[83] The population estimate based on the figures of Ryoichi Ishii, *Population Pressure and Economic Life in Japan*, London, 1937, p. 9. The figures as of January 1872, taken from the article "Jinko Shi" (History of Population) in the *Nihon Keizai Jiten*, p. 862, gives the population as 33,110,706. The figures for *samurai* households and total members of these households are taken from Fujii and Moriya, *Sogo Nihon Shi Taikei*, Volume XII, p. 348. The number of *daimyo* in the same year (1872) was 268.

[84] See Hippolyte Taine in *Les Origines de la France Contemporaine*, the first volume of which is *L'Ancien Régime*, sixth edition, Paris, 1878, p. 17. In note 1, pp. 529-30, Taine shows how he reached these estimates.

[85] Figures for Japanese clergy are taken from the *Résumé Statistique de l'Empire du Japon*, Number 2, Tokyo, 1888, p. 69.

slight indication of the strength of the declassed feudal elements in Meiji Japan as compared to revolutionary France.

The status of the *samurai* had become precarious at the close of the Tokugawa period, but now it was disastrous.[86] Although the *samurai* were a non-productive class under late feudalism, their swords had at least been at the service of their lords, but now the Restoration spelled their utter ruin as pure feudal retainers. Although the great leaders in the Restoration came largely from the lower *samurai*, yet this class, divorced as it was from any except small handicraft industry—to supplement the niggardly pittance paid them as stipends, *samurai* households commonly took to the hand manufacture of lacquer-ware, paper, twine, lanterns, and the like[87]—could not embody any new mode of production. The representative of the new mode of production which was gradually supplanting feudalism was, of course, the great *chonin* class. Its members were, however, so immature as industrial entrepreneurs and so inexperienced in statecraft that they had to rely on the state to develop industry and on the members of the former feudal class, especially the *samurai*, as administrators and statesmen.[88] Since the *samurai* were not anchored in the new society as were the merchants and peasants

[86] In 1869 the government relieved the *daimyo* of the obligation of supporting the *samurai* and maintained their stipend from the government revenue but at a reduced rate. La Mazelière, *op. cit.*, Volume V, pp. 124-5.

[87] Tsuchiya, *An Economic History of Japan*, p. 239.

[88] One evidence of their immaturity as compared for instance with the French merchant class at the time of the Revolution was the absence of even such a limited organ for political representation as the French *États-Généraux*, which played so vital a part in the early stages of the Revolution. In Japan there was lacking any such organ with the possible exception of the *Han Gimin* (people's assembly) in the Toba clan. Among the suggestions submitted to the Meiji Government at its establishment, the Toba clan urged the establishment of a national assembly modeled after its own administrative organization. This was composed of the *Han Giin* (clan assembly) with a *Gicho* (president of the assembly), *Fuku-cho* (vice-president) and the *Giin Kanji* (secretary of the assembly), and most interesting of all, it included a *Gimin* or people's assembly with a *Gimin-cho* (president). This assembly was probably a joint congress of *samurai* and popular representatives, the latter most likely drawn from the merchant and well-to-do landed classes. The Toba clan was one of the smallest, but its proximity to Kyoto, where the penetration of money economy was relatively deep, may have given the merchant class an exceptionally strong position there as compared to other clans. The above list of institutions in Toba comes from a study by Osatake Takeshi, "Gokajo no Goseimon fu Seitai Sho narabi ni Kanri Kosen" (The Five-Point Imperial Oath and Writings on the Political Organization together with the Public Election of Officials), in *Meiji Boshin* (Boshin being the year name for 1868 according to the sexagenary cycle), edited by Ichijima Kenkichi, Tokyo, 1928, p. 100.

(though in markedly different fashion), the great majority of them could not survive as an *independent and distinct* class. Yet they had to adapt themselves to the social change, and to trans form themselves into government officials, bureaucrats, petty traders, capitalists, professional soldiers, farmers, craftsmen, industrial workers, publicists, priests, teachers, anything in short but *samurai*. This problem of feudal warriors stranded in a modern society was one of major proportions, and it is small wonder that many *samurai*, deprived of all secure means of livelihood, longed for a return to the old order. Since the personnel in the Meiji Government was largely recruited from men of *samurai* origin, they made it one of their first responsibilities to find occupations for their less fortunate fellow clansmen as government officials, local administrators in prefectural and municipal governments, as petty bureaucrats, prison wardens, detectives, and policemen. Consequently the whole state apparatus was soaked through and through with *samurai* influence; to take but one example we might say without danger of exaggeration that the police force of modern Japan at its establishment was staffed almost entirely by former *samurai*. Itagaki Taisuke (later Count) had occasion to mention the position of the *samurai* in one of his many memorials: "In our country such people as the police for the most part are those who have come from the feudal classes."[89]

A smaller number, men like Shibusawa Eiichi, thanks to their own abilities and opportunities or to their adoption into *chonin* families became industrialists and financiers; some *samurai* from the favored anti-*Bakufu* clans were fortunate enough to be enlisted in the *Shimpeitai* or Imperial Army. The Government meanwhile did all it could with the limited means at its disposal to aid the *samurai*. Beginning in 1869, it adopted relief measures such as advancing small loans so that *samurai* could set up as modest traders or manufacturers, but above all it urged them to enter into new industries as foremen or managers or even workers, also to reclaim uncultivated land especially in

---

[89] Taken from the Memorials or Appeals to the Throne (*Josobun*) of Itagaki Taisuke appearing in *Meiji Bunka Zenshu* (Collection of Works on Meiji Culture), Yoshino Sakuzo, general editor, Tokyo, 1930, Volume III: "Meiji Seishi," (Meiji Political History), edited by Sashihara Yasuzo, p. 477. For a further account of ex-*samurai* in the gendarmerie and police force, see *infra*, Chapter IV, note 29.

Hokkaido, and so to become independent producers. These at
tempts met with indifferent success.[90]

The position of the *samurai* in the new society was by no
means uniform, and hence their influence was often conflicting
In the first place, many of this army of demobilized retainers
anticipated as the reward for their activity in the anti-*Bakufu*
struggles a greater opportunity to exercise their talents as war
riors and leaders, and the cry "promote men of talent" was
often on their lips. They saw the *samurai* of other clans rising
to high positions in government circles and they viewed with
dismay the rapid progress in modernization, the abolition of the
old-style dress, freedom of occupation, prohibition of sword
wearing, legal equality of all classes, universal conscription, all
measures aimed at the destruction of their caste privileges
These swiftly moving events together with their own economic
uncertainty aroused their furious resentment. Inheriting from
the repressive Tokugawa regime no traditions of concerted
political action but only the weapons of the vendetta and assas
sination, many of the more desperate *samurai* and *ronin* resorted
to terror as a means of government suasion.[91] Although not

---

[90] Yoshikawa, H., "Meiji Seifu no Shizoku Jusan," in *Meiji Keizai Shi Kenkyu*
pp. 580 *et seq*. Even after the return of the land registers in 1869, each clan
lord was left in control of his former territory, but now as a government
appointee. The *samurai* question, however, was not yet seriously tackled; (see
supra, note 86). The central Government began to pay more serious attention
to this question in 1871 with the abolition of clans and the establishment of
prefectures. The Government employed as many *samurai* as possible in prefectural
and municipal offices. Yoshikawa, *op. cit.*, p. 590. To facilitate, among other
things, the solution of this problem the Government promulgated the law of
freedom of occupation in December 1871, *ibid.*, p. 590. This law writes *finis*
to the *samurai* as a separate or privileged caste. Voluntary commutation of their
stipends came in the next year, *ibid.*, p. 592. A large scale project for settling
ex-*samurai* in Hokkaido was launched but enjoyed no lasting success, *ibid.*
p. 594. Most of these plans for settling *samurai* on the land ended in failure
for example, in Okayama prefecture of the 144 *samurai* engaged in land reclama
tion scarcely any remained to work on the land, *ibid.*, pp. 594-5. When com
pulsory commutation came in 1876, there were already a great many destitute
samurai, *ibid.*, p. 595. Both the inflation following the Satsuma Revolt of 1877
and their inexperience in trade and finance, together with the very small
capital which they received in exchange for their slender pensions left all but
a favored few in severely straitened circumstances. But the most enterprising
and those whose pensions had been larger succeeded in becoming pioneer
entrepreneurs in the field of spinning, weaving, tea and match manufacture
Ibid., pp. 624-5.

[91] Some of the most brilliant men of the early Meiji era fell victim to the
murderous attacks of these *samurai*. A few of the more prominent victims were
Omura Masujiro of *Kiheitai* fame, Vice-Minister of War in the Meiji Gov

always successful in achieving its immediate objective, terror became from the first a recognized though unwelcome instrument in the political life of Japan. It had been one of the only methods of protest under feudalism, and was carried over as such into this new society where the members of the government, largely former *samurai*, did not regard it as so alien to their tradition as to deserve repudiation and suppression.[92]

The Split Over a Korean Expedition

But it would be doing the great mass of the *samurai* a grave historical injustice to dismiss them all as fanatic terrorists. It must never be forgotten that the heaviest burdens of state were undertaken by the *samurai* of the four big clans—Sat-Cho-Do-Hi. Within the government circles however there was a growing division of opinion over the path along which Japan was to develop, whether by internal reconstruction and industrialization along Western lines or by immediate, forceful expansion. The most farsighted men in the government—Okubo, Kido, Iwakura—favored the former, and a large group made up of three distinct political shades favored the latter. This division was brought to a head over the agitation for a punitive expedition against Korea. The Hermit Nation, as it was deservedly called, had behaved churlishly toward a Japanese diplomatic mission in 1871, and the following year when the Under-Secretary for Foreign Affairs, Hanabusa Yoshichika sent some shipwrecked Koreans back by two Japanese warships, the Korean Government received its own nationals but insulted the Japanese who had brought them. Inflamed by such incidents, and coming out in support of the *Seikan Ron* (advocacy of a punitive expe-

ernment and assassinated by *samurai* of his own clan in 1869; the Councilor Yokoi Shonan killed in the same year because of his liberal views; Hirosawa Sanetomi, Sangi or Councilor of State, assassinated in February 1871. There was an attempt on Iwakura in 1874; and the great Okubo was murdered as an aftermath of the Satsuma Revolt in 1878. Some of these names are taken from a list of illustrious victims of *samurai* terror in the early Meiji period, given by Fujii Jintaro, *Meiji Ishin Shi Kowa* (Lectures on the History of the Meiji Restoration), Tokyo, 1929, pp. 269-70.

[92] An attentive observer of Meiji life and society, the French journalist Ludovic Naudeau, after summarizing the more important political assassinations in the first twenty years or so of the regime, describes the apotheosis of terror which not only exculpated but glorified such deeds. He cites the Rekishi Danwa Kai, a society which defended terror as a principle and sent letters to the survivors of such assaults asking whether they (the victims) were patriots. See Ludovic Naudeau, *Le Japon Moderne*, Paris, (no date), Chapter VIII, especially p. 89.

dition to Korea) various cliques agitated for an immediate invasion of Korea. The *Seikan Ron* was supported by three groups in opposition to the government: first the *samurai* opposition, representing the extreme right led by Saigo Takamori and including the future leader of liberalism, Itagaki Taisuke; second, a National Prestige Party personified in Soyejima Taneomi the Foreign Minister; and third, the Liberal Reformers led by Eto Shimpei, Oki Takato and Goto Shojiro on the left. The first group was the stoutest, most consistent champion of expansion. Its followers saw in such a campaign the means to solve such domestic problems as *samurai* discontent. After the abolition of the clans in 1871 and after voluntary commutation of pensions in 1873, the disintegration of the *samurai* class was of major concern to Saigo, the Bayard of that class. The rank and file of the army mobilized for the campaign against the *Bakufu* in 1867-8 and, led by Saigo, were the backbone of this party. The second party had its strength in the Foreign Office and its aims are self-explanatory. The position of the third group seems at first glance to be anomalous—a liberal party agitating for a war of expansion. Their motive seems to have been clouded by such considerations as a partisan opposition to a government in which Satsuma and Choshu were predominant and in which the clans of Tosa and Hizen, from which most of these liberal reformers came, were less generously represented. To them the expedition offered an opportunity of breaking up the consolidation of Satsuma-Choshu monopoly in government office, and for this reason alone, namely the attack on clan government, they were called liberal. (See section entitled Position of Liberal Opposition, *infra,* Chapter VI.) Without going into the details of this question, which was peacefully settled in 1873 by the Government leaders on their return from a mission to Europe and America, we may note in passing one or two points of historical interest which arise from this agitation for a Korean campaign. It shows, first of all, that the former *samurai* class as represented by Saigo, at any rate, wished to solve their own social problem by pressing the government into military action so that their experience as soldiers would once more restore to them their favored position as warrior leaders. Secondly the constitutionalism or liberalism of the third group was nothing more than a mask assumed to frighten the *Hanbatsu Seifu* (or "clan" government led by the autocratic Okubo) and to compel it to share the fruits of office with larger sections of the gentry or *samurai* class; in other words behind that mask was a face strangely resembling Saigo Takamori.[93] The only difference was that Saigo came from one of the favored clans and accordingly had no interest in breaking the clan monopoly or in extending social reforms; but had the less privileged clans held higher positions in the government as they desired, it is doubtful whether their motives would have differed greatly from Saigo's. This episode helps to bring out one of the great obstacles which stood in the way of the natural growth of political parties genuinely representing sectional interest in the country. Too often parties arose as mere temporary factions designed to embarrass or obstruct the government in the interests of a handful of disgruntled clan politicians. This characteristic has been eloquently described by the grand old man of Japanese parliamentarism, Ozaki Yukio. "Here in the Orient we have had the conception of a faction; but not of a public party. A political party is an association of people having for its exclusive object the discussion of public affairs of state and the enforcement of their views thereon. But when political parties are transplanted into the East, they at once partake of the nature of factions, pursuing private and personal interests instead of the interests of the State, as witnessed by the fact of their joining hands by turns with the clan cliques or using the construction of railways and ports . . . as means for extending party influence. Besides, the customs and usages of feudal times are so deeply impressed upon the minds of men here that even the idea of political parties, as soon as it enters the brains of our countrymen, germinates and grows according to feudal notions. Such being the case, political parties . . . are really affairs of personal connections and sentiments, the relations between the leaders and members of a party being similar to those which subsisted between a feudal lord and his liegemen."[94] Here again the speed with which the new Japan had to be constructed partially explains the strength of this feudal outlook in politics, and also, as a corol-

[93] The two-fronted attack upon the government from the extreme right (Satsuma Revolt) and, after its failure, from the left (the constitutional movement) has been described by O. Tanin and E. Yohan, *Militarism and Fascism in Japan*, New York, 1934, Chapter One, pp. 25-35. "At the same time large numbers of the samurai participated in the constitutional movement, which they also regarded as the method of bringing pressure to bear on the government for the purpose of rendering its foreign policy more active." *Ibid.*, p. 31.

[94] Ozaki Yukio, *The Voice of Japanese Democracy*, Yokohama, 1918, p. 93.

lary, it shows how the strong *samurai* influence in politics gave it a militarist and bureaucratic character.

Continued Opposition to the Government Ends in Civil War

Although the government of Okubo, Iwakura, Kido and Inouye successfully weathered the storm over the Korean question, they bowed before it when it appeared from the Formosan quarter. The reluctant permission given by the Government to the great Saigo's nephew Saigo Yorimichi to lead an expedition to Formosa in 1874 as a reprisal for the murder by Formosan aborigines of Ryukyu fishermen who were Japanese subjects, shows the very real strength of the *samurai* opposition. Foiled once over Korea, it was allowed to have its way in a less hazardous enterprise.[95] This expedition, however, did not succeed in quenching the flames of spreading *samurai* discontent. Saigo, after resigning as Minister of War in protest over the government's Korean policy, returned to his native Kagoshima, where like Achilles he sulked in his tent, deaf to all entreaties of the Government in Tokyo. But he did more than sulk, he organized "schools" (*Shi-gakko*) for Satsuma *samurai* to acquire proficiency in military science.[96] Following close on the settlement of the Korean question came the compulsory commutation of *samurai* pensions (August 15, 1876) which left many *samurai* without fixed income and added fuel to their resentment. So far from restraining the Satsuma *samurai*, their lord Shimazu Hisamitsu, the die-hard conservative critic of modernization, resigned from the Government and retired to Satsuma, where except for brief

[95] An incident of some significance arising from the Formosan expedition was the act of Saigo Yorimichi, leader of the expedition, in setting sail against the Government's instruction. In April 1874, the Governments of Great Britain and the United States protested to the Japanese Government over the proposed expedition. Terashima, who had replaced Soyejima as Foreign Minister, fearing the diplomatic consequences, sent Okubo to Nagasaki to stop the expedition. Saigo refused to yield but proposed that he take upon himself the full responsibility. After carrying out the expedition successfully—the well-known *fait accompli*—Saigo returned to Japan, but it was left to Okubo to go to China in order to settle the affair, a mission which he carried out with marked distinction and restraint. One notes at this early date the tendency of certain military leaders "to jump the gun." See R. H. Akagi, *Japan's Foreign Relations, 1542-1936*, Tokyo, 1936, pp. 71-2; also N. Ariga "Diplomacy" in A. Stead (ed.), *Japan by the Japanese, A Survey by Its Highest Authorities*, London, 1904, p. 168.

[96] For an account of the military schools of Saigo, see A. H. Mounsey, *The Satsuma Rebellion*, London, 1879, pp. 85-6, and La Mazelière, *op. cit.*, Volume V, pp. 155-6.

intervals he remained in seclusion for the remainder of his life. The first *samurai* rebellion broke out, not in Satsuma, but in Hizen in January 1874 under Eto Shimpei, followed by the outbreak of Maebara Issei in Choshu. Although both men and particularly the former were considered comparatively liberal, the slogans they fought under gave expression to the *samurai* desire for return to the old regime. These slogans were "War with Korea, Restoration of the *daimyo* and Expulsion of the Foreigner."[97] Finally the smoldering discontent broke out into serious rebellion in the great Satsuma uprising of 1877, which was suppressed after an epic and bloody struggle in which Saigo perished. It was the last in the series of threats to the new order, the last forceful attempt of the declassed *samurai* to drag Japan back to feudalism or at least to the rule of a federation of clans whereby each clan could be left to govern its own affairs.[98] Many older historians have interpreted the Restoration as nothing more than such a federation of Sat-Cho-Do-Hi clans supplanting the rule of the Tokugawa family.[99] The defeat of the Sat-

[97] Mounsey, *op. cit.*, p. 63.

[98] Westerners are often puzzled by the phenomenon of that fomenter of civil strife, Saigo, receiving honors in present-day Japan as the paragon of loyalty. While not doubting for a moment Saigo's devotion to the Imperial House, which, as he maintained, he was only trying to rescue from "unfaithful ministers," his policy can be interpreted partly as a crystallization of *samurai* discontent and partly as a typical feudal particularist movement in which loyalty to the clan clashed with loyalty to the central government. It is interesting to note that Shimazu of Satsuma always felt suspicion and hostility toward his retainer Okubo, the staunch advocate of centralized government, and regarded with benevolence the old fashioned loyalty of his other retainer, Saigo. What Saigo and his lord Shimazu expected from the Restoration was probably a federation of clans under the aegis of the Emperor with Satsuma as the center of gravity. Federalism was a very strong trend in the early days of the Meiji Restoration, and appears most clearly in a letter of a certain Nomura written in French to the Comte de Montblanc, dated November 10, 1867. "Je vous écris cette lettre pour être representé parmi les premiers que vous verrez accourir en vous criant: Victoire! Les préparatifs ont été longs, mais le *program* a été fidèlement suivi sur la base légale, révélée dans vos écrits et soutenu par vos actes. La confédération japonaise sous la présidence le (sic) Mikado est aujourd'hui dégagée de toute illusion. Sa Majesté le Mikado envoquera à Kyoto tous les daimyo japonais qui formeront un chambre souveraine. Cette chambre aura à prononcer sur toutes les questions d'intérêt général. La question des étrangers est acceptée au nom du Mikado sur les bases existant déjà dans les états du Kwanto . . . Sa Majesté le Mikado fera connaître les résolutions de la chambre fédérale par des décrets et des proclamations." This letter appears in Maurice Courant, *Les Clans Japonais sous les Tokugawa*. Conferences faites au Musée Guimet, Vol. 15, Paris, 1903-5, Part One, pp. 76-7.

[99] A. M. Pooley in *Japan at the Cross Roads*, London, 1917, p. 38, quotes several statements from Japanese sources to illustrate this thesis. "The *Bakufu*

suma rebels, however, proved that any such conception or ambition could no longer be reasonably entertained.

If these revolts are reactionary in character, aimed at the restoration of a modified feudalism, the reader may ask where the democratic or left opposition to the Government appears, if at all. The first phase of such democratic or anti-feudal opposition, though still inarticulate, was embodied in the revolts of the peasants and the city poor, as described above, which represented an attempt from below to extend more fully the benefits of the new regime. The feudal character of the *samurai* opposition is clearly indicated by the fact that, except where they were able to utilize peasant discontent for their own ends as in the revolts between 1874-7, they helped the government in suppressing peasant uprisings.[100] This is not at all surprising in view of the *samurai's* position in feudal society and his position in modern society as bureaucrat, policeman, or professional soldier. In both the old and new society he looked on the peasant from the point of view of the ruler, not of the ruled. After the decrease in the land-tax (1876), the increased strength of the state machinery, and the consequent falling off in peasant revolts, the liberal-democratic movement assumed an organized political form in the rise of the *Jiyuto* or Liberal Party in 1881.[101] But

was succeeded by a clan government." (Baron Shibusawa) "Mikado worship was established to further the political ambitions of the clan chiefs who were debarred from exercise of authority by the despotism of the Shogunate." (Count Soejima) "The Tokugawas were exchanged for Saigo, Kido, and Okubo. It was only a change in name." (Haga)

A Japanese writer has described the post-Meiji settlement in a similar vein. "When the Japanese feudal system was destroyed . . . there was set up in its stead, a bureaucracy that retained the spirit of the Shogunate. It is not too much to say that the political and social institutions of the new Japan were only another expression of the Tokugawa system." Quoted in Allen, *op. cit.*, p. 64.

[100] W. W. McLaren, *A Political History of Japan During the Meiji Era, 1867-1912.* New York, 1916, p. 96.

[101] In making a judgment as to who or what group was the standard bearer of democracy in Japan, one must examine the objectives and roles of various classes and groups before, during and after the Restoration. One of the ablest Japanese constitutional historians believes that a nascent democratic movement or trend can be discerned in the growing desire of the leading *daimyo* during the late Tokugawa period to win for themselves some sort of deliberative assembly to help shape national policies. He further states that the partial victory of this ambition, realized in 1853-4 when the *Bakufu* consulted the *daimyo* on the question of foreign intercourse, can be interpreted as a victory of the democratic idea over Tokugawa feudalism. See Osatake Takeshi, *Ishin Zengo ni okeru Rikken Shiso* (Constitutional Thought at the Time of the Restoration), Tokyo, 1929, Vol. I, pp. 14-17. (The author is indebted for this and another reference [*infra,*

we anticipate too much and we must return finally to the position and attitude of the former feudal lords in the new regime.

Anti-Feudal Policy of the Meiji Government: Its Attitude Toward the Feudal Daimyo and Landlord Class

The alternatives facing the new government were either to maintain feudalism, shifting the hegemony from the Tokugawa to some other clan or coalition of clans[102] or to establish a centralized state machinery embracing all parts of the country. Both the *foundation* upon which the new government rested, the merchant capitalist class, and its *leadership* supplied by the lower *samurai* and the former clan bureaucrats whose ambitions had been choked and whose loyalties dulled by the narrow confines of the clan horizon, were factors which guaranteed that the government would tread the second road leading toward the modern nation-state. Right from the start the new regime resolutely set about uprooting the old concepts of government. One must not be deceived by the outward form of Meiji reform but look beneath it to discover the content of its acts. For instance, even the attempt to model the constitution upon the Taika Reform (646 A.D.)—a pre-feudal code in the spirit of T'ang politi-

---

note 104] to Osatake's work just cited to a citation in Yanaga Chitoshi, *Theory of the Japanese State,* Doctoral Thesis, University of California, p. 251.) This view would seem hard to reconcile with the historical role of the *daimyo* at the time of the Restoration. With the usual warning against historical parallels, a comparison might be made to the motivation and outcome of Magna Carta. Most authorities are now agreed that the Barons' opposition to King John culminating in the Great Charter of 1215 was not a victory for representative or constitutional government in the accepted sense of these terms, but rather the victory of the feudal lords, of centrifugal forces, over 'the centralizing tendency of the crown. Its most famous clause, guaranteeing trial of every *freeman* by his peers under the laws of the land, excluded of course the great majority of the population at that time.

Similarly in Japan, the *Bakufu's* concession to the *daimyo* in 1853-4 indicates the patent weakness of its foreign policy and the loss of nerve by the Shogunate, and it also shows that the participation of the *daimyo* in government councils is a symptom of the fact that the Restoration would be carried through—under the Imperial flag it is true, but also by the alliance of the greater *tozama* (outside lords), some of whom at least were not adverse to maintaining a government under a coalition of clans in place of the Tokugawa monopoly. The early democratic movement in Japan, under whatever political name it went, is usually recognized as the *Minken-undo,* "People's Right Movement," which emerged shortly after the Restoration and became an organized political force about 1880 with a demand for a curb on clan government and for the granting of a representative assembly. This question is discussed again below in Chapter VI, note 1 and *passim.*

102 *Supra,* notes 98 and 99.

cal economy—was a groping after some anti-feudal philosophy of the state.[103] This is not at all surprising when one takes into consideration the fact that the political theories of countries other than China had as yet made very little impression on Japan,[104] or if one recalls "the Cult of Antiquity" in the French Revolution, when the most ardent Republicans and Jacobins could think of no better model for their ideals than those inspired by the heroes of the Roman Republic. In this sense the fundamental document of the Meiji Restoration, the Imperial Oath of March 14, 1868,[105] was an expression, in terms familiar and acceptable to all, of the anti-feudal aspirations of the masses of the people throughout the land, envisaging as it did the need for consulting public opinion and the administration of affairs for the benefit of the *nation* and the encouragement of foreign knowledge. All these clauses, particularly the first, aroused the highest expectations of a population long grown weary of feudal oppression, factional strife and obscurantism. The slogans under which the war of the Restoration was fought and won demonstrated the enmity of the leaders of the "outside" clans toward the Tokugawa rule, which some of them at least hoped to replace by government under their own aegis. But social forces were unleashed which the *daimyo* could not stem; these forces were steered by the lower *samurai* and *kuge* who had brought about the political revolution and who struggled to prevent the

[103] H. S. Quigley, *Japanese Government and Politics*, New York and London, 1932, p. 4.

[104] This is not the place to discuss the early influence of Western political thought in Japan, but a short and by no means exhaustive list of some of the first political works translated into Japanese might be of interest to the reader. Among pre-Restoration works was a translation of a Dutch work on the English Parliament by Aoji Rinso in 1927 (Osatake Takeshi, *Ishin Zengo ni okeru Rikken Shiso*, Vol. 1, p. 18). A Chinese version of Wheaton's *International Law* was introduced to Japan by Townsend Harris and was translated into Japanese and published in Kyoto in 1865. *Ibid.*, pp. 40-1. In 1868 several books on Western legal institutions were published, based on the lectures of Professor Vissering of Leyden which one of the first Japanese to study abroad had attended. (*Meiji Bunka Zenshu, op. cit.*, Vol. VIII, *Kaidai* or Bibliography, p. 2.) One of the first translations of a really important Western treatise was J. S. Mill's *Essay on Liberty* which appeared in 1871. The following year a partial translation of the *Allgemeine Staatslehre* by Bluntschli was published. Part of de Tocqueville's *Democracy in America* was translated in 1873 and Montesquieu in 1875. By 1877 a great spate of foreign political treatises appeared in Japanese, including works by Rousseau, Montesquieu, de Tocqueville, Mill, Spencer, von Mohl and Bluntschli, *Ibid.*, Vol. VIII, p. 589. For further data on this subject see *infra*, Chapter VI, note 38.

[105] This historic document appears in Quigley, *op. cit.*, Appendix I, p. 333.

feudal lords (whose economic and social roots differed not in the least from those of the Tokugawa regime) from re-establishing a feudal regime under different auspices. The *samurai-kuge* leadership in the *Hanseki-Hokan* (return of the land registers) in 1869 was the first move in driving a wedge between the *daimyo* and political power. This was rather a flank than a frontal attack since the lords were left in control of their clans except with regard to matters trenching upon coinage and foreign affairs. The behavior of Shimazu and other great lords leaves no doubt that the *daimyo* were taking alarm.[106] Before making a decisive move, the Government chiefs visited the most important *daimyo*. Iwakura and Okubo went to Kagoshima with a sword from the Emperor, a gift for the shrine of the late lord of Satsuma, while Kido went to Yamaguchi (Choshu), and later Okubo and Kido visited Kochi (Tosa).[107] More important, the Central Government had built up a small but loyal standing army recruited chiefly from the most dependable troops, many from Satsuma. The *coup de grace* was dealt the political aspirations of the feudal lords with the abolition of the clans in 1871.[108]

The question at once arises, why did not the feudal lords resist this infringement of their power, just as the Shogunate had fought against utter annihilation in 1867 and 1868? The answer is difficult but necessary for understanding the character of Meiji rule. It is generally asserted that the feudal lords surrendered their prerogatives voluntarily as a gesture of loyalty. This may have been true of some, but by far the greater proportion of the feudal lords made no such move. As for those who did make the offer, many of them were under the influence of the abler clan bureaucrats like Kido of Choshu and Itagaki of Tosa, who could in all honesty point out to their clan chiefs the advantages of such a move both from narrow personal interests (prestige, honors and the fruits of office) and from the broader view of national welfare. But whatever their hopes and ambitions, even the most stubborn champions of feudal separatism and privilege could not but see the handwriting on the wall, that it was impossible to maintain strongholds of local power free from the centralized government. Their most imaginative

[106] Mounsey gives a general summary of the very reactionary ideas of this great feudal lord. *op. cit.*, p. 100.

[107] *Meiji Seishi*, Volume II of *Meiji Bunka Zenshu*, p. 92.

[108] McLaren, *JGD*, pp. 32-3.

and idealistic retainers were sympathetic to the Imperial Government and wholeheartedly supported its policy, while those *samurai* who were discontented were not a sufficient force to fight against the central government troops which were the pick of the old clan armies. Furthermore, the government prepared the ground for this move by embarking on a campaign to rally public opinion in support of its move, and met with wide re sponse.[109] Had the lords revolted in the face of these unfavorable circumstances, the government undoubtedly could have mo bilized an army recruited from all classes which would fight valiantly—as they did against Satsuma *samurai* in 1877—to thwart the schemes of any rebellious lords. But most decisive was the guarantee of the continuation of the economic powei of the great feudatories in the form of government bonds granted them in exchange for their former revenues. The dif ference in the fate of the French nobility in the French Revolu tion and the Japanese feudal aristocracy from 1868 to 1873 is striking. The former suffered confiscation of their estates (with out compensation) which were auctioned off to become the property of landlords and peasant proprietors. Many of the aris tocrats turned to counter-revolution, while the new agricultural classes became the most devoted supporters of the new regime. In Japan, the feudal lord ceased to be a *territorial* magnate drawing his income from the peasant and became instead, by virtue of the commutation of his pension, a *financial* magnate investing his freshly capitalized wealth in banks, stocks, industries, or landed estates, and so joined the small financial oligarchy. This step was dramatic but not unexpected. Even before commutation the Government had taken pains to secure at least the neutrality if not the allegiance of these most powerful adherents of feudalism by dispensing lavish concessions with one hand, while undermining the bastions of feudal privilege and restriction with the other. To this end the Government as early as 1869 consented to pay the *daimyo* one half their normal revenue. This was altogether a most generous arrangement in view of the vicissitudes of the rice-harvest, the problem of peas-

[109] La Mazelière writes of this campaign "Malgré tant de difficultés, les chefs du gouvernement, n'avaient cessé de préparer l'opinion publique à la grande reforme; en juin 1871 ils fondèrent dans ce but le journal *Shimbun zashi*, dont les articles inspirés étaient violemment révolutionnaires dans le fond et dans la forme." La Mazelière, *op. cit.*, Volume V, p. 95.

ant recalcitrance, the expenses of public works in the clan, and the support of their *samurai*, from which risks and responsibilities they were now wholly relieved by the government. But such a settlement could not be made permanent since it imposed too heavy a financial load on the government, and since it left the feudal lords in control of their territory (for the return of the land-registers in 1869 did not mean the surrender of political power in the clan) and drawing a fixed sum from the central government, a situation not consistent with the idea of a modern state which the Meiji leaders were striving to construct. Thus the final compromise had to come as it did in 1873 when the decree on voluntary pension was promulgated. Under the altered and final capitalization scheme of 1876, the following rates of interest and time allowances for maturity of the bonds were fixed.[110]

Interest at 5 Per Cent		Interest at 6 Per Cent			Interest at 7 Per Cent		
Pensions	*Period of Maturity in Years*	*Pensions*		*Years*	*Pensions*		*Years*
Yen		*Yen*			*Yen*		
70,000 and over....	5	1,000 to 900....		7¾	100 to 75.......		11½
70,000 to 60,000....	5¼	900	800....	8	75	50.......	12
60,000 50,000....	5½	800	700....	8¼	50	40.......	12½
50,000 40,000....	5¾	700	600....	8½	40	30.......	13
40,000 30,000....	6	600	500....	8¾	30	25.......	13½
30,000 20,000....	6¼	500	450....	9	25 and under...		14
20,000 10,000....	6½	450	400....	9¼			
10,000 7,500....	6¾	400	350....	9½			
7,500 5,000....	7	350	300....	9¾			
5,000 2,500....	7¼	300	250....	10			
2,500 1,000....	7½	250	200....	10¼			
		200	150....	10½			
		150	100....	11			

On completion it was seen that the total claims when translated into public bonds amounted to 190,801,950 yen, divided thus:

Samurai (1874–76)..............	16,565,000 yen at	8%
Daimyo (1877).................	31,412,405 ” ”	5%
Daimyo and *Samurai* (1877).....	25,003,705 ” ”	6%
Daimyo and *Samurai* (1877).....	108,242,785 ” ”	7%
Shinto Priests (1877)..........	334,050 ” ”	8%
Samurai....................	9,244,005 ” ”	10%
Total....................	190,801,950	

[110] Henry Dumolard, *Le Japon, Politique Economique et Social*, Paris, 1905, p. 84.

Besides this, the sum of 20,108,507 yen was paid in cash, bringing the grand total of capitalization to 210,910,457 yen.[111]

It need hardly be said that in this final settlement of feudal
claims the greatest lords received a sufficient amount to become
members of the financial oligarchy in their own right, whereas
some of the very smallest feudal lords and the vast majority of
samurai were left with capital quite insufficient to raise them
above middle-class status. Perhaps it is not just a coincidence
that the most serious *samurai* uprising, the Satsuma Rebellion,
broke out shortly after the announcement (in August 1876) of
compulsory commutation.[112] This policy, however, succeeded
in removing the economic basis of the *daimyo* as local semi-
autonomous lords, while at the same time it insured the allegiance of these former feudal lords to the new society. It was
the final stage in the sealing of that peculiar union of merchants
and financial princes with the feudal or landed princes which
was already evident in the Tokugawa period. Thus the abolition of feudalism in Japan was no miracle, no contradiction of
the laws of historical process, but rather the logical outcome of
underlying, often invisible, but very real social forces. In a narrow sense the settlement can be summarized in the words of
McLaren. "A demonstration of armed force was made in the
sight of the feudal aristocracy, and at the same time an inducement involving monetary advantages to the *daimyo* at least, was
offered by the Government. Feudalism was thus partly driven
and partly lured to its own destruction."[113] But it was more
than that; despite the brave attacks launched against feudalism

[111] *Ibid.*, p. 85.

[112] Two Japanese economic historians indirectly connect these *samurai* uprisings with the commutations of their pensions, both voluntary (1873) and obliga-
tory (1876). As instances of *samurai* resentment they mention the attempt on the
life of Iwakura in 1874, the revolt in Saga in the same year, the uprising of the
Shimpuren (a secret society) in Kumamoto in 1876, the revolts in Hagi and Aki-
zuki (in which a leader of the former Choshu *Kiheitai* namely Maebara Issei was
involved), the incident at Shiambashi, all in the same year, and finally the great
Satsuma Revolt of 1877. Tshuchiya and Okazaki, *op. cit.*, p. 32.

[113] McLaren, *op. cit.*, p. 82. The commutation of pensions was not so favorable
for the *samurai* of course.

"As far as the *samurai* were concerned, the financial advantages of the pension
system were not nearly so great. Their nominal and actual revenues were equal,
and any dimunition of their incomes, which were small, meant hardship." *Ibid.*,
pp. 81-2. The decree authorizing this commutation of pensions is given in *JGD*,
pp. 557-60.

which reached a furious tempo in the years 1870-3 with the
recognition of the legal equality of all classes (warrior, peasant,
artisan, merchant, the abolition of feudal dress and of feudal
barriers, the disestablishment of Buddhism, the reform of the
calendar, the emancipation of the *Eta*, the rapid introduction
of Western thought and technique, the removal of the feudal
ban against the alienation and partition of land, the freedom of
crop and of occupation—despite these anti-feudal measures
of revolutionary and incalculable import, the government of
samurai and clan bureaucrats, confronted by mounting peasant
revolt, now found it politic to make peace on one front, the
front against feudalism, in order to concentrate its full strength
upon the other, the agrarian front. Relieved of the one front,
the Government could devote its energies to solving the agrarian
question, not simply by the use of naked force in suppressing
peasant unrest, but by strengthening the machinery of state,
by reforming administration, by concessions to the peasant proprietors (notably the reduction of the land tax in 1876), and by
the further consolidation of a landlord class which could become the political foundation for the Government on the countryside. This tendency becomes quite clear from the logic and
sequence of legislative acts. The commutation of *daimyo* pensions, while symbolizing the political compromise between a
former governing class and the new government resting largely
upon merchant and landed interests for its support, represents
at the same time a far-reaching social process in which the interests of usurer, landlord, merchant, financier and *ci-devant*
daimyo were melted down, transfused and solidified into a
homogeneous mass in which the original elements become in-
distinguishable. That the Meiji Government repudiated completely the social policy of the Shogunate, that it boldly opened
up the road for the development of capitalist economy can be
seen in the motivation of its reforms. The law (1872) which
swept away the prohibition against the sale in perpetuity in
land, the government policy of buying up of common lands, the
freedom of occupation and in the choice of crop testify to the
revolutionary victory of the right to private ownership in land.
The commutation of the land tax into a money tax collected on
a national uniform scale indicates a new tax relationship,
namely the impersonal cash nexus between government and

governed replacing the old irregular tax collected in kind according to the crop. Finally, all of these measures inevitably guaranteed the protection extended by the government to the new landlord class in its land-owning rights.

Another aspect of this same policy was the government guarantee of debts due this landlord-usurer class and incurred before the Restoration of 1868. This measure was of utmost importance to the money-lenders of Osaka with whom the impecunious *daimyo* were deeply involved. The government issued bonds in order to pay the bad debts of the deposed nobility to the *chonin* (but the debts of the Shogunate were not honored by the Meiji government). The underwriting of local debts added a burden of forty-one million yen to the government debt which was met by the issue of bonds.[114] These bonds not only secured the bad debts due the *chonin*, but supplied the bondholders with the funds for investment in industrial projects or in land.   This settlement had the effect of converting the greatest landlords and usurers into stockholders and bankers, as in the striking instance of Ichishima Tokujiro, a big landowner and money lender of Niigata, who established the Fourth National Bank in that city in 1873. The stockholders of the bank were mostly large landowners who were to play a leading part in provincial politics and administration.[115] We see at this early date that interlocking of landlordism, banking and government, which is one of the peculiar characteristics of the modern Japanese political and social organization.

The second great task was the unification of the national market. This meant the abolition of clan tariff barriers and tolls, the unification of the monetary and banking system—there were 1694 varieties of banknotes circulating in 1867—the freedom of trade and occupation, the abolition of the restriction on the growing of crops, all reform measures designed to allow the

[114] Andréadès, *op. cit.,* p. 36. He quotes the editor of the *Economiste Européen* in explanation of this debt settlement. "Les dettes des domaines subirent des traitements divers. Toutes les dettes antérieures à l'année 1843 furent déclarées non recevables. Les dettes contractées de 1844 à 1867 inclusivement et formant un total de 10,972,725 yens devinrent *l'ancienne dette* que le gouvernement s'engage à rembourser par annuités pendant une période de 50 années. Mais les 12,422,825 yens de dettes contractées par les daimyos pendant la période de transition, 1868-1871, furent converties en titres de *la nouvelle dette* de l'état rapportant 4% et amortissables en 25 années. Ces titres sont complétement remboursés depuis 1896." *Ibid.,* note to p. 36.

[115] Hirano, *op. cit.,* p. 268.

development of the national market and the participation of Japanese merchants in the international market.

Finally, the political unification of the country, achieved through the *Hanseki-hokan* (return of the land registers, 1869) and the *Haihan-chiken* (abolition of fiefs and establishment of prefectures, 1871), put an end to the feudal system wherein the autonomous *daimyo* exercised absolute sway over the land and the people inhabiting it through such means as the *corvée*, the prohibition of the flight of peasants, the restriction of occupation and of the choice of crop, and the right to seize the produce of the land by various legal or extra-legal measures. But this reform did not *uproot* so much as *stunt* the power of the feudal nobility after the fashion we have seen. In later years the same class, watered by the generous springs of pension commutation and warmed in the sun of nepotism, was to revive and push forth luxuriant shoots. The more obvious manifestations of this metamorphosis were the appointment of former feudal nobility to high government office and above all their emergence, after their temporary eclipse (when they together with the *kuge* were designated as *kazoku*, "flowery families"), as a peerage in 1884, with weighty constitutional powers exercised in the House of Peers after 1889. Shorn of feudal power over the land which for the most part came into the possession of peasant proprietors and the new landlord class, these lords were able through the funds granted them in 1876 and after to purchase large tracts of government lands put up for sale at fantastically cheap rates and so to become new landlords "writ large."[116] Some of them became stockholders and industrialists in the new society. The remarkably high share of banking capital held by these nobles in the National Banks in 1880 can be taken as an index of the great economic power which they were to wield in modern Japan. The following table gives the social division among shareholders in the National Banks in 1880.[117]

[116] Among the richest lords, were Shimazu Tadayoshi of Satsuma and Mori Motonori of Choshu, whose capitalized pensions were 1,322,000 and 1,167,000 yen respectively. *Ibid.*, p. 257. Some of the greatest plantations in Hokkaido were bought up by former feudal lords like Hachisuga, Nabeshima and Kuroda. *Ibid.*, p. 258.

[117] Horie, in *KUER*, July 1930, Vol. XI, p. 104. The relatively high proportion held by the *samurai* only indicates the great number of them. The average capitalized amount per *samurai* was very slight and quite insufficient for more than a year's livelihood. Thus, unlike the *daimyo*, only a few of them received sufficient capital to become bankers. industrialists and big *landowners*. The following table

SHAREHOLDERS OF THE NATIONAL BANKS IN 1880

Social Status		Amount of Shares Yen	Percentage of Total
Peers (mostly former *daimyo* and *kuge*)..		18,571,750	44.102
Samurai..........................		13,417,550	31.862
Commoners	Farmers...............	1,451,950	3.448
	Artisans...............	50,175	0.119
	Merchants.............	6,252,725	14.848
	Others...............	2,366,950	5.621
Total..........................		42,111,100	100.000

One would receive a distorted impression of the Meiji settlement if one were to regard the guarantee of debts to the *chonin* and the commutation of *daimyo* pensions as just a concession or a bribe to buy the support of these classes and nothing more. It must be emphasized again that although the personnel of the government was largely *samurai*, the new regime was underwritten and backed by the moneyed and landed classes; that with few exceptions the *daimyo* saw the advantages to be gained in coming to terms with the new regime, a compromise which their former relations with the *chonin* made quite natural. The creation of the National Debt fund through debt-guarantee and capitalization of pensions performed a revolutionary function in breaking down the feudal limitations imposed on the accumulation and utilization of capital which were among the chief obstructions to the development of capitalism under the *Bakufu*. The capitalized pensions were intended to pay off over a short

shows the total amount of bonds held by the *shizoku* in various prefectures at the time of capitalization and the amount left in their hands ten years later. (1884.)

Prefectures	At Time of Bond Issue (1874) (in tens of thousands)	1884
Kyoto......................	239 yen	66
Aichi......................	651	247
Nagano....................	220	66
Iwate.....................	94	7
Akita.....................	270	25
Ishikawa..................	812	163
Toyama...................	113	37
Tottori....................	334	34
Okayama..................	167	74
Hiroshima.................	215	35
Wakayama.................	107	78
Fukuoka..................	840	119
Total....................	4,062	951

See Tsuchiya and Okazaki, *op. cit.*, p. 33.
Thus only 23 per cent of their capitalized pension remained in the hands of the *samurai* of these provinces.

period the annuities which otherwise would become a permanent charge on the government. The bonds issued in August 1876 by the National Banks, established by Okuma Shigenobu, the Minister of Finance, for this purpose, reached the sum of 174 million yen. In this way the former pensioners received in a lump sum though at a discount what they would have received over a long period of time. This capital, easily converted into investing capital, at one stroke transformed feudal or immobile claims into mobile or transferable claims and linked former semi-isolated communities with the financial hub, and through the chain of banking drew those communities into the orbit of a nation-wide economy.[118]

Conclusion: Factors Which Conditioned the Establishment of a Modern State in Japan

Such in its social and political outlines was the Meiji settlement which laid the foundation for a modern state in Japan. It was carried out under the brilliant leadership of *samurai* bureaucrats who, in the teeth of opposition directed against them even by members of their own class, wisely pursued the path of internal reconstruction (a task which the tenacity of the outmoded *Bakufu* regime had magnified a hundredfold), in preference to the path of foreign conquest which at that early date, before the creation of factory industry or a modernized army and navy and before winning recognition as a great power, might have brought disaster in its train. The statesmanship of men like Okubo, Iwakura, and Kido during the crisis over the Korean question in 1872-3 merits the highest praise of their countrymen.

This bureaucracy, moreover, had to work not only with lim-

[118] "In 1871 in consequence of the abolition of clans and establishment of prefectures, the government had to bear all the debts of the clans. To convert these debts into new national bonds was the idea of the writer (Shibusawa) of the time. In 1873 the Finance Department decided to issue two kinds of bonds, called 'old bonds' and 'new bonds' and, in the following year, that any *shizoku* or *samurai* who wished to surrender the hereditary pensions and receive bonds in place of them, should be given eight years' pension in bonds. Subsequently in 1874 all hereditary pensions were abolished and Kinroku bonds given in commutation. But the amount to be issued for this purpose reached the enormous amount of 174 million yen and on that account the matter required most careful consideration. Another apprehension was that the barons and *shizoku*, who had been accustomed to live on their pensions, might by selling these bonds lose their means of support, in which case it was very probable that they might do something to disturb the peace of society." Baron Shibusawa Eiichi, Chapter XXI (Development of Banking) in *Fifty Years of New Japan*, Volume I, pp. 501-2.

ited resources, but in the shadow of the foreign menace which since the middle of the century had persistently loomed over the country in the shape of military aggression, and in the much more sinister form of foreign capital which had taken quite deep root in the port cities during the early years of the Meiji era. That this foreign danger was not imaginary has been indicated in the foregoing chapter; proof of it lay in the existence of extra-territoriality in Japan until 1899, while tariff autonomy was not fully achieved until 1910. Like Nehemiah, they had to build with sword in one hand and trowel in the other. In their anxiety to gain complete national independence and to escape once and for all from the threat of foreign encroachment, they had to concentrate on military problems at great sacrifice to social and political reform. The historical legacy from Tokugawa society did not permit of a social transformation taking place *from below* through democratic or mass revolutionary process, but only *from above*, autocratically. The new structure was built from the top downwards, upon the ruins of the old; moreover, the burden of this task as far as government revenue was concerned, was shouldered by the agricultural community, at whose expense also the accumulation and centralization of capital was carried out; such being the case the government had no choice but to retard the tempo of anti-feudal consciousness which was sweeping the countryside.

The instrument in all this was a state which was autocratic but never so inflexible as to be in danger of cracking. It was only through an absolutist state that the tremendous task of modernization could be accomplished without the risk of social upheaval which might attend the attempts to extend the democratic method in a nation which had emerged so suddenly and so tardily from feudal isolation. The machinery for the epochal changes accompanying the Restoration was a government formed from the ablest, most self-sacrificing of clan military bureaucrats who utilized to the full and with remarkable dexterity those autocratic powers which they steadily strengthened. In looking back to the stormy years of that period, whatever one may think of the words "military" and "bureaucrat," it seems an incontrovertible fact that these military bureaucrats were the spearpoint of advance, the vanguard of modernization, in the establishment of a modern state in Japan. In the words of

one Japanese writer: "It is not fair to the bureaucrats to condemn them as destructive reactionaries. They did much good.
In a period of transition someone must take the helm, and they
were expert pilots. But the period of transition is now over."[119]

[119] Iwasaki Uichi, *The Working Forces in Japanese Politics*, New York, 1921,
p. 52. On the later role of bureaucracy, see Chapter IV, The Key Industries and
the Bureaucracy, and Chapter VI, The Question of "Military versus Civil" in the
Japanese Government.

EARLY INDUSTRIALIZATION

Before industrialization on a nation-wide scale can take place, there must exist two prerequisites, an adequate supply both of capital and of labor. In expanded form these fundamental prerequisites can be conveniently summarized as, (1) a sufficiently high level in the production and circulation of commodities and in the division of labor, (2) a certain accumulation of capital in the hands of the producers, and (3) the existence of an adequately large body of free labor—free in the sense of being untrammeled by any ownership of the means of production and hence ready to offer themselves in the labor market. To grasp the distinguishing features of Japanese industrialization we can perhaps do no better than trace these three preconditions for the rise of industrial capitalism as they existed in Japan.

Since this paper is not intended to be a systematic and detailed study of the economic development of modern Japan, it would take us too far afield if we were to enter into a rigorous historical investigation of all three prerequisites. Accordingly it will be sufficient to bring forward a few facts to illustrate the first condition; the second, which is more important in its shaping of Japanese capitalism, will receive fuller treatment; while the third, the creation of a labor market, will be reserved for the next chapter, where it will be treated as one of the consequences of the agrarian settlement.

Production and Circulation of Commodities

In the works of such writers as Takekoshi, Honjo, Tsuchiya, Kokusho, and Takizawa there is abundant material to show how high a level trade and handicraft manufacture (as distinct from machine manufacture) had reached in the Tokugawa period. Although rice was still the *standard* for exchange, money had become predominant as the *means* of exchange, especially in towns and cities. What made this great trading activity possible was production for the market, that is production over and above the needs of the producer which naturally kept pace with the steady rise in the productivity of agriculture and with the advance in the division of labor. The demand for goods was stimulated in turn by the rapid growth of cities attendant upon the concentration of *samurai* in castle towns and the brisk movements of transport and trade activities which were connected with the *sankin-kotai* system. How great this demand for goods must have been can be surmised from the population of Edo, which was, at the turn of the eighteenth century, probably the greatest city in the world, numbering from 1,300,000 to 1,400,000;[1] Osaka, even in 1665, had a population estimated at 268,760;[2] and Kyoto, the busy hive of skilled handicraft trades in Japan, was considered by the observant traveler Dr. Engelbert Kaempfer in 1691 to be the greatest manufacturing center in Japan with the most diverse trades and industries.[3]

Division of Labor

The division of labor, which Adam Smith maintained was the chief cause of increasing its productivity, had advanced far enough in this period for there to be a distinct line of demarcation separating the production of raw materials and the manufacture of commodities.[4] Specialization was noticeable in the crafts so that the builder of a house would have to secure the services of the craft guilds of carpenters, sawyers, painters, plumbers, roof-thatchers, bricklayers, plasterers, masons and

[1] Tsuchiya, *Economic History of Japan*, p. 193. He gives the population of London, regarded as the greatest city in the Western world as between 500,000 and 700,000 in 1700, and 865,000 in 1801. Takizawa, *op. cit.*, p. 52, gives an even higher estimate for the population of Edo. In 1723, according to a contemporary record used by Takizawa, it was 526, 317 (excluding *samurai*), and in 1787 it had jumped to 2,285,300. That these figures are too high would seem to be borne out by the estimate of Takekoshi which is very close to Tsuchiya, 1,367,880 at the end of the 18th century. Takekoshi, *op. cit.*, Vol. III, p. 133. A convenient summary by Professor S. Koda of urban population in the Tokugawa period is to be found in "Materials on Japanese Social and Economic History: Tokugawa Japan," edited by N. Skene Smith, *TASJ*, Second Series, Vol. XIV, June 1937, pp. 35-6.

[2] Takizawa, *op. cit.*, p. 53. For the population of other cities in Tokugawa Japan, see Tsuchiya, *op. cit.*, p. 193.

[3] Engelbert Kaempfer, *History of Japan, 1690-1692*, English translation by J. G. Scheuzer, Glasgow, 1906. See the paragraph entitled "Description of Miaco" (Kyoto), Volume III, pp. 20-2.

[4] For further data on the specialization in manufacture and the division of labor in the Tokugawa period, see Tsuchiya, *op. cit.*, pp. 175-84.

mat-layers.[5] In time, of course, the nature of guild exclusiveness became a brake on productivity which thus required their abolition (which was effected once and for all after the Restoration); but what is important for the division of labor in this period was the sharp difference between the producer and the seller of goods, the former organized into craft or workmen's guilds, the latter into the monopolistic wholesalers, the *Tokumi Donya*, and the *Kabu Nakama* or Federation of Guilds.[6]

Together with this went regional specialization, replacing the old clan self-sufficiency, never complete even in remote times. Yamagata Hoshu wrote in 1820, "There are provinces that abound in rice, others in grain, others in cloth, and still others in paper and timber and so forth. Thus, most of the provinces have come to produce one or two kinds of goods in large quantities and do not make other things themselves."[7]

The division of labor, was, however, restricted by the prevalence of widespread household industry dominated by trading capital and including the manufacture of porcelain, lacquer, silk, cotton, brass, and articles of wood and bamboo, straw matting, *sake,* and *shoyu.* The chief commodities produced for the market were largely in the hands of peasant or poor *samurai* households which worked at such tasks to supplement their meager family income. We shall see in the next chapter, how the invasion of cheap foreign commodities, especially cotton yarn, together with the products of Japanese machine manufacture, ruined the household industry of thousands of these primitive hand producers, thus accelerating the division of labor and the creation of the home market.

[5] William A. Spurr, "Business Cycles in Japan before 1853," *American Journal of Political Economy,* Vol. XLVI, No. 5, October 1938, p. 663.

[6] On workmen's guilds in the Tokugawa period, see the chapter of that title (XXVI) in Takekoshi, *op. cit.,* Vol. III, pp. 242-73, and Takizawa, *op. cit.,* pp. 63-4. On the *Tokumi Donya,* see Takekoshi, *op. cit.,* Vol. II, pp. 498-566, and Takizawa, *op. cit.,* pp. 58-60; 104-5. On the *Kabu Nakama* (Federation of Guilds), see Smith, editor, "Tokugawa Japan," *TASJ,* Second Series, Vol. XIV, June 1937. pp. 78-116. An authoritative account in Japanese of the traders guild is the "Tonya Enkaku Shoshi" (Short History of the Tonya), Vol. VIII, pp. 769-89, in *Nihon Sangyo Shiryo Taikei* (An Outline of the Historical Materials for Japanese Industry, by Takimoto Seiichi and Mukai Shikamatsu, Tokyo, 1927. This account emphasizes the difference between Osaka as the central market or entrepôt of Japan and Edo as the chief center of consumption. This account lists the names of *Tonya* in Japan during the Tokugawa period and explains how they secured their charters for monopoly trade by the payment of a fee called *myogakin* to the authorities, whether clan or *Bakufu.*

[7] Quoted in Spurr, *op. cit.,* p. 663.

Accumulation of Capital

As to the second condition, the accumulation of capital in the hands of producers, all our evidence points to the conclusion that the chief agents in the accumulation of capital during late feudalism were traders and usurers, and in this connection the role of the Osaka *fudasashi* (rice brokers and agents) was particularly important. Commercial capital, severely hampered by Tokugawa isolation, had to batten exclusively upon internal trade, which was as highly organized as the restrictions of feudal economy permitted. Chief of these restrictions was the overlapping of agriculture and industry (*i.e.*, household industries) and the consequent narrowing of the home market.

Commercial capital as it existed in Tokugawa Japan was accumulated in the hands of a few great traders and privileged money-lenders, like the Mitsui, Ono and Konoike families, and one can estimate roughly the extent of such accumulation from the inventory of the huge fortune confiscated by the *Bakufu* from Yodoya Saburoyemon the great rice merchant in Osaka during the Genroku period (1688-1702).[8] We know that a few merchant princes under the protection of the *Bakufu* and powerful feudal lords succeeded in accumulating a respectable pile if we may judge by the size of *goyokin* (forced loans).[9] But barred as they were from any chance to reap profits from overseas adventure, or to feed upon colonial plunder and trade which enriched the great companies and merchants of Western Europe under the mercantile system, Japanese merchants had to be content with working the very limited market for all it was worth in collaboration with the *Bakufu* or clan governments, and with speculating on the rice market, in general, rather modest operations which retarded the rate of accumulation when compared to the great trading nations of Europe. We might say

[8] "The confiscated property included 50 pairs of gold screens, 3 toy ships made of jewelry, 373 carpets, 10,050 *kin* of liquid gold, 273 large precious stones and numberless small stones, 2 chests of gold, 3000 large gold coins, 120,000 *ryo* of *koban*, 85,000 *kwamme* of silver, 75,000 *kwan* of copper money, 150 boats, 730 storehouses, 17 storehouses for jewelry, 80 granaries, 80 storehouses for beans, 28 houses in Osaka, 64 houses in other places, a rice stipend for one *daimyo* amounting to 332 *koku* and 150 *chobu* of cypress forest." Takizawa, *op. cit.*, p. 103. Another indication of wealth, not just in capital, however, is given in a long list of names with the amount of wealth possessed by each. Takekoshi, *op. cit.*, Volume II, pp. 360-2.

[9] On the size of *goyokin*, see Honjo, *op. cit.*, pp. 328, 331, 333, 336, 342-3. One should distinguish between the amount levied by the government and the amount actually paid by these great houses.

that Tokugawa policy had so constricted Japanese mercantilism as to prevent it from reaching its full-blossomed, most profitable and characteristic stage, namely that period when monopoly trade between an overseas colony and its metropolis is regulated to profit the latter at the cost of the former. In Japan the prevailing type of mercantilism was also of a monopoly character, but was closely knit to the "clan reform" movement described in the last chapter, and was in the main a type of mercantilism which exemplifies the metropolis-colony relationship between the city (metropolis) and surrounding countryside (colony) characteristic of primitive European mercantilism.[10] Like the European system, the Japanese relied upon monopoly as well as on intervention and protection by the state whether *Bakufu* or *han,* and since it was a phase in the period of the accumulation of capital, it was likewise marked by a hunger for bullion and a "fear of goods."[11]

European and Japanese Mercantilism Compared

In pre-Tokugawa Japan foreign trade, piracy, even the beginning of colonization—*e.g.,* Yamada Nagamasa (1578-1633) in Siam—and above all Hideyoshi's Korean expedition pointed to a policy of mercantilism which corresponded to the trading, piratical and colonizing activities of contemporary Europe and England in particular. The long years of seclusion thus did not merely hamper Japanese economic growth; it retarded it both absolutely and relatively so that, as Mr. Orchard justly observes,

[10] Maurice Dobb, *Political Economy and Capitalism, Some Essays in Economic Tradition,* London, 1937, p. 232, note 2. "The various monopolistic provisions of the merchant guilds, reinforced frequently by a policy on the part of the town governments, amounting to a sort of "colonialism" with regard to the surrounding countryside, gave rise to an exploitation—relation of this sort . . ."

[11] The great German mercantilist Johann Joachim Becher expressed this typical "fear of goods" as follows: "It is always better to sell goods to others than to buy goods from others, for the former brings a certain advantage, and the latter inevitable damage." Quoted in Eli F. Heckscher, *Mercantilism,* London, 1935, Vol. II, p. 116. For an analysis of this mercantilist "fear of goods" and its corollary, the hunger for bullion which characterized Japanese mercantilism as well as European, see *ibid.,* Vol. II, pp. 117-18.

One of the pioneer advocates of Western intercourse in the Tokugawa period, Honda Rimei (or Toshiaki), writing at the end of the 18th century, displays a surprising comprehension of mercantilist principles which he advocated without any direct knowledge of European mercantilist works. He summed up in a phrase perhaps the essence of mercantilism when he wrote: "Foreign trade is a war in that each party seeks to extract wealth from the other." Quoted in Honjo Eijiro, "Japan's Overseas Trade in the Closing Days of the Tokugawa Shogunate," in *KUER,* April 1939, Volume XIV, p. 5. See also *supra,* Chapter III, note 78.

18th century Japan ought to be compared, not to 18th century England on the eve of its great industrial revolution, but rather to 16th century Tudor England, overwhelmingly agricultural and possessing widespread domestic handicraft industries.[12] Even so, the comparison is still generous toward Tokugawa Japan, because Tudor England had already laid the foundations of her overseas trade (in the great trading companies of the 16th century), and of her naval expansion under Henry VII; she had even begun to acquire colonies (Newfoundland, discovered and claimed in 1497), and by successfully challenging Spanish naval supremacy she was well on the way to securing control of vital trade routes to the Indies and the Americas. To express it briefly, the Meiji Restoration had to begin where Hideyoshi left off. But since the 250 years of isolation had left deep marks on Japanese economy and society by stunting its national growth, Meiji Japan had to wrestle with those accumulated disabilities inherited from Tokugawa practices. The Restoration was not merely a continuation of Hideyoshi's policy of trade expansion, for the simple reason that in the 19th century Japan was faced with a struggle for existence as an independent power against the menace of foreign capital. It was a race to overtake the advanced Western nations with their machine technology and armaments, and Japanese economic and even political independence were at stake; Japan had to enter the race with the handicap of a tariff fixed by the unequal treaty system which lasted for half a century. Meiji economic policy was a blend of the old mercantilism, with its state protection, and the new style monopoly. This new monopoly was linked organically to the pre-existing mercantile monopoly in Tokugawa Japan so that to a large extent the same favored merchant families with banking interests now became privileged directors of banks and industries. Thus a Japanese economic historian, Dr. T. Nagai, can call the Meiji statesmen the last of the mercantilists, while an American authority, Dr. H. G. Moulton, considers them to be the first planners of a national economy.[13]

[12] John E. Orchard, *Japan's Economic Position*, New York, 1930, pp. 71-2.

[13] Both T. Nagai and H. G. Moulton are referred to in this connection in R. Ishii, *Population Pressure and Economic Life in Japan*, London, 1937, p. 20. Although the idea of national planning is not synonymous with monopoly, perhaps it is possible to regard the policy of state subsidy and special favor extended to a few big financial houses as "planning" in contrast to the classical Manchester laissez-faire policy with its opposition to any form of state intervention. Another

In other words, one might say that the mercantile system with its monopoly of trade and reliance on the absolutist state (as in 16th-17th century France and England) was the crutch with which capitalism learned to walk. Grown to full strength, European capitalism discarded the crutch, absolute state power, and finding it a hindrance, turned against it and destroyed it. In Japan the immature capitalist class was unable to dispense with this crutch of absolutist power and relied upon it even more completely in the Meiji era than it had under the *han* or *Bakufu* regimes.

The feverish haste of the Meiji leaders to accomplish in a generation what had taken other nations a century or more to do was now to be checked by the gulf which separated Japanese primitive feudal technique from the industrial technique of the most advanced nations. To leap over this gulf, rather than to plod along the intervening valley road taken by pioneer nations would require time to train a great body of skilled labor and to amass a large store of capital. Japan still lacked the former in the early Meiji era, and as for the latter, only a very few wealthy families had a sufficient accumulation to enter the field as entrepreneurs in factory industries, a condition which incidentally favored monopoly or highly centralized capital right from the beginning of Japanese capitalism. But these few financial magnates who were, as we have seen, very close to the Government, showed hesitation in risking their capital in enterprises which demanded at the very outset such an immense outlay of capital, and before there was any clear indication of the profitability of

Japanese writer has referred to the early Meiji period as mercantilist. Professor Yosio Honyden, "Der Durchbruch des Kapitalismus in Japan" in *Industrialisierung Japans*, Weltwirtschaftliches Archiv, 46 Band, Heft 1, Jena, July 1937, p. 29.

This mercantile monopoly system carried out by bureaucratic statesmen required the autocracy of absolutism in the political sphere for its rapid progress, and was therefore antagonistic to "liberal" capitalism which never had a chance to grow in Japan. The similarities and differences between the old (mercantile) and new (finance capital) monopoly systems are explained in Dobb, *op. cit.*, Chapter VII, pp. 226-72.

Another Japanese writer Itani Zenichi says, "Okubo, who exercised extreme mercantilism in the early Meiji period up until 1877, can be compared to Colbert of France." Quoted in Horie Yasuzo, *Nihon Shihonshugi no Seiritsu* (The Formation of Japanese Capitalism), Tokyo, 1938, p. 252.

Royama Masamichi in "Problems of Contemporary Japan." *Occasional Papers of the University of Hawaii*, Number 24, January 1935, p. 14, explains how the Meiji government followed the same mercantilist policy on a national scale as the more advanced clans had in late feudal Japan.

such undertakings. The lag in distance between primitive Japanese technique and the best Western methods of production created very hard conditions for the genesis and growth of private capital in industry. Although a wide field for industrial investment lay fallow, the merchant princes were reluctant to become pioneers in working this field; so the government with the aid at first of *goyokin* (loans) from these same magnates and together with its limited revenues, chief of which was the land tax, had itself to develop industry. Thus, early Japanese capitalism may be described as a hothouse variety, growing under the shelter of state protection and subsidy. Big private capital preferred to remain in trade, banking and credit operations, particularly in the safe and lucrative field of government loans,[14] while small capital had no inducement to leave the countryside where trade, usury and, above all, high rent—averaging almost sixty per cent of the tenant's[15] crop—prevented capital invested in agriculture from flowing into industrial channels.

Predominance of Banking Capital in Japan

For the purpose of facilitating exchange and credit as well as centralizing the available capital, the great financial houses under government advice and protection formed the *Tsusho Kaisha* (Commercial Companies) and *Kawase Kaisha* (Exchange Companies), regulated by the *Tsushoshi* (Commercial Bureau established in 1869) and replacing the short-lived *Shohoshi*.[16]

[14] The rate of interest on *goyokin* in the early Meiji was 1.5% per *month* with land tax as security. Honjo, *op. cit.*, pp. 335-6. The same author gives a table showing the principal and interest on *goyokin*, *ibid.*, p. 336.

[15] "Indeed the condition of tenant farming is far from being satisfactory, for according to investigations made in 1887, out of ten parts of the products of puddy (paddy?) fields throughout the country the landowners obtain about six and the tenant-farmers only four, while in regard to the upland fields the relative ratio was 4½ parts and 5½ respectively. . . . The steady increase in population far beyond that of the tillage of land . . . keeps rent high because tenants have to compete for leases. . . . In extreme cases the share of harvest that falls to the lot of the tenant farmers is barely sufficient to pay the cost of the manure applied to the fields." *Japan at the Beginning of the Twentieth Century*, published by the Imperial Japanese Commission to the Louisiana Purchase Exposition, Tokyo, 1904, p. 90.

[16] For details see Baron Shibusawa Eiichi, "Development of Banking in Japan." in *Fifty Years of New Japan*, Vol. 1, pp. 487-8. The close relations of these great financial houses with the government were maintained and strengthened in the Meiji era. The same authority writes, "The families of Ono and Shimada, had played a very important part in the finances of the Shogun and various *daimyo*, and even after the Restoration they had very intimate relations with the government and the public." *Ibid.*, p. 496.

From this very early interest in credit and banking operations to the exclusion of other fields of investment, private capital in Japan was given a great start by the government's assumption of the old clan debts. Merged with the financial power of the old feudal nobility—a power transformed and multiplied by pension commutation and capitalization—private capital has always favored banking as the chief outlet for capital investment. And to this day, banking capital is overwhelmingly predominant over industrial capital. This preponderance is seen in the following table:[17]

AUTHORIZED CAPITAL OF ALL LIMITED COMPANIES BEFORE THE
JAPANESE-CHINESE WAR

Activity	End of 1877 (,000 yen)	End of 1883 (,000 yen)	End of 1893 (,000 yen)
Agriculture	—	1,053	2,542
Trading	454	35,904	57,616
Manufacturing	—	14,725	68,259
Railways	—	12,080	57,945
Banking	24,981	75,375	111,635
Total	25,435	139,137	297,997

Banking capital, while growing out of all proportion to industrial capital, by the end of the 19th century gave a striking example of concentration, in this way continuously strengthening the position of the financial oligarchy or *Zaibatsu*.[18] In Japan the concentration of capital, as distinct from its accumulation, was accelerated by the Government's policy of subsidy and artificial encouragement. The speed with which concentration of capital was affected in Japan came from (1) the generally low level of accumulated capital, (2) the need for large amounts of capital to begin industrial enterprises run on the latest Western scale, (3) the adoption of the joint-stock company system in Japan right from the beginning of industrialization (1869, the *Kawase Kaisha*) and (4) competition with advanced foreign countries also favoring a high concentration of capital. In those industries which turned out products to compete either in the home or international markets with the products of other capitalist countries, trusts or cartels were formed in the very

[17] S. Uyehara, *The Industry and Trade of Japan*, London (revised), 1936, p. 271. See also S. Doke, "Economic Developments in Japan since the Meiji Restoration, from its Statistical Point of View," in *Bulletin de l'Institut International de Statistique*, Tome XXV, 2 ième livraison. Tokyo, 1931, p. 224. The same authority writes, "the total number of companies in 1884 was 2392 of which 1094 being banks (*sic*)." *Ibid.*, p. 223.

[18] Ishii, *op. cit.*, p. 26.

course of the industrial revolution, notably in the textiles in the 1880's. Japanese concentration of capital, of course, has not been unique in its tendency to grow through big capital swallowing small especially in times of economic crisis. This is the most characteristic method by which the *Zaibatsu* or financial clique comprising notably the Mitsui, Mitsubishi, Sumitomo and Yasuda companies has strengthened itself in recent times. The absorption in 1927 of the Suzuki Company by the Mitsui is an outstanding example. But as Professor Allen points out, their impregnable position lies, not just in their size or their close government connections, but in their pre-eminence both in finance on the one hand and industry and commerce on the other. Thus this triple aspect gives them an immense competitive advantage.[19] But the citadel of their strength is finance, the foundations of which were firmly laid in the early Meiji period.

In Japan, banking and loan capital, leaning heavily upon the state for support, was used in turn by the government to create those branches of industry requiring a greater capital investment, while at the same time small capital tied to domestic industry had to get along as best it could with under-capitalization and high interest rates. Small companies would use up their capital on hand in building and equipping a factory and then find that to commence operations they had to resort to the banks for a loan. The rate of interest at the end of the 19th century was as high as ten, twelve, fifteen or even eighteen per cent, while interest on deposits was seven to eight per cent. Unable to meet their financial obligations on such terms, these small companies by the end of their first year became mortgaged to the banks.[20] In this way small and middle capitalists were

[19] G. C. Allen, "Concentration of Economic Control in Japan," in the *Economic Journal*, London, June 1937, pp. 271-86.

[20] Dumolard, *op. cit.*, p. 151. "Dans de pareilles conditions il n'est pas étonnant que la plupart des affaires soldent leur bilan annuel par des pertes, comme le montre par exemple le tableau suivant qui vise les filatures de coton.

Années	Nombre des Compagnies	Compagnies Réalisant des Bénéfices	Compagnies en Perte
1893	40	29	11
1894	45	28	17
1895	47	41	6
1896	63	41	22
1897	74	33	41
1898	72	42	30
1899	70	30	40
1900	70	27	43
1901	70	25	45

Il est à remarquer que le manque de capitaux s'affirme surtout dans les industries purement japonaises." *Ibid.*, pp. 151-2. (Italics mine E. H. N.)

obliged to undertake only those types of enterprise which were left over from the sphere of interest of big capital, such as the small, peculiarly "Japanese" industries, porcelain, silk, lacquer, straw, *sake, shoyu* and the like, which require less capital equipment and do not have to compete with foreign production. But in time these small industries have fallen more and more into the power of banking and loan capital, a trend which has continued up to the present day.[21]

In most nations, during the formative stage of capitalism banking capital has usually been distinct from industrial capital, but in Japan industrial capital did not develop independently; the state initiated industrialization, developed it and turned it over at amazingly low rates to a few private enterprises, mostly representatives of the great banking houses. In this process no new class of industrial capitalist was created; what took place was only the strengthening of banking and usury capital (including the more affluent nobility) and its partial transformation into industrial capital. This smothering of the seeds of an independent class of industrialists is a reflection of the immature, hot-house character of capitalism in Japan and of its serious weakness in this respect compared to the strongest capitalist nations. Here again it may be helpful to emphasize the effect of high rent in agriculture acting as a strong inducement to keep private capital tied to the land rather than invested in industrial enterprise with its greater risks and its lower return on the money invested.

Role of Foreign Capital in Early Japanese Industrialization

We have noted the foreign menace to Japan during the chaotic years at the close of the *Bakufu*, a danger not so much of military invasion as of the more insidious penetration of foreign capital within the economic strongholds of the nation, which might easily dwarf or strangle its free development as in China. Al-

---

[21] "The influence of the Zaibatsu (financial clique) extends far beyond the confines of the concerns which they directly or indirectly control. This extension is brought about by several methods. . . . First, through their control over the credit machinery of the country they are able to dictate policy to their debtors to no small extent. Secondly, through the operations of their trading companies they are able to bring under their sway, not merely the larger firms who sell through these channels, but also the multitude of very small producers and local factors and merchants who depend on those trading companies for both working capital as well as for a means of reaching the market." Allen, in *Economic Journal* (cited), p. 278.

though future economic development was already jeopardized by the unequal treaties negotiated by the *Bakufu* whereby Japan's tariff autonomy was forfeited for half a century, these leaders did their utmost to avoid further entanglement in the meshes of foreign capital. Therefore in spite of the anemia of domestic capital they resisted the temptation to seek heavy foreign loans which might well have compromised the nation's economic independence.

From the Restoration until the end of the century only two foreign loans were contracted. The first was a loan of £1,000,000 (to be exact, £913,000) at 9 per cent floated in London in 1870 to help in the construction of the first railway, from Yokohama to Tokyo. The second was also floated in London in 1873, a loan of £2,400,000 with interest at 7 per cent, and was intended to help the government meet the cash needs for pension commutation and capitalization.[22] The first loan was redeemed in 1881, the second in 1897, and until a London syndicate purchased in that same year (1897) 43 million yen of bonds through a contract with the Bank of Japan no foreign capital was introduced into the country. In view of the desperate need for working capital in the early Meiji period[23] we cannot but ask why no further efforts were made to secure foreign capital. Perhaps the most authoritative answer was given by Sakatani Yoshiro, writing in 1897 as Director of the Bureau of Computation of the Department of Finance, and later one of the financial leaders in the Government.[24] He gives four reasons. The first was the depreciation of non-convertible notes. Despite the Government's attempt to cancel these non-convertible notes, they kept increasing in

[22] These details on foreign loans are taken from Y. Sakatani, "Introduction of Foreign Capital" in *The Far East* (English edition of the *Kokumin-no-Tomo*), Vol. II, No. 9, September 1897, p. 399. Another authority gives these figures in yen as follows: for the first loan 4,880,000 yen, and for the second 11,712,000. Kinosita Yetaro, *The Past and Present of Japanese Commerce*, New York, 1902, p. 119.

[23] Some idea of the plight of Government finance on the morrow of the Restoration can be gained from these few figures:

Year	Government Receipts	Government Expenses
1868	3,665,000 yen	30,505,000 yen
1869	4,666,000 yen	20,786,000 yen

The deficit was met largely by the *goyokin* (forced loans) of the big merchants. F. F. Evrard, "Coup d'Oeil sur le Situation Financière du Japon," in *The Far East*, Tokyo, September 1897, Vol. II, No. 20, p. 406. A fuller table giving "extraordinary" revenue, such as forced loans and *Dajokan* notes and covering 1868-71, appears in Honjo, *op. cit.*, p. 333.

[24] Sakatani, in *The Far East* (cited), pp. 399-403.

volume until they reached dangerous proportions in 1877, when the Government had to increase the issue of notes to meet the huge expenses incurred in suppressing the Satsuma Revolt, with the result that in the next year the notes depreciated and became subject to constant fluctuation. Furthermore, the excess of imports over exports precipitated a heavy efflux of specie. In 1886 the Government began the conversion of notes until the difference between silver and notes disappeared. This situation made Japan an unattractive field for foreign investment.

The second reason was the difference in monetary standards. Foreign nations were on the gold standard—Japan was on a *de jure* silver standard from 1871 to 1878; thereafter, bi-metallic, until October 1899, when it went on the gold standard. Thus the variations in the ratio between gold and silver made foreign capital cautious about investing in Japan.

Thirdly, the unequal treaty system did not allow foreigners to engage in business in the interior, while extraterritoriality made commercial and financial relations between Japanese and foreigners extremely complicated and so acted as a deterrent to the free import of capital.

Fourth and most decisive, was the fear of both government and people of the dangers arising from a late-awakening nation's dependence on foreign capital. Our authority, Sakatani, mentions specifically the unhappy experiences of Egypt and Turkey, which had mismanaged foreign capital introduced into their countries and so had invited foreign intervention. Those keen observers of past and present events, the Meiji statesmen, were determined not to fall into a similar error. By the end of the century none of these four reasons, some of them appreciated by potential foreign investors and the last by Japanese statesmen, was any longer valid, so that the Government had no fear of foreign capital. But by that time (1897) the flotation of 200 million yen worth of railway bonds was largely subscribed by Japanese capitalists who were now strong enough to absorb the lion's share of such gilt-edged securities.

How deeply the national consciousness was stirred over the question of foreign loans can be seen from the words of Viscount Inouye Masaru regarding railway development. "To be more precise, the people generally disliked the railway because of the heavier burden it would throw upon their shoulders by causing additional taxes. Many even of the governmental officials stood on the side of opposition, some of them crying out 'to make (sic) a foreign loan is to sell the country.' They did not understand what a foreign loan was."[25]

The result of the prudence shown by Meiji statesmen in regard to foreign capital was to accentuate certain characteristics of Japanese capitalism: the predominant position of state enterprise supported by the financial oligarchy, the retardation of the tempo of industrialization, and the heavier tax burdens on the population, particularly on the agricultural community.

The History and Influence of Strategic Industries

At this point, although it will take us away from our immediate subject, the accumulation of capital, and though it presupposes logically the succeeding question of the creation of a labor market, it may nevertheless be well to illustrate that unique feature of Japanese industrialization just referred to, i.e., monopolistic and state control of strategic industries—*strategic* whether because of their connection with naval and military defense or because of their importance in export industries intended to compete against foreign products and hence requiring subsidy and protection.

With the fate of China before its eyes as an ever-present warning of foreign menace, and with the tumultuous years following the war for the Restoration adding considerable danger to the regime from agrarian discontent and *samurai* insurrection, the Meiji Government devoted its energies to the centralization and modernization of the standing army and the police system. These forces for defense against foreign invasion and internal disturbance had begun to be built up haphazardly in the last few years of the *Bakufu*, when under the impact of foreign relations, the Shogunate itself undertook to acquire new military equipment on the French model, Satsuma on the English, Kii on the German, and other clans again on the Dutch.[26] The armies of the clan-coalition which overthrew the Shogunate were enlarged and reformed on the French model,[27] while the navy with strong Satsuma influence adopted the English system

[25] Viscount Inouye Masaru, "Japanese Communications: Railroads," Chapter XVIII in *Fifty Years of New Japan*, Vol. I, p. 431.

[26] Prince Yamagata Aritomo, "The Japanese Army" in *Fifty Years of New Japan*. Vol. I, p. 201.

[27] *Ibid.*, p. 202.

from the first.[28] This army, originally composed exclusively of ex-*samurai* and enlarged by the conscription of 1873, was the core of the future standing army. At the same time, the police system was hurriedly unified and enlarged, being of vital importance in maintaining law and order in the critical transitional years and in serving as the bulwark of absolutism in its struggle against liberalism in later years.[29] The armed forces, reorganized after the Meiji Restoration, were merely a skeleton without flesh and blood and would have been helpless without modern industries and a transportation system. Consequently, since the problem of defense was foremost in the last few years of the *Bakufu* and the first years of the Meiji era, the keenest minds were concerned with such questions as the creation of trade and industry, not for their own sake, but rather to establish those industries which one might conveniently call *strategic*, as the *sine qua non* of a modern army and navy, the creation of which was the central problem of the day. To put the sequence of emphasis in logical order, the Meiji leaders thought somewhat as follows: "What do we most need to save us from the fate of China? A modern army and navy. On what does the creation and maintenance of modern armed forces depend? Chiefly on heavy industries, engineering, mining, shipbuilding, in a word *strategic* industries." Thus the first stage of industrialization in Japan was inextricably interwoven with the military problem, and it fixed the pattern for its later evolution. This pattern was indeed already apparent before the end of the Shogunate.

Western military industries were first introduced by such

---

[28] Admiral Count Yamamoto Gombei, "The Japanese Navy," in *Fifty Years of New Japan*, Volume I, p. 224.

[29] Baron Oura Kanetake, "The Police of Japan," in *Fifty Years of New Japan*, Vol. I, pp. 281-2. "Soon after the Restoration the country was thrown into a whirlpool of disturbance. . . . Risings occurred in many places, and bloodshed and pillage kept the people in a state of constant apprehension and alarm. Nothing was more urgent at that time than a strong constabulary, and the government, at once recognizing this, created a force in the first year of Meiji (1868), *Shichu Torishimari*, or 'town constables,' in the city of Yedo (Tokyo), and those who had discharged the duties of police under the old government were appointed to the same work under the new. But this force was soon disbanded, and soldiers from the various fiefs were summoned to the office of city police. In the next year (1869) soldiers chosen from the clans were organized into a brigade of *Fuhei* or 'city guards' under the control of the Governor of the prefecture of Tokyo. Again in 1871 another change took place: three thousand *Rasotsu* (patrol men) were enlisted for the protection of the citizens, the city guards being disbanded at the same time. Thus a body of police was systematically formed for the first time in our country."

clans as Satsuma, Hizen, and Choshu. The first reverberatory furnace (used in the making of cannon) was set up by the Saga clan (Hizen) in 1850 and was ready for use in 1852.[30] Cannon had been made by that same clan on the Dutch model as early as 1842.[31] Reverberatory furnaces were built in rapid succession in Satsuma (1853), Mito (1855) and also for the Shogunate (1853), thanks to the labors of its greatest military reformer, Egawa Tarozaemon[32] whose services were not valued at their true worth by the obscurantist *Bakufu*.[33] In Satsuma a factory equipped with machinery for cannon-boring was completed in 1854; two iron-smelters were built in 1852 and six ships equipped with cannon between 1853 and 1856.[34] In Choshu an iron foundry was first built in 1854, and a shipyard where cannon could be mounted on ships was opened in 1857.[35] An iron foundry and gunsmithy were built in 1840 by the Mito clan on the Dutch model under the supervision of Tani Zenshiro at Kanzaki.[36] In 1855, after surmounting great difficulties in securing suitable materials and without having seen any of the models introduced into southern Japan, this clan constructed a reverberatory furnace, following the instructions of Dutch textbooks.[37]

In 1855, the *Bakufu* commenced work on an iron foundry completed in 1861; in 1857 it built a steamboat, and in 1865 established with French help the famous Yokosuka Iron Foundry and dockyards.[38] Thus under the necessity of modernizing mili-

[30] *Meiji Kogyo Shi* (History of Meiji Industry), edited by a committee under the chairmanship of Tanabe Sakuro, Tokyo, 1929, volume entitled *Kahei* (Military Industry), p. 15.

[31] *Ibid.*, p. 13.

[32] *Ibid.*, p. 16.

[33] For a brief outline of the difficulties in the way of military reform under the *Bakufu* with which the name Egawa Tarozaemon (1801-55) is connected, see Yamagata Aritomo, *op. cit.*, pp. 199-200.

[34] *Meiji Kogyo Shi*, pp. 19, 20, 21.

[35] *Ibid.*, p. 28.

[36] Takasu Yoshijiro, "Bakumatsu Sui-Han Seiyo Bummei Yunyu Hanashi" (The Story of the Introduction of Western Culture into the Mito Clan at the end of the *Bakufu*) in *Bungei Shunju*, Tokyo, March 1939, Volume XVIII, No. 5, p. 295.

[37] *Ibid.*, pp. 296-7.

[38] Tsuchiya and Okazaki. *Nihon Shihonshugi Hattatsu Shi Gaisetsu*, p. 145. The contract for this foundry and shipyards was drawn up in 1865 by an able technician and manager, Verny, working under the guidance of the French minister Léon Roches. Its construction was to last four years at a total cost of 2,400,000 piastres (yen?) and was to employ 2000 workmen. Actual construction commenced in 1867, and was not completed until 1871; despite the political

tary industries, the *Bakufu* introduced machine production on a limited scale in the strategic industries.

The Meiji Government inherited the problems of the Tokugawa regime, and accordingly it had first to perfect its military preparations; hence Japanese machine production was cradled during those days of military urgency in the strategic industries. Technology was still at a pre-capitalist stage; the spirit of enterprise among the capitalist class was still timorous, and capital accumulation on a very low level. For these reasons and on strategic grounds as well, it was necessary for the state to undertake the centralization and further development of these industries. The Meiji Government confiscated the *Bakufu's* military establishments and came forward as the chief entrepreneur in mining and heavy industrial production. For instance the Tokyo arsenal founded by the *Bakufu* and known as the Sekiguchi arsenal was taken over by the new government in 1870.[39] Foreign instructors were engaged in order to raise the technical level of arsenal workers as rapidly as possible, and such institutions as the *Juho Kyoikujo* were established for training in the manufacture of guns.[40] The Osaka arsenal was opened in 1870 with machinery taken from the Nagasaki Iron Foundry belonging formerly to the Shogunate.[41] Foreign instructors for the Yokosuka shipyard had been used even under the *Bakufu*, but the number was increased when these famous shipyards were confiscated by the Meiji Government, which by 1881 was employing 1,861 persons (Japanese) in one of the largest factories in Japan at the time.[42] Other great shipyards in the country were also taken over by the government; the Nagasaki in 1871, later sold to the Mitsubishi; and the Ishikawajima shipyards, first built by the Mito clan in 1854, acquired by the *Bakufu*, then confiscated by the Meiji Government and later, like the Nagasaki shipyards, put up at public sale by the government.[43] Engineering, technical and

revolution of 1868, Verny faithfully discharged his duties to the new government under the terms of the contract.

These details on the history of the most famous of Japanese naval shipyards are taken from an article "L'Arsenal de Yokosuka," unsigned editorial in the *Far East*, Tokyo, November 1897, Vol. II, Number 11, pp. 546-55.

[39] Kobayashi Ushisaburo, *Military Industries of Japan*, New York, 1922, pp. 20-30.

[40] Tsuchiya and Okazaki, *op. cit.*, p. 146.

[41] Kobayashi, *op. cit.*, p. 35.

[42] Tsuchiya and Okazaki, *op. cit.*, p. 147.

[43] *Ibid.*, pp. 147-8.

naval schools were founded with foreign instructors, while the best students were sent abroad to master the technique required in these key industries.[44]

Mining followed much the same lines. The government confiscated all the mines formerly operated by the *Bakufu* and clan governments and later sold the greater part of them to those financial circles close to it. The government's policy has been concisely stated by a Japanese authority: "At that time (the Restoration) ten important mines namely Sado, Miike, Ikuno, Takashima, Ani, Innai, Kamaishi, Nakakosaka, Okatsura and Kosuka were worked by the Government itself to obtain quick development, but after having been fairly started, they were transferred to the hands of private persons. Nowadays all mines except some few of iron and coal which serve some special objects are in private hands."[45] In order to increase production the government employed some of the best foreign experts they could secure.[46]

Transportation and communication were developed at a rapid pace thanks to the restless energy of the Meiji leaders. These activities were jealously watched to safeguard the interests of the state. The history of railway construction in Japan has been told many times; its task of opening up the home market is of particular importance. Although private capital was used in its development, the first lines were built by government enterprise with a loan of £913,000 from London. Toward the end of the century private capital in railways exceeded govern-

[44] *Ibid.*, p. 148.

[45] Furukawa Junkichi, "Mining," in *Fifty Years of New Japan*, Volume I, p. 610.

[46] Furukawa gives the names of the more famous foreign technicians and advisers; they include English, French, Germans and Americans. *Ibid.*, p. 609.

Among the most important mining enterprises taken over from the *Bakufu* or *han* governments by the Meiji Government, excluding those already mentioned, were the Ikuno silver mine (1868) and Sado gold mine (1869), both confiscated from the *Bakufu*, the Kozaka silver mine (1869), the Takashima coal mine (1872), the Daikatsu and Mayama gold mines (1873) and the Kamaishi iron mine, all taken over from various *han*. The Miike coal mine was at first the enterprise of the Miike clan; under the new regime it was first loaned out to the *shizoku* (ex-samurai) as a means of bettering their economic position, but was finally confiscated outright by the Government. In industry, besides those plants already mentioned, there were the Yokohama Iron Foundry and the Akabane Engineering Works, comprising the smelting-works given by the Saga clan to the *Bakufu* and confiscated by the Meiji Government. The Sakai Spinning-Mill, once the property of the Kagoshima clan, was taken over by the Government in 1872. Horie, *op. cit.*, pp. 245-6.

A list of eleven mines confiscated by the government and the dates of their sale into private hands is given by Tsuchiya and Okazaki, *op. cit.*, pp. 151-2.

ment, but in 1906 all but narrow-gauge lines were national-
ized.[47] Looking at it from the politico-military view, we must
note that the railroads were regarded as one of the most useful
instruments in national unification, and their strategic value
has never been neglected by the military wing of the government. For instance, in 1892 when the law for railway construction was passed establishing the principle of government ownership, a supervisory council was set up; this was called the
Tetsudo Kaigi, composed of twenty members, several of whom
were military men, and its first president, General Kawakami
Soroku, was perhaps the greatest strategist of his day.[48] A most
interesting example of military strategic considerations over-
riding commercial motives appears in the discussion regarding
the construction of the Nakasendo line traversing mountainous,
thinly populated country. Difficulties and expense seemed so
great that the plan was temporarily abandoned, and, in the
words of the authority on Japanese railroads, Viscount Inouye,
"But this was objected to (i.e. abandoning this route) by military men who insisted upon the advantages of the Nakasendo
from a strategical point of view."[49] This consideration loomed
large from the first in the task of weaving the web of transportation and communication.

One or two references to government documents will illustrate the attention paid to the strategical aspect of the telegraph
and telephone systems. In response to request for private ownership of telegraph lines, a proposal urging rejection of the request came to the *Dajokan* (Council of State) on August 2, 1872,
which read in part: "In the West there are countries where private lines are established for the purpose of communication;
but *the private lines often bring inconvenience in regard to secrecy of Government*. Besides, communications have a bearing

[47] The political, military and economic reasons for nationalization are given by
Watarai Toshiharu in *The Nationalization of Railways in Japan*, N. Y., 1914,
pp. 57-62.

[48] Kobayashi Yoshimasa, *Nihon Sangyo no Kosei* (The Structure of Japanese
Industry), Tokyo, 1935, p. 189, and p. 190, Note 3.

[49] Inouye, "Railroads," in *Fifty Years of New Japan* (cited), Vol. I, p. 441. In
another place he writes, "At this time, Prince Yamagata and other high officials
of the Army insisted upon the necessity of connecting Takasaki and Ogaki, and
subsequently, the Prince submitted to the Emperor his opinion to that effect."
Ibid., p. 439.

See also Minister of War Terauchi's answer to the query, "What danger is there
in the present system of private railroads regarded from the point of national
defense?" Watarai, *op. cit.*, p. 55.

on intercourse with other countries, so henceforth it is desirable to put an end to privately-owned lines and in the future make all lines government undertakings." This proposal was accepted.[50] That the value of the telegraph in modern warfare was so precociously grasped by the Meiji government may be seen in the effective· use they made of it to outmaneuver the Satsuma rebels in 1877.[51]

Private ownership of telephonic communications was similarly rejected. "At that time (1889), however, the Government was not in a position to open the service for public use, and an attempt was started to set up a private telephonic service. The Government decided, however, in favor of making it an official undertaking as in the case of the Telegraphs, and in 1890 the Telephone Service Regulations went into force."[52]

These few quotations from official or semi-governmental sources are intended to illustrate, not the main objectives in the modernization of the country through new industry, railway and telegraphic communications, but the special attention paid from the first to their *strategic* importance, which in turn arose from the *political necessity* of throwing up a rampart of defense around Japan to ward off the danger of attack which had been hanging over the country ever since the beginning of the 19th century, while at the same time guarding against internal disturbance which might arise from the excessive burdens laid upon the population in paying for this modernization. This condensed and one-sided account of the fostering of the strategic industries does not imply that there was anything sinister in the industrial policy of the early Meiji Government, nor is it intended to prove that modern Japan was planning from the start to embark on foreign conquest. But it is meant to show how political necessity, whether of foreign or internal origin, inevitably made the founders of new Japan sensitive to the strategic aspect

---

[50] *Meiji Zenki Zaisei Keizai Shiryo Shusei* (Collection of Historical Materials on Finance and Economy in the Early Years of the Meiji), edited by Tsuchiya Takao and Ouchi Hyoei, Tokyo, 1931, Vol. XVII, p. 215. (Italics mine E. H. N.)

This account goes on to describe the close network of lines established at an early date between the Department of Interior, the Department of Justice, the Metropolitan Police Bureau and Branch Police Stations. *Ibid.*, pp. 223-35.

[51] *Ibid.*, p. 222. "It was the Saigo Rebellion in 1877 that aroused the country to the importance of the Telegraph Service such as it was then." Baron Den Kenjiro, "Japanese Communications: The Post, Telegraph and Telephone," in *Fifty Years of New Japan*, Vol. I, pp. 418-19.

[52] *Ibid.*, p. 421.

of the industrialization of the country. It is to the credit of these Meiji leaders that, understanding the trend of the times, they resolutely set about reshaping the defenses and economic foundations of the country. In contrast we might note the utter incapacity of the Manchu Dynasty to accomplish a similar task in China. It was no fault of the Chinese themselves that they were unable to prevent the Western powers from penetrating the crumbling defenses of their empire; on the contrary, every patriotic attempt to modernize the country met with ruthless dynastic suppression. It is, however, to the lasting shame of the foreign dynasty then ruling over China, that it preferred to make a deal with foreign powers at the expense of national integrity in order to maintain its own precarious position as ruler of an estranged and sullen people. The unpatriotic policy of the Manchu Dynasty is reflected in the Chinese aphorism, "It is better to make a present to friendly states than to give it to your domestic slaves."[53] The logical end of this policy was strikingly seen when China was defeated by Japan in 1894-5. It was then discovered that the revenues marked for the creation of a modern fleet and for national defense had been used by the Old Buddha, the Empress Dowager, and her representative Prince Ch'un, on her pet project, the Summer Palace near Peking.[54] When this Chinese fleet intended for national defense met the Japanese navy, it had only one round of ammunition per gun. This incident vividly illustrates the gulf which separated the policy of the Ch'ing rulers, who thought more of their dynastic security and comfort than of Chinese independence, from the Meiji program of national reconstruction. This contrast might

[53] The original of this much paraphrased saying comes from a remark of Prince Ch'un's at a meeting of the Council when called to discuss the French campaign in Tonking and the growing discontent and revolt in Southern China. This diehard conservative, the favorite Councillor of Tzu Hsi said: "It were better to hand over the Empire to the Foreign Devils, than to surrender it at the dictation of these Chinese rebels." Quoted in J. O. P. Bland and E. Backhouse, *China Under the Empress Dowager*, London, 1912, p. 166.

[54] It is difficult to apportion the just balance of blame for this scandalous misappropriation of funds. One authority, while not absolving the Old Buddha, states that the chief agent of corruption was Prince Ch'un. Another authority places the blame upon the egregious rascal Li Lien-ying, the Chief Eunuch, whose truly enormous peculations were made possible by Tzu Hsi's indulgence toward him. J. O. P. Bland and E. Backhouse, *op. cit.*, pp. 169 and 195. Thus it would appear the safest course to single out not one member of the court, but impartially to condemn Tzu Hsi and her entourage—in short the Manchu Dynasty, of gross corruption and negligence.

serve to illustrate a fable entitled, "How can foreign rulers ever be patriots?"[55]

Starting Point of Japanese Industrialization Conditioned by Military Necessity

One aspect of the preceding major point is that in Japan, because of this concern with strategic industries, the normal order of the starting point and succeeding stages of capitalist production was reversed.[56] In the classical type of capitalist development the starting point is the production of consumers goods, chiefly by light industries such as the great textile mills of Lancashire which began to be important in the first quarter of the 18th century. Only when the light industries are nearing maturity does the production of capital goods become significant.

[55] These casual remarks are not to be taken as an attempt to formulate a serious norm for comparing Chinese and Japanese society in the Nineteenth Century. The possible value of the reference to Prince Ch'un and dynastic corruption in China is not to give the *reason* for the *difference* in the divergent paths trodden by China and Japan, but, by recounting a rather well-worn incident, to remind the reader how divergent in actual fact were those paths. I would be the first to admit the danger lurking behind the use of a term such as patriotism with regard to Imperial China; the concept of nationalism was as foreign to even (or perhaps especially) an educated Chinese of the last century as that of money was once to the American Indian. Pre-modern Chinese society consisted of thousands of cell-like, semi-autonomous communities living largely off the soil, governed as little as possible by an easy-going, leisure loving mandarinate; this society could produce a stubborn culture-consciousness, and hence even anti-foreign sentiment, but not *nationalism*. Chinese society was thus *sui generis*, making all comparison with other types of society hazardous if not disastrous to the impetuous student. To pass judgment on the failure of China under the Ch'ing to achieve an industrial society, and to contrast this with Japan's successful industrialization, the student should by all means eschew such touchstones as patriotism, and apply himself to a rigorous examination of the native characteristics of Chinese society, to the inter-relationship of merchant-usurer-official-landlord. He should probe into the reasons why merchant or state capital stopped so far short of developing into industrial capital; he must study Chinese society *as a whole*.

Scientific studies of Chinese society have not as yet progressed far enough for the non-specialist to venture upon generalization. However, should the reader be interested in pursuing this subject further, he is strongly recommended to read a recent study by E. V. G. Kiernan, *British Diplomacy in China 1880-1885*. Cambridge University Press, 1939. In Chapters XV and XVI the author ventures some penetrating *obiter dicta* on the reason why Nineteenth Century China failed to evolve "normally" into a modern capitalist society. Further bibliographical references to the subject will be found in his footnotes. (See also *supra*, Chap. II, note 53.)

[56] We are here contrasting the reversal in the order of industrial development, not the order or sequence in the *industrial revolution* which in Japan did not begin, at the earliest, until the 1880's when the textile industry shot up at record pace. What some call the second industrial revolution, marked by the great expansion in heavy industry, took place during and after the World War.

Heavy industries in England did not assume importance comparable to the light branch until the invention of the lathe at the end of the 18th century. This normal order of transition from light to heavy industry was reversed in Japan.[57] Before the first introduction of cotton spinning machines in Japan in 1866,[58] even before the importation of foreign fabrics, engineering works and arsenals had been established. Cannon were cast as early as 1844 in Mito,[59] and engineering works were established, as we have seen, in 1856 for military and naval purposes in southern Japan. Reverberatory furnaces, arsenals, foundries and shipyards were built in Satsuma, Saga, Choshu and also in the *Bakufu* domain in the fifties. The first silk mills to be equipped with modern machinery were not built until 1870 with the filature of Maebashi, on the Italian model, and the French model mill at Tomioka in 1872, with Italian and French technical supervisors.[60]

This reversed order brought about a certain deformity in Japanese technological growth. From the first the strategic military industries were favored by the government, and technologically they were soon on a level with the most advanced Western countries. We have noted how the arsenals in Nagasaki were originally under Dutch supervision, the Yokosuka shipyard arsenal and iron works under French, and other shipyards under English care. These foreign technicians trained the Japanese so that in time native workers were technically as literate as their foreign tutors. In the textile industries foreign managers and assistants were also employed: English in the Kagoshima spinning mill, French in Tomioka and Fukuoka, Swiss or Italian in the Maebashi filatures. For training in engi-

[57] The military-political significance of industrialization is generally recognized by most authorities. For a convenient summary of this aspect of industrialization, see Horie, *Nihon Shihonshugi no Seiritsu*, pp. 270-1.

[58] The first spinning factory with machinery was set up by the Satsuma clan in Kagoshima. Shimazu Tadayoshi (1840-97) son of Hisamitsu, in March 1864 instructed the two clan *yonin* Shinnon Hisanaga and Godai Tomoatsu who were leaving on a trip for Europe, to buy spinning machinery there. Machinery arrived in 1866, and the factory was ready for work in 1867. The manager was an Englishman, who had six assistants of the same nationality and two hundred Japanese working under him. Tsuchiya and Okazaki, *op. cit.*, p. 267.

[59] Orchard, *op. cit.*, p. 92.

[60] Yosio, *Der Durchbruch des Kapitalismus in Japan*, (cited) p. 32, note. Tsuchiya and Okazaki say that the Maebashi filature was under Swiss supervision and the Gumma mill at Tomioka under French. *Op. cit.*, pp. 299-300.

neering, government technical schools were established with foreign instructors, while the best Japanese students were sent abroad to master the most up-to-date technique, to replace foreign advisers on their return.[61] In this way the military key industries were technically advanced while those industries which were not of strategic value, or did not compete against foreign articles in the international or home market were left in their primitive handicraft stage of development.

It was the Meiji policy to bring under government control the arsenals, foundries, shipyards and mines formerly scattered among various *han* or *Bakufu* domains, then to centralize and develop them until they reached a high level of technical efficiency, while at the same time initiating other strategic enterprises such as chemical industries (sulphuric acid works, glass and cement factories); and the last step was to sell a large portion of these industries to the handful of trusted financial oligarchs. But control over the most vitally strategic enterprises, such as arsenals, shipyards and some sectors of mining was kept in government hands.

Change in Industrial Policy and the Law for the Transfer of Government Factories

This peculiarity in early Japanese industrialization—the predominance of state control over industrial enterprise—is reflected in the manner in which the government, while retaining and strengthening its control over the key industries, disposed of the peripheral or less strategic industries by selling them into private hands. This change in government industrial policy from direct control to indirect protection was symbolized in the promulgation of the *Kojo Harai-Sage Gaisoku* (Regulations or Law on the Transfer of Factories) on November 5, 1880. The reason given by the government for the change of policy appears in the preamble. "The factories established for

[61] The burning desire of Japanese leaders to overtake Western technique, particularly in the vitally important sectors of industry, is reflected in the words of Okubo when he visited the Kagoshima Spinning Mill in 1869, "I went to see the Iso spinning-machine; the way it operates is marvelously smooth and delicate, and no words can describe it. What a difference there is between the intelligence of foreigners and ours (so that) we must sigh with shame." Quoted by Horie, *op. cit.*, p. 253.

The role of foreign experts in Japanese industrialization is described by Orchard, *op. cit.*, pp. 90 *et seq.*

encouraging industries are now well organized and business has become prosperous, so the Government will abandon its ownership (of factories) which ought to be run by the people."[62] Although the preamble expresses the belief that various enterprises created and fostered by the government could now be turned over to private ownership to operate at a profit, it was admitted elsewhere by Matsukata that many projects under direct state control were not at all profitable, but on the contrary threatened to become a drain on the revenue rather than a source of profit for the exchequer.[63] The gradual disposal of government-owned factories, chiefly, as we shall see, of enterprises not strictly military, left the government free to devote its finances and administrative energy more exclusively to the military or strategic industries. Without making this distinction, an American authority has described this change of policy. "There are few modern industries in Japan today that do not owe their existence to government initiative. In most cases the government has endeavored to withdraw from the industries as soon as possible and to turn them over to private companies, but in some cases that has been impossible and the government has continued as an active agent in manufacturing."[64]

The general tendency described above should not be interpreted too strictly, as if the new policy ushered in by the law for the sale of factories divided Japanese industries into two sharply defined groupings, the one related to the armament industries where government control was maintained, and the other embracing all the remaining non-strategic industries which were suddenly to be exposed to the vicissitudes of pure *laissez-faire*. The distinction to be made is rather in the *different form* of paternalism adopted by the government after 1880; that is to say, the government retained paternalism as before, both in the military and non-military enterprises after the sale of government factories, but in a form appropriate to each of these two sectors of industry. The *Noshomusho* (Department of Ag-

[62] From *Meiji Zaisei Shi* (History of Meiji Finance), Volume XII, p. 231, and quoted in Horie, *op. cit.*, p. 262.

[63] Matsukata's statement to this effect appears in his "Shiheiseiri-Shimatsu" (Circumstances Concerning the Regulation of Paper Currency) in *Meiji Zenki Zaisei Keizai Shiryo Shusei*, Volume XI, pp. 215-16.

[64] Orchard, *op. cit.*, p. 90.

riculture and Commerce), established in April 1881, was the government organ fashioned to realize its new policy.[65]

As indicated above, the first transfers were made in the non military industries. The model cotton-spinning mills set up by the government in 1881 in Hiroshima and Aichi with the most up-to-date English machinery were sold to Hiroshima prefecture (1882) and to the Shinoda Company (1886) respectively.[66] The Shinagawa Glass Factory was handed over to the Ishimura Company in 1885, and the Shimmachi Spinning Mill to the Mitsui in 1887 and the Fukuoka filature to the same company in 1883; the Fukagawa Cement Factory was leased to the Asano Company in 1883, and sold outright the following year.[67]

In the sphere of railroad construction, government ownership of lines was partially abandoned in 1880, and the next year the Nippon Railway Company was founded, receiving generous government loans and subsidies during the most active period of railroad construction.[68]

The role of government subsidy is most spectacularly demonstrated in sea transportation. Long before the law for the sale of factories, the government gave *gratis* to Iwasaki Yataro, the founder of the Mitsubishi Company, the thirteen ships used for military transport in the Formosan expedition of 1874; and this was soon followed by another stroke of fortune for the company, the purchase of the Yubin Jokisen Kaisha, a semi-govern-

[65] During the period of government initiative in industrial development, when every detail of financial, political or technical nature had to be studied and settled by the government, the organ of control was the short-lived but enormously important and successful *Kobusho* (Department of Industry). Its responsibilities were the following: (1) to establish an institution for technological education; (2) to foster the industrial arts with suitable rewards, and to make industrial production prosper; (3) to supervise and manage all mining enterprises; (4) to construct and keep in repair all railroad and telegraph lines, as well as lighthouses; (5) to build and repair the naval and mercantile ships; (6) to undertake the refining and casting of copper, iron and lead ores for use in various enterprises, and to engage in machine construction; and (7) to undertake land and sea surveys. See the "Kobusho Enkaku Hokoku" (Memorandum on the History of the Department of Industry), in *Meiji Zenki Zaisei Keizai Shiryo Shusei*, Vol. XVII, pp. 10-11.

Although short-lived (1870-85) the *Kobusho* acted as the indispensable co ordinating agent in the process of industrialization imposed from above. The new department, the *Noshomusho*, established in 1881, effected the gradual and smooth transfer of industries into private hands, also maintaining that type of paternalism necessary under the changed circumstances.

[66] Kobayashi Yoshimasa, *Nihon Sangyo no Kosei*, p. 104.

[67] *Ibid.*, p. 104.

[68] Inouye Masaru, "Japanese Communications: Railroads," *loc. cit.*, pp. 437-9.

mental fleet, for 320,000 yen.[69] In the government's desire to build up a strong mercantile marine it favored this company from the beginning by giving it a yearly subsidy of 250,000 yen, starting from 1875 and lasting for fifteen years.[70] To bolster the monopoly position of this company, the government enacted in 1876 the *Gaikokusen Norikomi Kisoku* (Rules regarding the Boarding of Foreign Ships), thus delivering a crushing blow to the P. and O. hopes of obtaining a monopoly in its newly opened Yokohama-Shanghai service.[71] In the period immediately following the promulgation of the law for the sale of factories the government temporarily abandoned its policy of favoring exclusively the Mitsubishi Company, and with a view to stimulating sea-transport through competition, it established a rival line, the Kyodo Un'yu Kaisha, in 1883, thereby precipitating a bitter struggle with the Mitsubishi.[72] Mobilizing all its financial resources, as well as its wide-spread political agents and allies, the Mitsubishi succeeded in effecting amalgamation with the Kyodo Un'yu Kaisha in 1885, forming the world-famous Nippon Yusen Kaisha. The government now threw its full weight behind this great monopoly firm, granting it a yearly subsidy of 880,000 yen.[73]

After disposing of some of its model factories in the non military industries, the government gradually turned over some of its mining and shipbuilding enterprises to private hands. Among the most notable transfers in this sphere was the lease (in 1884) and sale a few years later of the great Nagasaki shipyards to the Mitsubishi Company.[74] In 1896 the same company acquired the Ikuno silver mine and the Sado gold mine.[75] The Mitsui Company secured a large share in the confiscated *Bakufu*

[69] Kobayashi, *op. cit.*, p. 170. Also Karl Rathgen, "Japan's Volkswirtschaft und Staatshalt," in G. Schmoller (ed.), *Staats und Socialwissenschaftliche Forschungen*, Leipzig, 1891, Vol. 45, X, pp. 296-7.

[70] Kobayashi, *op. cit.*, pp. 170-1.

[71] An account of this rivalry and of the Mitsubishi victory is to be found in an editorial, "The Development of Navigation in Japan," in the *Far East*, Tokyo, Vol. I, No. 6, pp. 3-4.

[72] The Kyodo Un'yu Kaisha was also established partly as a naval defense measure. *Cf.* Iida Tadao, *Iwasaki Yataro* (Life of Iwasaki Yataro), Tokyo. 1937, pp. 221-47.

[73] Kobayashi, p. 171.

[74] For further details on the growth of Mitsubishi enterprises largely through government aid, see G. C. Allen, "The Concentration of Economic Control in Japan." *Economic Journal,* June 1937, pp. 271-87.

[75] Tsuchiya and Okazaki. *op. cit.*, p. 151.

and *han* enterprises, including textile mills and the famous Miike coal mine.[76] The Furukawa Company bought from the government the Ani gold mine in 1880 and the Innai gold mine in 1894.[77]

One could go on describing the process of transfer of large sections of government-controlled industry into the hands of the financial oligarchy. Among Japanese scholars there is considerable controversy regarding the real motivation of the government in its sale of these industries.[78] But there is no doubt that this policy greatly enhanced the power of the financial oligarchy, especially in view of the ridiculously low prices at which the government sold its model factories.[79] But what is most striking in this process is that, from their favored position as financial supporters of the new regime, a few families, such as the Mitsui, Mitsubishi, Sumitomo, Yasuda as well as the lesser Kawasaki, Furukawa, Tanaka and Asano, have continually strengthened their advantage through such measures as the purchase at low rates of the well-organized government industries. But most important is the position of the smaller circle of financial oligarchs, the *Zaibatsu*, made up of the first four companies

[76] Allen, *loc. cit.*, p. 273.

[77] Tsuchiya and Okazaki, *op. cit.*, p. 152. Other transfers of government enterprise were the Hyogo Dockyard, leased to the Mitsubishi in 1883 and sold to the Kawasaki Company in 1886; the Nakakosaka Iron Mine, sold to the Sakamoto Company in 1884; and the Kosaka Silver Mine, sold to Fujita in 1886. Kobayashi, *op. cit.*, pp. 103-4.

[78] Various explanations of this act have been summarized by Professor Horie. (1) To avoid competition between government and private enterprise (The Taiyo Magazine). (2) To avoid the charge of unfair subsidy or nepotism; on the eve of the opening of the Diet the government wished to appear to be abandoning paternalism and adopting laissez-faire (Takahashi Kamekichi). (3) By selling industries to favored monopolistic companies, the government hoped to gain more flexible control over the key industries (Kobayashi Yoshimasa and Yamada Moritaro). Professor Horie does not advance any new interpretation of his own but would seem to favor (2). Horie, *op. cit.*, pp. 262-3.

[79] The following table will give an indication of these low prices of sale. The price of transfer is compared only to the expenditures of the Department of Industry on the enterprise concerned.

Name of Company	Price of Transfer	Government Expenditure (Kogyohi)
Furukawa Cement Company	250,000 yen (including the price of the land)	468,000 yen
Innai Mine	75,000 yen	195,000 yen
Kosaka Mine	200,000 yen	547,000 yen
Shinagawa Glass Factory	80,000 yen	189,000 yen

See Mori Kiichi, *Nihon Shihonshugi Hattatsu Shi Josetsu* (Introduction to the History of the Development of Japanese Capitalism), Tokyo, 1934. p. 263.

in the above list, which, through the tremendous leverage given by their interlocking control over banking on the one hand and industry and commerce on the other, have been able to swallow lesser industrial concerns.[80]

As stated above, the government policy of selling some of its enterprises into the hands of the favored financiers left it free to concentrate on purely military industries which were kept strictly under government control as formerly. After the suppression of the Satsuma Revolt, the government resolutely set about expanding its armament industries; despite retrenchment in other state expenditures in this period (1881-7) there was a sharp increase (over 60%) in military expenditures and (1881-91) naval estimates (200%) as seen in the following tables:[81]

MILITARY EXPENSES

Year	Ordinary	Extraordinary	Total
1878............	6,409,005	220,739	6,629,744 yen
1881............	8,179,712	559,060	8,738,772
1884............	10,764,593	771,190	11,535,783
1887............	11,842,619	565,917	12,408,536

NAVAL EXPENSES

	Total of Ordinary and Special Expenditures
1871.................	886,856 yen
1881.................	3,108,516
1891.................	9,501,692

These projects required the import of expensive finished and semi-finished military equipment. But in this sphere of enterprise profit or loss was of no account, and strategic consideration was everything. However, this great expansion in the armament industries had the effect of stimulating the drive for self-sufficiency in Japanese industry. The military industries thus became a mold which shaped the pattern of Japanese heavy industry.

The policy of keeping a tight control upon military industries while maintaining paternalism of appropriate sorts over other types of enterprise has continued down to the present and is one of the most distinctive characteristics of the history of

---

[80] This point is emphasized by Allen, in *Economic Journal* (cited), pp. 278-9.

[81] Yamagata Aritomo, in *Fifty Years of New Japan*, Vol. I, p. 215; Yamamoto Gombei, *ibid.*, p. 230. For the naval expansion of 1882 and the naval bonds of 1886, see Yamamoto, *ibid.*, p. 224.

Japanese industrialization. It can be traced back beyond the days of the Restoration to the time when feudal lords took a sudden interest in acquiring modern Western military equipment long before they thought of engaging in other forms of industrial enterprise.

Let us for the moment trace very briefly the effect of this unique government control over key industries as it affects the importance of the bureaucracy.

The Key Industries and the Bureaucracy

The scarcity of accumulated capital in the Tokugawa period, the technical backwardness of Japanese industry, Japan's poverty in raw materials and the restriction on the tariff made it exceedingly difficult for private capital to compete with foreign capital on the home market and, at a later date, on the international market unless it received from the start generous state aid in the form of subsidies.[82] This tendency was strengthened toward the end of the century as other nations advanced from *laissez-faire* to monopoly, creating conditions favorable to state intervention and to the interlocking of state and monopoly capital in Japan. The merging of private and state capital, particularly in those branches of industry close to war economy, such as transport, steel, and machine-making, gave new strength to the bureaucracy, placing it politically on an equal if not superior level to its partner, private monopoly capital. It is generally agreed that in the early Meiji period government-controlled enterprise provided wide scope in the employment of the declassed *samurai* who formed part of the new bureaucracy as managers, administrators and departmental officials.[83] From the middle of the Meiji era, when a large number of state enterprises was turned over to private corporations and party politics rose on a very limited scale, the bureaucracy went into eclipse. But in recent years, since the Great War and more especially since the Manchurian Incident, the growth of military industries implies the importance of state enterprise and the conse-

[82] The absence of tariff autonomy, although it has been referred to in various connections above, had the immediate effect of necessitating state subsidy and protection of industry, and deserves fuller attention than can be afforded here. There is however, excellent material on this aspect of Japanese industrialization, notably the article by Herbert M. Bratter, "Subsidies in Japan," in *Pacific Affairs*, May 1931, Vol. III, pp. 377-93, and Orchard, *op. cit.*, pp. 89-90.

[83] The relation of the old feudal classes to the new state enterprises and their employment in them is explained in Horie, *op. cit.*, pp. 270-3.

quent resurrection of the bureaucracy.[84] In the responsible task of administering these gigantic state enterprises the bureaucracy, which had been unobtrusively consolidating its power even in past days when it was in relative obscurity, although it has not yet assumed such direct leadership as in the Meiji period, now acts not only as the custodian of Japan's most vital economic activities, but with one hand in the military camp and the other in that of finance capital, it also attempts to reconcile the conflicts between these camps. In this mediating role it has shown signs of emerging from its temporary cloud to take over once more government leadership as in the early Meiji but under greatly changed circumstances.[85]

In fine, the features conditioning Meiji policy were, first, the insufficient accumulation of capital which necessitated state enterprise and facilitated the centralization of capital and economic control in the hands of the financial oligarchy. Even after state enterprise was partially abandoned, the government policy of subsidy was maintained if not strengthened. This policy was partly the outcome of the treaty system, whereby after the first commercial treaty of 1858 the tariff was restricted to a low rate and still further reduced by the tariff convention of 1866. Tariff autonomy was secured through the general treaty revision of 1899 and went into force in 1910. Second, it was the military aspect of industrialization dictated by the international situation and internal forces which caused those sections of industry most closely connected with defense to remain even to this day under close state supervision. Finally, we note the policy of transference of certain branches of industry to a narrow circle of large banking houses whose position, fortified at the time, has continued to dominate Japanese industrial activity to the present day.

With respect to technical development in Japanese indus-

---

[84] In the census of 1925, the number of workers employed in state enterprises in manufacturing, mining and transport was 523,000 out of a total of 2,770,000 employed in these same industries—or one-fifth. The capital invested in state enterprises in these industries was 2,968,000,000 yen out of a total of 10,014,000,000 yen, or 30%. In these industries on which a war economy depends, the state owns 66.5% of total investments in transport, 51% of total investments in iron and steel, and 13% in machine-making. See O. Tanin and E. Yohan, *When Japan Goes to War*, New York, 1936, p. 104.

[85] For a short but suggestive comment describing this recent revival of the bureaucracy, see Minoru Uchida, "Japan as a Totalitarian State," (Open Discussion) in *Amerasia*, May 1938, pp. 133-6, especially p. 134.

trialization, two distinct tendencies stand out in bold relief. There is, first, the growth of those branches of national economy most closely linked with military enterprises in a wider sense—engineering, shipbuilding, mining, railways and the like —where the government maintained strict control, backed by politically favored and trusted financial houses. These industries, most highly developed in the technical sense and fashioned after the most up-to-date Western models, were the pride of the state bureaucracy which jealously guarded them even after large parts were acquired by private capital. Secondly, we note the development of "left-over" industries engaged in the manufacture of typically Japanese products both for the home and foreign markets. These industries have been dominated by the capital of small traders and usurers, and have been compelled to remain at a primitive stage technically, employing to a large extent domestic and female labor.

CHAPTER V

THE AGRARIAN SETTLEMENT AND ITS SOCIAL CONSEQUENCES

The agrarian settlement of the early Meiji, which is basic to the understanding both of modern agricultural conditions and of Japanese society as a whole, merits a volume rather than a chapter; hence its treatment here will be highly condensed and perhaps arbitrary. Modern Japanese agriculture with its unique tenant-landlord relations, with its small scale of operation and primitive agricultural technique, received its final shaping in the early years of the Meiji period. It is a subject not only of intrinsic interest, but also it is the source from which flow many other social phenomena, such as the beginning of the labor market, the formation and limitations of the home market for the disposal of manufactured goods, the creation of a surplus population in the form peculiar to Japan, the growth and characteristics of the Japanese labor movement, and the position of female labor. Of the social phenomena listed above it is our intention to treat only two or three, in particular the creation of a body of free labor (which is the last of the three pre-conditions for industrialization listed in the last chapter), the nature of surplus population in Japan, and the significance of domestic or supplementary household industry. But first we must consider the central problem, the actual land settlement of the early Meiji period.

The Trend Toward Private Ownership in Land

Annexation of land by a new landlord class had been going on surreptitiously under the feudal regime; it was legally recognized following the Meiji Restoration. After their emancipation from feudalism the peasants became nominally free-holders. but this process actually opened the way for the dispossession of the peasantry, since the removal of the ban prohibiting the sale and division of land legalized the various mechanisms for the unlimited acquisition of land by forced sale, mortgage and the like. So we can say that the Restoration brought genuine

136

emancipation to the peasant *qua* landholder but not necessarily *qua* cultivator. At the beginning of the Meiji era most of the peasantry were independent cultivators, and although accurate figures do not exist, it has been estimated that shortly after the Restoration tenant land occupied 30 per cent of the area cultivated.[1]

The removal of the ban against the sale of land in 1872 was a step in the direction of a modern land tax, as can be seen by the report of the *Okura-sho* (Department of Finance) to the *Dajokan* (Council of State) in September 1871. "Now that political power is wholly restored to the Imperial Court, at a time when various affairs of state are unified, it is necessary to establish a uniform law relating to tax legislation which is so vital a matter to the state. . . . Abandoning ancient laws and permitting sale and purchase of real property, it would be better to enforce a land tax derived from a unified system of land rent. But above all one must guard against the hasty enactment of the law, and on this account *one should first permit the permanent alienation of landed property and after that establish a simplified law for tax collection.*"[2] One more quotation may illustrate the importance of the freedom to alienate land for tax revision.[3] In the memorial of 1871 written by Kanda Kohei, one of the chief architects of land tax revision, we read: "There are those who oppose tax revision; they say 'in old times people were allotted land according to the size of the household (or

[1] This proportion of 30% tenant land is based on sectional estimates made at that time and later. For instance, in the survey of eighteen prefectures in 1883, tenant land was 34.2% of the total cultivated area, and in the same prefectures this proportion had risen to 38.09% in 1887. See Tsuchiya and Okazaki, *Nihon Shihonshugi Hattatsu Shi Gaisetsu*, p. 220. A survey of sixteen other prefectures in 1884 gives the proportion of tenant land as 39.8%. *Ibid.*, p. 221. Another estimate made from a study of local statistics gives the proportion for all Japan as 30.6% in 1872, the year before land tax revision. Hirano, *Nihon Shihonshugi Shakai no Kiko*, p. 55.

[2] (Italics mine E. H. N.) The excerpt is taken from the *Okura-sho's* (Department of Finance) *Chiso Kaisei Reiki Enkaku Satsuyo* (An Outline History of the Regulations for Land Tax Revision), quoted in Ono Takeo, *Ishin Noson Shakai Shiron* (An Historical Essay on Village Society at the Restoration), Tokyo, 1932, p. 189.

The law of September 1871, granting freedom of crop, was also a step toward the regularization of private property in land.

[3] See Maki Kenji, "Meiji Shonen ni okeru Tochi Eitai Kaikin" (The Removal of the Ban on the Permanent Alienation of Land in the Early Years of the Meiji Era), in *Rekishi to Chiri* (History and Geography), Volume XX, No. 6, Tokyo, December, 1927, pp. 450-82. The author shows how this measure was the first step in the recognition of private ownership of land, a tendency strengthened by land tax revision. *Ibid.*, pp. 463-64.

according to the census), and it prevented alienation of land and evened up the gap between rich and poor. If we suddenly allow the sale and purchase of land now, it would be contrary to established law and would cause great harm.' The answer to this question is as follows: Here we have a wise and there a foolish man, and again here is a diligent and there an idle man. The one who is wise as well as thrifty becomes rich, while he who is idle and wasteful becomes poor; if we prevent the annexation of land and try to level the rich with the poor, it means stinting the rich to give to the poor, and gradually that would assume such proportions as to submerge the wise and thrifty while encouraging the idle and wasteful."[4] Here we have the perennial parable of the idle poor and the diligent rich, used to give weight to the argument that feudal "paternalism" and communal responsibility must now bow before the unrestricted right of the individual to own landed property. The wheels of history were inexorably moving in the direction of the legalization of private ownership of land, and in every age and country the small man, whether tenant, customary holder, or peasant proprietor, has been crushed beneath those wheels. Japan was no exception.

Land Tax Revision of 1873

Since the Land Tax Revision of 1873 fixed once and for all the framework within which modern Japanese agrarian relations are confined, it is perhaps worth spending a few pages on an examination of its form and content.

Before it was possible to establish a uniform land tax assessed according to the value of land and not by the feudal system of sharing the produce between lord and peasant, it was necessary that each piece of land whether worked by tenant or independent cultivator should have a recognized owner. In other words, the proposed land tax entailed the fullest recognition of the private ownership of land. We have seen some of the measures logically leading up to this revision, and these were to be supplemented now by the distribution of certificates of landownership known as *chiken*. The first lot were issued in January 1872, another series in February and finally a third in July of the

[4] *Meiji Zaisei Shi* (History of Meiji Finance), compiled and edited by the Meiji Zaisei Shi Hensan Kai (The Committee for the Compilation of the History of Meiji Finance), Tokyo, 1904, Vol. V, p. 319.

same year.[5] This system of *chiken* served as an entering wedge in the drive to uproot the old feudal land system and to gain recognition for the concept of private ownership of land, while at the same time it provided the basis for an assessment of the

[5] These *chiken* or certificates present some delicate questions in law which do not concern us here. The early *chiken* system acted as a scaffolding for building the system of private property in land; moreover, since it has not been treated fully in foreign literature, it may be of some service to describe briefly the details relating to these certificates of land ownership.

In December 1871, an edict from the *Dajokan* (Council of State) abolished in Tokyo what was known as *bukeji* and *choji* (*samurai* land and townsmen's land), which under the Tokugawa had been exempt from tax. This abolition was a step toward the legal recognition of the land in question as the property of an individual who would in the future be responsible for the land tax assessed according to the value of the land. In the following January (1872) regulations were issued to Tokyo-Fu by the *Okura-sho* (Department of Finance) which laid down the principles for the issuance of *chiken* to owners of the former *bukeji* and *choji*. Tokyo was chosen as the first place in which to begin this experiment since private ownership of land had been recognized longest there. Despite the ban on alienation of land, first promulgated in 1643, land had been freely transferred in Edo within the *chonin* and *samurai* classes. Another reason for choosing this locality first was that formerly it had been tax-exempt; and by issuing *chiken* for holdings, the government clearly intended to show that in the future all such land would be taxed. This precaution was taken to avoid any charge of partiality.

The second issue of *chiken* was on February 24 of the same year, just nine days after the removal of the ban against permanent annexation of land. *Chiken* were now given to those who had bought land since the new regime, and the purchasing price was used as the basis for the first estimate of land values.

The third distribution of *chiken* came in July of the same year, when the trend toward private ownership of land had demonstrably gathered momentum and when those in possession of land who had not yet received *chiken* were anxious to obtain the legal recognition of their proprietary rights. In this third distribution many points of technical difficulty arose concerning proof of ownership, especially where no recent transaction of land had taken place, and amid the welter of claims and counter-claims it was only natural that chicanery and sharp practice succeeded in some cases in carrying the day. At any rate it is not surprising that there were many discontented people after the final distribution had been made, since the claims often had to be substantiated by the not too exact records of customary and traditional land-rights kept by the village headmen (*shoya* or *nanushi*). The latter, being human and, indeed, more sympathetic to the landlord's than to the peasant's outlook, often inclined their ear more favorably to the claims of the well-to-do usurer and landlord than to the poorly articulated demands of the peasant whose memory of customary practice and tenure was, despite his illiteracy, as long as his family history and as good proof, he believed, as any piece of paper. The inevitable dissatisfaction which followed the distribution of *chiken* in some quarters reached the proportion of angry demonstrations and riots.

The village common lands were registered at first as village land and were finally made state property in July 1889.

For the details given above, the chief source of reference has been Ono Takeo, *Ishin Noson Shakai Shiron*, a sub-section entitled "Chiken Seido" (The Chiken System), pp. 185-203.

land according to its sale value, before the land survey of the Empire could be carried out (1875-81). Indeed, transactions in land (sale and purchase) served as the chief basis for the issuance of *chiken*. These certificates or *chiken* remained as the sole proof of landownership until the law of March 22, 1889 was passed, when the government recalled all duplicate copies of *chiken* and in return, proof of landownership was henceforth established by registration in the *daicho* (registers) kept in the *ku-saibansho* (sub-district court) and certified by the *chian saibansho* (justices of the peace, since reorganized under another name).[6]

The revision of the land tax was not a hasty make-shift measure but a reform which occupied the best minds in the government over a long period of time. The names of Inouye Kaoru, Okuma Shigenobu, Kato Kozo, Kanda Kohei and Matsukata Masayoshi are notable in this connection. After a patient, exhaustive review of all relevant memoranda, and after many deliberations of committees and assemblies, the act of revision was promulgated early in 1873. The legislators saw that the most urgent need for stable government revenue was a unified system of taxation—a tax that was easy to collect and difficult to evade, and above all a tax that would not fluctuate according to the harvest. Kanda Kohei expressed well the inadequacy of the old system when he wrote in his memorial of 1870, relating to land tax revision, "If we follow the same tax-legislation as in the past, in the first place it would be troublesome; in the second it would be likely to bring reduced revenue since it would invite cheating and evasion; moreover, such legislation shows no regard for the people's interests, and as a matter of law it has loopholes which would bring loss to the state finances."[7] The question of tax revision was debated before a specially convoked session of prefectural officials in 1873, when three views were argued. The one which finally prevailed urged a thorough change in the land tax, rather than bothering to patch up the old system. Under the guidance of Vice-Minister of Finance Okuma Shigenobu (in charge of the Department during Okubo's asbence in Europe), this plan was carried out, involving a change from a tax in kind to a money tax collected according to

6 *Ibid.*, p. 186; and La Mazelière, *op. cit.*, V, p. 113.
7 Quoted in Tsuchiya and Okazaki, *Nihon Shihonshugi Hattatsu Shi Gaisetsu*, p. 50.

the value of land which was to be assessed in a nation-wide survey.[8]

The three basic principles of the land tax were: (1) whereas formerly the norm for tax payment had been the harvest, now it was to be the value of land; (2) the rate of taxation was to be 3 per cent of the land value (reduced in 1876 for a short time to 2½ per cent) with no increase or decrease for good or bad years, an adjustment possible under the paternalistic feudal regime; (3) the tax was to be collected in money, not as formerly in kind.[9] This tax at 3 per cent of the land value actually meant a reduction from the old feudal tax if the local tax at 1 per cent were not included.[10] But it cut deeper than this; it meant a qualitative as well as quantitative change from the feudal tax system. These points of difference can be summarized as follows: first, the diverse forms of levy which were imposed both arbitrarily and by custom under the *Bakufu* and *han* governments were now unified under a national central government. Secondly, in former days the *direct producers*, irrespective of whether they were tenants or independent cultivators, were the

[8] *Ibid.*, pp. 56-7. The principle adopted for assessment in the land survey following tax revision was to determine the "legal value" of land by the average yield of each piece during five years at the average price of rice, etc., prevalent in the locality. This sum was then capitalized and accepted as the basis of the land tax. Revaluation was to take place every six years, but this plan was not carried out. It will be seen from the above that the principle of land evaluation did not differ fundamentally from the feudal idea of capacity to pay according to the yield of the land. For the above, see Ono Yeijiro, "The Industrial Transition in Japan," in *Publications of the American Economic Association,* Baltimore, January, 1890, Volume 2, Number 1, pp. 32-3.

[9] For the makeshift system of taxation which survived the Restoration up to 1873 and which, though a continuation of the old feudal tax, was collected on a national instead of fief basis. See Chapter III, note 77, *supra.*

[10] The official account says: "Under the old *(Bakufu)* regime the land tax was 5:5 (that is five parts to the lord or state and five to the people), but there were exceptions, so in reality often the rate was 3:7 (three to the state and seven to the people). But now the land tax was fixed at 3 per cent of the land value; therefore if one puts the harvest at 100 the tax will be 24 or 25 per cent, so it means a decrease of 4 to 5 per cent." *Meiji Zaisei Shi,* Vol. V, p. 336. If we add the local tax of 1% to the land tax there is actually very little difference from the old feudal tax as far as the rate is concerned.

This fact is also attested by the leading authorities—for example, Ono Takeo's estimate to be found in Ikemoto, *op. cit.,* pp. 263-4, where detailed examination of the rate of taxation ends with the categorical statement, "Dans ce cas nous constatons que, par suite de la révision, *la charge de l'impôt foncier diminua brusquement*" (italics in original). *Ibid.,* p. 264. This was even before the reduction of the rate from 3 to 2½% in 1876.

For a table illustrating the share of state, landlord and tenant in the various transitional stages of the early Meiji period, see note 29, *infra.*

tax-payers, but now only the *landowner,* whether independent producer or absentee landlord, paid the land tax. Thirdly, under the *ancien régime* the tax was fixed according to the yield, or according to the type of soil; but after revision it was fixed at the uniform rate of 3 per cent of the land value without regard to bumper or lean years. Finally, the former payment of the tax in kind, principally in rice, was now changed to a money payment.

The Meiji leaders saw the necessity of taking this step in order to get rid of the fluctuations caused by the variations in the harvest as well as in the price of rice or other agricultural products which had been used as payment for a tax in kind. In other words, by providing for a *constant* source of revenue, they were making possible a modern budgetary financial system. In a country still agricultural and lacking tariff autonomy it was natural that the very considerable burden of military expenditures as well as of capital outlay for model industries and the maintenance of a large body of bureaucrats should be made dependent on the land tax, and it was important that this revenue should not fluctuate. We saw how removing the ban against permanent annexation of land—a measure bound to come in time—logically preceded and blazed the way for the new tax system, because it was absolutely essential for the guarantee of the new tax system that revenue from the land should cease to depend on the paying capacity of each landowner; in other words someone legally identifiable as the owner has to be responsible for the tax on every acre of land regardless of who works it. There is another fundamental difference from the old system. Under feudalism the principle governing the amount of tax paid by the peasant was to appropriate as much as possible, leaving the producer enough for only the barest subsistence, or, in the phrase current in that age, "to see that the peasants had just enough to live on and no more."[11] The system of collection was based upon the group responsibility of the village divided for administrative convenience into teams of five men,[12] and by this method peasant privation was at once deepened and universalized. But under the new government the burden of payment shifted from producer to landholder; the peasants were now freed from the oppressive bondage of feudalism and at the

[11] See Sansom, *op. cit.,* p. 457.
[12] *Gonin-gumi,* see Chapter III, note 80, *supra.*

same time deprived of the "paternal" consideration of their lord whose problem it was to see "that they neither died nor lived." In the new society they were free to choose their own fate; to live or die, to remain on the land or sell out and go to the city. In this way the majority of the rural population, while released from the tyranny of feudalism, were not at the same time accorded state protection in the same way as were the landlords by the guarantee of the right to private ownership of land. The position of the small landowner working his own piece of land was precarious in the extreme, subject to all the vicissitudes of nature (bad crops, storms, blight) and of society (fluctuations in the price of rice) and yet unable to escape the responsibility of paying a fixed amount of cash every year to the government as tax. To meet this demand the peasant proprietor could give up the struggle to remain on the land, dispose of his tiny plot by sale, or resort to the village usurer and so enter upon the long uphill path of debt payments, which might end at any time in foreclosure.[13] Furthermore, with the low level of capitalist development prevalent in the countryside, the sudden requirement to turn from 25 to 30 per cent of his proceeds into money in order to meet the land tax[14] placed a heavy burden on the small isolated cultivator, living off his pigmy-sized farm, who was not yet swept into the main reaches of the national market. By being thrust from a position of comparative self-sufficiency to one of dependence on the market, the peasant was forced to sell his rice as soon as it was harvested, and thus exposed to all the dangers arising from price fluctuations which did not affect to the same extent the position of the large land-

---

[13] "Ensuite le paysan, mis en possession de la terre sans avoir rien fait pour l'acquérir, n'en a pas compris la valeur, il a continué de vivre d'une manière imprévoyante, *l'impôt foncier fixé et payable en argent lui a paru plus dur que la quote-part due sur la récolte au seigneur feodal, il s'est endetté et la terre a passé pour une grande part aux mains des usuriers.*" La Mazelière, *op. cit.*, Vol. V, p. 132. (Italics mine E. H. N.)

[14] "In a rice field of 1 *tan*, let the crop be one *koku* and six *to*, and let the price of rice be three yen per *koku*; then the gross return will be 4.80 yen. If we substract the cost of production, fertilizer, seed, etc., amounting to 72 sen or 15% of the total, and subtract the land tax estimated at 122.4 sen and the local tax of 40.8 sen, we have a remainder of 244.8 sen." This is the theoretical estimate made by the Department of Finance in a study of land value and average production. *Meiji Zaisei Shi*, op. cit., Vol. V, p. 346.

Thus the land tax alone, amounting to a fraction more than 1.22 yen, is a quarter of the gross proceeds of the field estimated in money (4.80 yen), which with the additional local tax (a fraction over 1.63 yen) becomes 30% of the gross proceeds.

lords who could store rice in granaries.[15] Here we are speaking of the small producer who owned his land and accordingly paid the land tax himself. The tenant still paid rent, for the most part in kind, to the landlord who, after deducting the amount to be forwarded to the government as land tax, pocketed the remainder as clear profit. Thus the Land Tax Revision acted as a mechanism hastening the already inevitable trend toward the dispossession of the peasantry and the accompanying concentration of land in the hands of the landlord class. Let us look for a moment at the extent and rate of its progress.

Dispossession of the Peasantry

From 1883 to 1890, 367,744 agricultural producers suffered forced sales for arrears in the payment of the land tax. Among these, 77 per cent failed to pay their land tax because of poverty. The total amount in arrears was 114,178 yen, or an average amount of 31 sen per person; the area of land auctioned or confiscated was 47,281 *chobu* (115,838.45 acres) with a total land value of 4,944,393 yen. In round figures, the value of land confiscated or sold was 27 times the amount in arrears.[16] The whirl-

---

[15] In the peculiar arrangement whereby the tax was paid in money and the rent in kind, the superior position of the non-cultivating landlord as compared to that of peasant proprietor can be theoretically illustrated as follows. The landlord's share of the produce is the rent (rice) less the land tax (money). Thus the land tax being constant, his share will depend on the size of the crop, the current price of rice and the costs of production (the market price of seed, fertilizer, implements, etc.). The hazards of the cultivating proprietor, arising from the greater number of fluctuations and variables, make the position of the peasant proprietor more vulnerable than that of the landlord. This is a theoretical exposition which may explain one aspect of the process of increased tenancy during the Meiji era. The effect of the fluctuation of rice in displacing the peasant proprietor is discussed by Miki Shozaburo, *The Labor Problem in Japan,* unpublished MS. in Columbia University Library, 1900, pp. 3-4. This author conveniently gives a table, reproduced here, showing the fluctuations in the price of rice from 1873 to 1894. *Ibid.,* pp. 4-5.

INDEX OF FLUCTUATIONS IN THE PRICE OF RICE, 1873-94
(1873 = 100)

1873	100	1884	110
1874	152	1885	138
1875	149	1886	125
1876	107	1887	103
1877	111	1888	105
1878	133	1889	125
1879	166	1890	186
1880	220	1891	146
1881	221	1892	151
1882	184	1893	154
1883	131	1894	165

[16] These figures come from a study of a German agricultural expert, Paul Mayet,

wind speed of peasant expropriation can be imagined from some further data on mortgages and compulsory sales, taken from a study by P. Mayet. Since such statistics for the early Meiji period are rather difficult to obtain, we will reproduce some of them here. For the province of Okayama we have the following table.[17]

OKAYAMA PROVINCE

Year	Mortgages on Houses and Land		Compulsory Sales		Bankrubtcies	
	Yen	Persons	Yen	Persons	Yen	Persons
1879	2,881,300	63,577	105	9	5,699	52
1880	4,123,940	78,023	259	24	2,916	54
1881	5,322,164	86,470	1,798	40	5,132	84
1882	6,097,271	107,574	7,481	106	22,342	199
1883	7,072,120	137,008	21,414	520	58,811	493

This will give us an impression of the intensity of expropriation in one prefecture, and when we turn to a national survey we can see its extensive sweep. "An official report on mortgages for *all Japan* in the 14th year of Meiji (1881) reckons them at 141,000,000 yen as compared with an assessed value of only 123,-000,000 yen, and that with a number of about 2,000,000 mortgages. The mortgages taken up, therefore, average only about 72 yen, a fact which shows the immense need which Japan has for mortgage credit in small sums, such as cannot be satisfied by any great central office."[18]

Peasant distress was also analyzed by a French observer who reported that "en 1884 la valeur déclarée des hypothèques dans le vieux Japon s'élevait à 16.3% de la valuer totale des propriétés telle que l'établissait l'estimation légale et la valeur réelle des hypothèques y compris les hypothèques non déclarées était bien supérieure."[19]

---

employed by the Japanese government as adviser on agricultural insurance. The study is in Japanese (translated into Japanese by Saito Tetsutaro and others) and is entitled "Nihon Nomin no Hihei oyobi sono Kyuji Saku" (The Impoverishment of the Japanese Peasantry and a Policy for Its Remedy). This appears in the *Nihon Sangyo Shiryo Taikei* (Outline of Source Materials for Japanese Industry), Tokyo, 1926, Vol. II, pp. 424-5.

[17] Paul Mayet, *Agricultural Insurance*, translated from the German by Rev. Arthur Lloyd. London. 1893. p. 61.

[18] Mayet, *op. cit.*, p. 64. This general summary of mortgages in Japan in 1881 is broken down into detailed figures according to *fu* and *ken* (city and prefectures), giving the number of *cho* (1 *cho* = 2.45 acres), the value according to the land assessment, the amount advanced and the number of mortgages. *Ibid.*, p. 65.

[19] La Mazelière, *op. cit.*, Vol. V, p. 132.

These figures indicate the dominating position held by usurers' capital in the Japanese countryside, and the role it played
in dispossessing the peasantry.[20] Its power is reflected in the
manifestoes and political handbills circulated in Izu by the
"Debtors' Party," the *Shakkinto* (the name for local parties of
impoverished peasants formed to oppose wholesale eviction).
According to these notices, interest at 13 per cent was considered
a philanthropic rate, and the postponement of repayment from
three to five years was held to be equally generous.[21]

The decade from 1880 to 1890, when the revised land tax was
in full operation, was the period of the most spectacular shifts
in landownership in Japan, and the fastest tempo in this social
revolution was reached in 1884-86. La Mazelière writes, "Dans
le vieux Japon (y compris les villes) le montant des ventes
s'élevait en 1884 à 4.8% de la valeur totale des propriétés, en
1886 à 5.1% . . . En vingt ans la totalité de la propriété aurait
changé de mains, et cela immédiatement après la depossession
complète de tous les anciens propriétaires; ce furent là au point
de vue économique et social des épreuves plus graves que celles
qu'a subies la France sous la Révolution."[22]

If we examine the figures for the decrease in the number of
those qualified to vote (i.e. those who paid a land tax of five
yen or more) and of those eligible for office (i.e. paying ten yen
or more), although it will not give us any indication of the increase in the number of tenants, it will show the steady worsen-

[20] Mayet, *op. cit.*, pp. 3-5. "The fixed and high money land tax becomes oppressive for the agriculturist as soon as in any year the product of the two factors,
'saleable produce' and 'price of sale,' falls below the average assumed by the
Land Tax Reform. Then the farmer incurs debt. But he can only obtain short
credit at high rates of interest without repayment by instalments, and unsecured
against a sudden notice of repayment, whereas, by its very nature, agriculture
requires long Credit at low rates of interest with gradual repayment of Capital by
instalments, and secured against any sudden recall of the whole capital at once.
So, for the want of such arrangements the agriculturist falls into the hands of the
usurer. . . ."

"Inasmuch as Japanese agriculture is in want of suitable facilities for mortgage-
debenture, insurance, and saving, it is unable to cope with the high and constantly uniform money land tax. Ten thousands of country people have consequently been ruined during the past years, and helplessly delivered over to the
blood-sucking usurer, and hundreds of thousands will so fall into his hands during
the next decades." From the Introductory Letter of Mayet to Count Yamagata
Aritomo, Minister of the Interior, Mayet, *loc. cit.*

[21] *Ibid.*, p. 68.

[22] La Mazelière, *op. cit.*, Vol. VI, p. 133.

ing in the position of small and middle peasant proprietors which is one of the phenomena preparing the way for continual peasant expropriation. The following tables give us this information.[23]

Year	Number Qualified to Vote by Payment of Tax of Five Yen or More	Relative Decrease 1881 = 100
1881.............	1,809,610	100
1882.............	1,784,041	94
1883.............	1,718,020	94
1884.............	1,682,419	93
1885.............	1,637,137	90
1886.............	1,531,952	84
1887.............	1,488,107	82
1888.............	1,505,183	83
1889.............	1,462,183	81
1890.............	1,409,510	78
1891.............	1,175,045	64
1892.............	1,120,643	62
1893.............	1,118,508	61
1894.............	1,083,697	59

Year	Number Eligible for Office Through Payment of Ten Yen or More	Relative Decrease 1881 = 100
1881.............	879,347	100
1882.............	878,840	99
1883.............	871,762	99
1884.............	849,244	97
1885.............	840,965	96
1886.............	809,880	92
1887.............	802,975	91
1888.............	803,795	91
1889.............	814,022	93
1890.............	755,412	86
1891.............	621,382	71
1892.............	593,273	67
1893.............	589,803	67
1894.............	574,269	65

By 1892 in Japan proper including Hokkaido the area of land worked by tenants had risen to 2,031,958.5 *chobu* (4,978,278.33 acres) or 39.99 per cent of the total cultivated area.[24] Figures

[23] Table taken from Hirano, *op. cit.*, pp. 71-2. It should be stated for the sake of clarity that the electorate did not determine the Diet, but the *Fu-ken Kai*. For details see McLaren, *JGD*, pp. 272-6. The first session of the Diet took place in 1890, with the elector having to pay a direct national tax of at least 15 yen for a period of not less than one year preceding the time fixed for making the list of electors.

[24] Tsuchiya and Okazaki, *op. cit.*, p. 221. The table from which the above state-

for the number of tenant households are not particularly illuminating because of the large number which are part tenant and part owner, but here too the data indicate a noteworthy shift from peasant proprietorship to tenancy or part-tenancy.[25]

ment is taken may be reproduced here since such statistics for the early Meiji are not easily available in a Western language.

Year	Area Cultivated by Independent Producer	Tenant Land	Total	Per Cent of Tenant Land to Total Cultivated Land
1883 (for 3 *fu* and 33 prefectures)	2,160,599.5 *cho*	1,255,107.7 *cho*	3,415,707.2 *cho*	37.00
1887 (Japan proper, including Hokkaido)	2,795,707.3	1,813,465.4	4,609,172.7	39.34
1892 (Japan proper, including Hokkaido)	3,049,046.3	2,031,958.5	5,081,004.8	39.99

Another authority gives the percentage of tenant land from 1873. In 1873 the proportion of tenant land was 31.1%; it increased to 36.75% in 1883, to 39.34% in 1887, and to 39.99% in 1892. Note how the greatest increase came in the years immediately after Land Tax Revision. See Azuma Tosaku, *Meiji Zenki Noseishi no Shomondai,* (cited) pp. 89-90.

25

Year	Number of Cultivator-Owner Households	Number of Pt.-Tenant Pt.-Owner Households	Number o Tenant Households
1883 (for 3 *fu* and 28 prefectures)	1,706,476	1,676,634	951,266
1888 (for 3 *fu* and 28 prefectures)	1,477,722	2,000,345	954,498

PERCENTAGE OF TOTAL AGRICULTURAL HOUSEHOLDS

1883	39.83	38.65	21.94
1888	33.34	45.13	21.53

Tsuchiya and Okazaki, *op. cit.,* p. 222.

Note in this period the big decrease in the number of cultivating owners. A large number dropping out of the category of cultivating owner probably shifted at first to that of part-tenant and part-owner rather than to that of pure tenant, indicating the zig-zag, uneven pace of peasant expropriation.

Recent figures for tenancy are given in the following table:

DISTRIBUTION OF LANDED AND TENANT FARMERS IN
1910, 1920 AND 1930
(Percentages of Households)

Farmers	1910	1920	1930
Landed	33.4	31.3	31.1
Part-tenant	27.4	28.1	26.5
Tenant	39.2	40.6	42.3

This table comes from *Hompo Nogyo Yoran,* Tokyo, 1931, p. 33. and is cited in Ishii, *op. cit.,* p. 154. The ratios of tenant acreage since 1914 are as follows:

CHANGES IN THE PROPORTION OF TENANCY IN DRY AND WET FIELDS, 1914-34
(By area)

	Wet Fields		Dry Fields		Total	
	Proprietor	Tenant	Proprietor	Tenant	Proprietor	Tenant
1914	49.0%	51.0%	60.1%	39.9%	54.5%	45.5%
1921	48.4	51.6	59.1	40.9	53.7	46.3
1926	48.9	51.1	59.8	40.2	54.2	45.8
1931	47.6	52.4	61.1	38.9	52.7	47.3
1934	46.8	53.2	60.1	39.9	52.9	47.1

Comparison of Peasant Dispossession and Its Effects in Japan and England

A similar process of peasant expropriation accompanied the change to capitalist relations in the countryside in England during the enclosure movement for grazing in the 16th century and the far more sweeping enclosure movement for cereal crops in the 18th century. The economic forces at work brought about a sharp decrease in the number of small owners who lacked either capital or holdings sufficiently great to keep pace with the new improved scientific agricultural production for the market, whose household industries were ruined by the new machine industries of Lancashire, and who consequently were forced to leave the land and migrate to the city. In England this movement was accompanied not only by the concentration of land in fewer hands, but also by the very considerable increase in the scale of farming.[26] In Japan, however, this process was very complex, and, unlike the English enclosures of the 18th century, it did not precipitate a wholesale exodus of peasants to the cities in the years immediately following the Land Tax Revision. On the contrary there has been no absolute decrease in the number of agricultural *honke* (or households) working the land.[27] The answer to the apparent contradiction of a peasantry which suffered expropriation on the large scale described above, yet which

This table is taken from Tohata Seiichi, *Nihon Nogyo no Tenkai Katei* (The Process of the Development of Japanese Agriculture), Tokyo, 1936, (revised and enlarged edition), p. 74.

[26] "From 1765 until 1815 the price rose almost continuously . . . There was naturally a great desire to grow as much corn as possible and the small farms were thrown into the large ones for that purpose.

"The era of the large corn-growing farm had set in and lasted until nearly the end of the nineteenth century, often of course combined with stock raising." W. H. R. Curtler, *The Enclosure and Redistribution of Our Land*, Oxford, 1920, p. 28.

"During that period (1760-1875) the attention of English farmers was mainly fixed on corn-growing, which is most economically carried on on large farms where business methods and machinery have fullest scope. The small farm was looked upon by all agricultural authorities with disfavor." *Ibid.*, p. 241.

"Between 1793-1850 we get the disappearance of the small farm and the rise of the large one . . .

"The large farm being thus definitely established as the typical feature of English agriculture, it proceeded to new triumphs." L. C. A. Knowles, *The Industrial and Commercial Revolutions in Great Britain during the Nineteenth Century*, London, 1921, pp. 363-4; 368.

[27] The total number of households working on the land in 1910 was 5,497,918, and in 1937 the number was almost the same, 5,574,879. *Norin Tokei* (Statistics for Agriculture and Forestry), published by the Statistical Bureau for the Minister of Agriculture and Forestry, Tokyo, 1939, abridged edition, p. 18. See also p. 160. *infra.*

remained on the land as tenants or part tenants, cannot be given merely by pointing to the well-known fact that in the early and middle Meiji years there were as yet no highly developed industries which could absorb a dispossessed peasantry, because even after the industrialization of Japan there still remains a constant or rather steadily increasing number of agricultural households on the land. The answer would seem to lie rather in the Japanese tenant-landlord relations with excessively high rent and consequent atomization of land. The high rent characteristic of Japanese landlordism has made the non-cultivating landowner interested exclusively in collecting rent[28] and has deterred him from using his capital to enter agricultural enterprise as a capitalist.[29] In England the fulfillment of capitalist development

[28] "It must be pointed out in this connection, too, that in Japan the landlords are required to pay only the land taxes; all other farming expenses are met by the tenants. Thus, agricultural rents in Japan, although perhaps not as extremely high as in other Oriental countries, are exorbitant when compared with those of the old agricultural nations in the West. According to the record in *Nihon Nogyo Nenkan* (The Japan Agricultural Yearbook), the Japanese rate is 7 times that of England, 3.5 times that of Germany, about 4 times that of Italy, and 3 times those of Denmark and Holland." Ishii, *op. cit.,* p. 155.

[29] The following table gives a simplified and convenient analysis of the division in the proceeds from the land going to the State, to the landlord and to the tenant.

	State	Landlord	Tenant	Total
Division under feudalism, when share averaged 5 to state and 5 to people and when tax was paid in kind	50%	18%	32%	100%
On eve of Land Tax Revision (1873)	34	34	32	100
1874–76, based upon average price of rice	13	55	32	100
After tax reduction in 1877 and based upon price of rice for 1878	12	56	32	100
1878–87, based upon average price of rice	11.5	56.5	32.0	100

The first line is taken from Mori, *op. cit.,* p. 167, the remainder from Hirano, *op. cit.,* p. 30. In passing, we might note again how the landlords' position was strengthened both at the time of tax revision (1873) and of tax reduction (1876). For recent times we are told the following: "Investigation proves, it is said, that 54 per cent of the crop from tenanted land goes to the landlord, taking the country as a whole." Daniel H. Buchanan, "Rural Economy in Japan," in the *Quarterly Journal of Economics* (Harvard), Vol. 37, August 1923, p. 571. This statement is roughly borne out by a table based on an elaborate survey of rents undertaken by the Bureau of Agriculture between 1915 and 1920:

AVERAGE RATIOS OF RENT OF PADDY AND UPLAND FIELDS
TOTAL VALUE OF PRODUCTS, 1915–1920 (Percentages)

Paddy Fields

Fields	Rent Paid by	High	Usual	Low
One-crop fields	Rice	53.3	51.0	46.9
Two-crop fields	Rice	57.4	55.0	52.9

Upland Fields

Rent Paid by	Percentage	Rent Paid by	Percentage
Rice	40.0	Barley-Beans	40.6
Beans	35.0	Money	27.6
Rye	26.0		

in agriculture left the land concentrated in the hands of fewer
individuals who, after driving off the old customary tenants
through acts of Parliament enforcing enclosure, increased the
unit of cultivation and worked the land for profit as a capitalist enterprise.[30] The old semi-feudal customary tenant was
forced off the land in England once and for all, and he had to
seek employment with all his family in the rapidly growing city
industries. In Japan, however, because of the attractively high
rent, the landlord or usurer has not been intent on driving off
all the old tenants or peasant proprietors for the sake of taking
over the enterprise himself; he has preferred to leave the peasant
household working its tiny farm in return for an exorbitant
rent. With the ruin of the old time-honored household industries and the increasing pressure of over-population on the
countryside following the removal of feudal restrictions on the
birthrate,[31] and with the rise of a modern factory industry,
younger members of the family, in particular the women, left
the countryside for the city in the hope of supplementing the
meager family income. What is of particular significance in this
city-ward movement is that the overcrowding of the agricultural family, its desperate financial plight aggravated by the
ruin of domestic industry, coincided with the rise of the textile
industry which was the core of the first Japanese industrial

In the same survey in search of the prevalent rent-ratio for the years 1915-20 it
was found that the median rent on one-crop fields was 50.2% and on two-crop
fields 54.6%. These tables appear in Ishii, op. cit., p. 156.

[30] "It followed therefore when the mediaeval village disappeared in England the
peasant, as a rule, sooner or later, disappeared with it . . .

"This was the result at which the enclosing landlord aimed. He held that
production was hampered not merely by the system of common fields and co-
operative control, but also by the wide distribution of rights of property and
rights of common. He believed that the best work was done by laborers who
depended on their wages and had nothing to distract them from their duty to
their employer. This relationship he considered the best for production and
production was everything." J. L. and Barbara Hammond, The Rise of Modern
Industry, London, 1925, pp. 87-8.

"In other countries the capitalist system was confined for the most part to
industry; in England it began by overspreading the village as well as the town."
Ibid., p. 90.

For the earliest English enclosure for grazing rather than cereal production,
see R. H. Tawney, The Agrarian Problem in the Sixteenth Century, London, 1912,
especially "Transition to Capitalist Agriculture" in Part Two. The author
minutely records the first big wave of peasant expropriation in England which
was not completed until the end of the 18th century. The second type of enclosure is described above in note 26, supra.

[31] Ishii, op. cit., Chapter III, pp. 32-47—especially Part I, "Movement for Abolition of Abortion and Infanticide," pp. 31-47.

revolution and has remained a vitally important sector of industry, especially for the export trade. This situation made possible the recruiting of female labor from the overcrowded villages and the consequent lowering of labor costs in the textile industry. It has created an industrial working class composed of an unusually high percentage of female labor. The following table will illustrate its extent.[32]

Year	Total Workers	Women Workers	Percentage of Women Workers in Industry
1882	51,189	35,535	69%
(In five-year averages)			
1895–99	425,602	252,651	59%
1900–04	472,955	291,237	62%
1905–09	637,043	391,003	61%
1910–14	828,942	592,320	71%

(These figures cover only factories employing over ten workers and exclude government-owned factories.)

The other important consequence of the agrarian settlement insofar as it affected the migration to the city is that, in contrast to what obtained in England, those members of the peasant household, whether younger brothers or daughters, went to the city only for short periods, returning to the village because of unemployment, or for marriage, or to help out during harvest time. The uprooting of the old self-sufficient customary tenant in English society propelled the whole tenant family city-wards

[32] Kobayashi, op. cit., p. 257.
In 1919 the total number of factory workers was 1.777,171, of which 911,732 or slightly more than 50% were women. In 1924 there were 992,835 women workers out of a total of 1,789,618, again slightly more than 50%. Figures from Nihon Teikoku Tokei Nenkan (Statistical Year Book of the Japanese Empire), 45th issue, 1926, p. 124.

ANALYSIS OF WORKERS IN THE TEXTILE INDUSTRY
ACCORDING TO AGE AND SEX

1899

	Male	F male	Total	Percentage
Over 14 years of age	15,373	47,921	63,294	83.7
Under 14 " " "	1,202	11,111	12,313	16.3
Total	16,575	59,032	75,607	100.0
Percentage	21.9%	78.1%	100.0%	

1909

	Male	F male	Total	Percentage
Over 20 years of age	13,317	27,141	40,458	45.1
20 to 16 " " "	2,990	24,476	27,466	30.6
16 to 14 " " "	1,042	11,883	12,925	13.9
14 to 12 " " "	462	6,914	7,376	8.2
Under 12 " " "	44	1,512	1,556	2.2
Total	17,855	71,926	89,781	100.0
Percentage	19.9%	80.1%	100.0%	

Table taken from Tsuchiya and Okazaki, op. cit., p. 291.

and when a slack season set in, they had to remain idle in the city since their ancient country home had long since disappeared. In Japan, however, they returned to their ancestral village when unemployed. This solution to the problem of unemployment, even though it arose as a natural and not preconceived consequence of the agrarian settlement, is one of the reasons which drives landlords and industrialists together rather than against each other, as occurred, for instance, in England during the agitation for the repeal of the Corn Laws. The reason for this coincidence of landlord and industrialist interest lies in the fact that the burden of the upkeep of the unemployed is largely removed from state and employers, while at the same time the resulting overcrowding of the village bids up the rent rate.

Minute-Scale Farming in Japan: Its Cause and Effects

Unlike the English experience, the expropriation of the peasantry in Japan did not mean the consolidation or extension of the average unit of land cultivated. On the contrary (despite an infinitesimal increase in the average unit of land cultivated), the extension of tenancy was accompanied by continued atomization of the average unit of land worked by a peasant household. Comparative figures from the early Meiji period are as follows:

In 1874 an examination of the 3 fu (i.e., the 3 great urban areas, Tokyo, Osaka and Kyoto) and 27 prefectures (not including Hokkaido) revealed that the average unit of cultivation (both dry and paddy fields taken together) per peasant household was 9 tan, 6 se, 16 bu (2.353 acres), and thirty-five years later this unit, still excluding Hokkaido, was virtually the same, being 9 tan, 7 se, 10 bu (2.384 acres).[33]

[33] Tsuchiya and Okazaki, using government sources, op. cit., p. 430. The total number of peasant households in that year (1909) was 5,407,203, cultivating a total area of 5,617,624.6 cho (1 cho = 2.45 acres). These same authorities give a table, ibid., p. 431, showing the variation in the unit of cultivation according to district in 1909.

AVERAGE AREA OF CULTIVATED LAND PER HOUSEHOLD, 1909

District	Rice Fields	Dry Fields	Total
All Japan (including Hokkaido)	0.535 cho	0.504 cho	1.039 cho
Hokkaido	0.253	3.159	3.412
Tohoku	0.883	0.623	1.521
Kwanto	0.460	0.595	1.055
Hokuriku	0.813	0.307	1.120
Tokai	0.450	0.330	0.780
Kinki	0.559	0.160	0.719
Chukoku	0.489	0.238	0.727
Shikoku	0.378	0.475	0.853
Kyushu	0.481	0.557	1.038

The minute parcelation of land characteristic of Japanese agriculture thus remained even after the recognition of the principle of private land ownership and after the rapid increase in tenancy. The reason for this is to be found in the unusually high rent, which, as we saw, was for rice fields as much as 60 per cent of the harvest.[34] This question is so important in Japa‑ nese agrarian relations that at the risk of undue repetition we will analyze it further. As long as those who possess capital and land, namely the merchant, usurer or rich peasant, can expect so high a return on capital sunk in the land, they have no incen‑ tive to turn themselves from parasitic landlords into agricul‑ tural entrepreneurs, working the land for profit on agricultural produce grown for the market and hiring their former tenants or others as wage laborers. As agrarian relations exist in Japan. a landlord who is sure of such a high return on his money would be foolish to undertake the risks of enterprise for a profit which might well be at a lower rate than rent. In a word, the exorbi‑ tant rent cuts into or discourages the entrepreneur's profit. The result is that land remains as it was in feudal times, parceled into minute lots and worked by a prolific peasantry whose increasing numbers make for competition in leases, thus safeguarding the high rate of rent. This in turn tends to atomize the unit of land

---

For 1914 the figures for all Japan, including the comparatively large-scale type of farming in Hokkaido as well as Okinawa, are as follows: total number of peasant households, 5,456,231; total area of land cultivated (both paddy and dry fields), 5,815,695 *cho*, giving an average unit of cultivation of 1.065 *cho* (2.61 acres). These figures are abstracted from *Nihon Teikoku Tokei Nenkan* (Statis‑ tical Year Book of the Empire of Japan), compiled by the Statistical Bureau to the Ministry of Interior, 45th issue, Toyko, 1926, pp. 76, 79.

It is important to note that the average unit of cultivation for rice land taken separately is much smaller than the average for both dry and rice fields taken together, as can be seen from the table above. The largest unit of rice fields is in the Tohoku district with 0.883 *cho*, or slightly less than two acres.

[34] How high this rent was can be seen in the following table comparing the landlord's share on a field of one *cho* at the time of the Land Tax Revision and later.

LANDLORD'S SHARE IN THE PRODUCE FROM A FIELD OF ONE CHO

Year	Tenant's Ren in Koku of Rice	Price of Rice per Koku	Ren Converted into Money	Total Land and Local Tax	Landlord's Net Income
1873	.757 *koku*	4.89 yen	3.70 yen	1.85 yen	1.85 yen
1881 (after land tax was re‑ duced to 2½%)	.661	10.29	7.01	1.56	5.45
1885	.761	6.30	4.79	1.55	3.24

Tsuchiya and Okazaki, *op. cit.*, p. 218. In passing we should note how the land tax reduction of 1876 helped to increase the landlord's income. From the above it appears that the rent is consistently over 60% of the gross proceeds from the land.

cultivated. To this must be added the passionate attachment of the peasant for land which has been consecrated for him by the toil of countless forebears. In his struggle to remain on the land as proprietor or part proprietor, the peasant sells a few *tsubo* of land at a time to cover his tax arrears, to meet his debt to the village usurer or to tide himself over a lean year caused by poor crops, loss of draught animals or some other natural calamity. He surrenders each square yard of land unwillingly, like an outflanked army fighting a hopeless but determined rear-guard action, and the result is that he has to cut down his scale of operations still more on the land that is at his disposal. This is of course only an imaginative case, but it illustrates in part the effects of high rent as a deterrent to the development of pure capitalist relations in agriculture, while the extreme pressure of population on the countryside has the effect of maintaining and in some cases even diminishing the minute scale of operations which existed from feudal times. As a Japanese authority has said: "The farmer himself knows how inconvenient and disadvantageous such an agricultural system is, but substantial improvement is often impossible in a short time on account of the fixed conditions of ownership or tenancy." And again: "On the ruins of feudalism, land-ownership has been divided into small sections; the scale of agriculture management is as small as ever; family labor is still available, no fundamental change has occurred in these old conditions. Japanese agriculture still retains its old form."[35] Thus the peasant, marshaling his whole household to keep on a subsistence level, intensifies agriculture by making the most of every square foot of land at his disposal. This parcelation or atomization of Japanese agriculture is thus an outcome of the land settlement of the early Meiji period and the peculiarities of Japanese topography, and has the effect of intensifying and diversifying agricultural production, but acts as an insurmountable barrier to any attempt at large-scale mechanization or at revolution in agricultural technique. The atomization of land and the peculiar arrangement arising from the Meiji agrarian settlement, whereby an extraordinarily high rent is paid in kind and a heavy tax is paid in money, and above all the effect of high rent which discourages holders of capital from entering agricultural production as entrepreneurs, have

[35] S. Nasu, *Land Utilization in Japan,* Japanese Council, Institute of Pacific Relations, Tokyo, 1929, pp. 81, 83.

left a distinctive mark on Japanese agrarian relations. This can be analyzed best by examining the actual social relations of the Japanese tenant farmer.

Social Character of the Japanese Tenant Farmer

The Japanese tenant farmer is not a capitalist entrepreneur as in other countries, but a cultivator paying a large percentage of his produce in kind to the landlord. Nor is he an agricultural wage laborer receiving a cash wage from a landowner who takes both the risks and profits of the enterprise. The Japanese tenant is a mixture of the two. He resembles the English tenant farmer inasmuch as he shoulders all the risks of agricultural enterprise, but in spite of this the profit from the enterprise is taken by the landowner; so in this respect the Japanese tenant resembles an agricultural day-laborer. The wage of this agricultural semi-proletarian is not a money wage but a payment in kind which depends upon the size of the harvest and subsequent fluctuations in the prices of agricultural products. In a good year the share of the tenant increases somewhat, but since the demand for agricultural products is relatively inelastic, the price of the product falls drastically especially at harvest time. Thus it is possible for the money income of the tenant to decrease despite a good crop. The price of industrial goods on the other hand, which the tenant must buy back, has nothing to do with the harvest but is influenced by other economic forces such as the state of the international market. In a year of poor crops, this price of cereals will rise, but scarcely anything remains of the raw product in the hand of the producing tenant who, especially if he cultivates a very small farm, may actually be compelled to buy back the cereals which he grew. Thus the Japanese tenant-farmer manifests the double nature of capitalist-tenant (who takes the risks of the entrepreneur) and of agricultural proletarian (inasmuch as the landlord, by reason of the high rent, takes a large part of the profits of the enterprise). One aspect is so closely intertwined with the other that it is inaccurate to describe him either as pure tenant or pure proletarian. Here we see again the Janus head of the Japanese peasant, formed by his social relationships. As we noted in Chapter III, this double aspect makes the Japanese peasant at once more conservative and more radical than the French or English farmer. A foreign observer has commented upon this characteristic of the Japa-

nese peasant, as follows: "Yet the 'discontent and radical tendencies' that we usually associate with an urban proletariat are
there 'mainly confined to the rural population.' "[36]

The Question of a Stagnant Surplus Population and the Creation of the Labor Market

From this analysis it appears that the process of growing land
lordism on the one hand, and the divorce of the peasant proprietor from the land on the other cannot be explained as the
consequences of capitalist development in agricultural productive relations, which was the driving force behind the English
enclosures of the 18th century. This process of peasant expropriation, as well as the separation of industry from agriculture
(that is to say, the ruin of domestic industry), moved faster than
the development of capitalist enterprise in agriculture or of
urban industry. That the process of peasant expropriation described above advanced more rapidly than the development of
capitalism both in agriculture and industry is attested by the fact
that during the quarter-century following the Land Tax Revision the dispossessed peasantry were not converted to any large
extent into an agricultural or industrial proletariat, but became
tenants, part-tenants or proprietors of exceedingly small farms,
depending for a bare subsistence upon domestic supplementary
industries, such as spinning, weaving or sericulture.[37] This vast
body of small peasant proprietors, tenants and half-tenants, cultivating in ever larger numbers minutely parceled plots of land,
historically forms the reservoir of Japanese stagnant and potential surplus population.[38] The atomized, minute-scale cultivation
is quite inadequate to give them a net income sufficient to eke
out even a bare subsistence, so their women folk must engage in
some form of domestic industry while the men seek part-time
employment as coolies working on roads, railway construction
and the like. That section of stagnant surplus population which
was not afforded the protection of the family system was forced
to seek its livelihood in the cities. Those who could not enter

[36] W. R. Crocker, *The Japanese Population Problem*, New York, 1931, p. 93.

[37] This point is well demonstrated by Kazahaya Yasoji in his recent monograph
Nihon Shakai Seisaku Shi (History of Japanese Social Policy), Tokyo, 1937, pp.
22-3.

[38] The expressions, stagnant surplus population and potential surplus population, are self-explanatory and have been borrowed from Kazahaya's treatise referred to above in note 37. The next paragraph is largely based on the analysis
and description by the same authority, *op. cit.*, pp. 17-25.

the factories became rickshaw-men, longshoremen, coolies, in a word the lowest stratum of unskilled labor. This class includes also those who were driven out of small-scale domestic industry by the introduction of new machine techniques or whose labor became superfluous through the employment of female and child labor. This stagnant surplus population is semi-employed at the best, and its condition of livelihood is marked by irregularity of work, insecurity of employment and, when employed by extremely long hours of work and very low wages. This stagnant surplus population tends eventually to drift back from the city to the natal village, aggravating the already congested condition of life in the countryside and acting as a depressing factor on the standard of living in the village. The extreme pressure of population on the land prevents many of them from becoming cultivators, so they must seek a living in some form of domestic industry;[39] with the decline of the latter, the unbearable pressure compels them to send their daughters to the textile mills in the city to earn enough—or so they hope—to keep the family debt from reaching ruinous proportions. The population which is expelled from all participation in the process of production in agriculture, and has not succeeded in being enrolled as part of the industrial proletariat, becomes *fluid* as soon as its numbers are sufficient. And just as water tends to seek the lowest level, so this fluid surplus population is compelled to seek the lowest level—that is to say it flows into the most poorly paid types of employment, dragging down with it the general wage level. In a country like Japan, where the development of city industry even though rapid in speed was not widespread, the larger part of the surplus population could not be absorbed by industry. Furthermore, when the overseas labor

[39] The continual increase in the proportion of agricultural households engaged in domestic or household industry (despite the ruin of certain types of old domestic industry such as cotton-spinning and sugar-making) was a result of this extreme pressure of population in the countryside. The new type of domestic industry to which the peasantry turned was sericulture. The increase in the proportion of agricultural households engaged in domestic or supplementary industry is seen in the following table:

Year	Per Cent Total Households Engaged Only in Agriculture	Per Cent Agricultural Households Engaged in Additional Industry	Total
1884 (3 *fu* and 26 prefectures)....	54.21	16.39	70.60
1904 (all Japan)................	44.89	19.49	64.38
1909.........................	40.73	18.79	59.52
1919.........................	37.78	19.90	57.68

Tsuchiya and Okazaki *op. cit.*, p. 442.

market, an outlet which helped to solve the surplus population problem in certain European countries at the end of the 19th century,[40] is blocked by immigration exclusion, this surplus population could do nothing but await employment with the further advance in industrialization or seek new opportunities in household manufacture. It is correct to say that the existence of this vast reservoir of stagnant or potential surplus labor has attracted small-scale manufacturers to the countryside. Since the pressure of population in agriculture closes the door of agricultural employment to a great proportion of this stagnant population, the only means of subsistence left to them is industry whether urban or domestic. But large-scale urban industry did not develop to a level sufficient to absorb the reservoir of labor. partly because of factors conditioning the rise of Japanese industry, but to a large extent because of this very pre-existing reservoir of stagnant surplus population. In other words, many Japanese enterprises have been able to dispense with expensive factory equipment simply by distributing piece-work jobs to the households of those living in that limbo lying between agricultural employment, which is closed behind them, and urban industry which has not yet opened before them. In this way Japanese entrepreneurs have gained a certain flexibility in their wage fund, awaiting the sporadic rise and fall of market demands without the risk of deterioration or obsolescence of stock and factory equipment during slack times. This is another instance where mutual interests drive landlords and industrialists together.

Another important consequence of the Meiji agrarian settlement was the creation of a labor market, the third prerequisite for the development of capitalism. The creation of a labor market in Japan was marked by the formation of a reservoir of potential stagnant labor drawn largely from a dispossessed peasantry whose absorption into industries was retarded by the slower pace in the development of large-scale industry. That such absorption took place is not denied, but the extent to which a surplus population was left stagnating in the countryside and in the cities is an important factor limiting the standard of living and the wage level of Japanese labor.

[40] On the extent of European emigration in the 19th century, see A. M. Carr-Saunders, *World Population*, Oxford, 1936, pp. 49-50. This authority estimates that at least 65 million Europeans moved overseas between 1821 and 1937. *Ibid.*, p 50.

Before leaving the subject we may note the gradual movement of part of the agricultural surplus population into industry, and the slow but steady relative increase in the industrial population. In the period stretching from 1894, when the process of peasant expropriation was almost completed and the first industrial revolution was at its peak, until the eve of the Great War (1913) the total population which can be considered as gainfully employed increased from 24,428,109 to 30,026,403 (i.e., from 100 to 123), while in the same period industrial workers increased from 381,390 to 916,252 (i.e., from 100 to 240).[41] Although the number of agricultural households increased absolutely from 1887 to 1913, it decreased relatively. The proportion of agricultural households in all Japan was 71 per cent in 1887 and only 58 per cent in 1913, while the ratio of agricultural households to industrial workers decreased from 11.1:1 to 6.4:1.[42]

Creation of a Home Market and Its Limitations

The expropriation of land from the peasants following the Land Tax Revision and the gradual creation of a labor market described above were social phenomena with far-reaching consequences. Among the most important *sequelae* was the creation of the home market for the disposal of manufactured goods by the separation of the labor power of the peasant from the means of production, thus making him dependent to a greater extent on the commodity market. The first step in the expansion of this home market came with the thorough commercialization of rice and other agricultural produce.

Rice had always been the most important agricultural product and at the time of the Restoration its cultivation occupied the labor of at least 80 per cent of the population. Already under the Tokugawa regime it had become commercialized to a limited extent (e.g., the feudal lords' conversion of rice into money through rice-brokers), but since it brought only a negligible cash return to the peasant, it did not yet signify the crea-

[41] Abstracted from government statistics in Kazahaya, *op. cit.*, p. 40. The various percentages gainfully employed in 1930 were as follows: agriculture 47.7%, manufacturing and mining 20.2%. From a table in Ishii, *op. cit.*, p. 77.

[42] Kazahaya, *op. cit.*, p. 41. This proportion is given in expanded form. *Ibid.*, p. 42. For further details on the trend toward urbanization and the relative increase of urban as compared to agricultural population, the reader is referred to Ishii, *op. cit.*, pp. 69-74.

tion of a wide home market. Conditions changed radically after the Restoration, when the government by its Land Tax Revision stabilized its financial receipts by, amongst other methods, converting the tax in kind into a money tax. The peasant proprietor or landlord now had to convert rice into money to meet the new tax, thus hastening the trend toward the commercialization of rice. This was followed by the government act removing the ban on the export of rice as well as exempting it from the export tariff.[43] Thanks to the government policy of maintaining a fairly high price for rice and allowing its export, production of rice was stimulated and the peasantry were drawn more and more deeply into the eddies of a commercial or money economy.[44]

Advancing *pari passu* with the commercialization of agricultural products went the decline in the old domestic (*heimat*) industry, particularly in cotton-spinning. Although in the first few decades after the Meiji Restoration, great numbers of peasants were forced off the land either to seek employment in the city or to stagnate in the village, the separation of agriculture from industry (which is one of the destructive prerequisites for the creation of a home market for manufactured goods) could not be thoroughly or extensively carried out through a mere shift in landownership or even through the increased pressure of population in the villages. The real impetus for the creation of the home market was given by the import of cheap, machine-manufactured commodities from the advanced capitalist countries which directly attacked the handicraft textile industries of

[43] To control the sharp rise in the price of rice the *Bakufu* had since 1854 (the opening of Japan) forbidden the export of rice, but the Meiji Government reversed this policy, attempting to check the outflow of specie and encouraging the export of raw materials, including rice, in the hope of raising the price of agricultural products and so helping as best it could the agricultural population which had to bear the heaviest burden of taxation.

In 1874, following the Saga Revolt and the Formosan Expedition, the price of rice rose so steeply that in May the ban on its export was reimposed, only to be raised again in March 1875 and to remain so in the future. See Horie Yasuzo, "Meiji Shoki no Koku-nai Shijo" (The National Market in the Early Years of the Meiji Period) in *Keizai Ronso* (Economic Review), Vol. XLVI, No. 4, April 1938, pp. 635-6.

[44] In connection with this question of export of agricultural products one should emphasize the part played by the export of raw silk and tea in augmenting the money income of the peasantry and widening the commodity market in the village. In the late Tokugawa period a sharp decline in the old domestic industries set in and was accelerated after the Restoration, causing a shift in peasant supplementary industry to sericulture. Horie, *loc. cit.*, p. 138.

the village. Of such imports the most important for our imme
diate purpose were cotton fabrics and cotton yarn which entered
Japan in ever greater quantities, as illustrated by the following
table.[45] (1 *kin* = 1.32 lbs.)

Years	Quantity Cotton Fabric Imported (1,000 kin)	Quantity Cotton Yarn Imported (1,000 kin)	Per Cent Value Cotton Fabrics to All Imports	Per Cent Cotton Yarn to All Imports	Total Per Cent Fabrics and Yarn
1868-72	3,631	3,607	16.02	15.91	31.93
1873-77	5,092	3,853	19.53	14.49	34.02
1878-82	5,125	6,982	15.71	20.79	36.50
1883-87	2,771	6,129	8.48	18.69	27.17

It is scarcely realized abroad how universal was the domestic
production of cotton in Japan throughout the later feudal and
early Meiji periods. A standard work on the history of Japanese manufactures says: "During the Bunroku period (1592-
1595) Southern Barbarians (Spanish and Portuguese) re-intro-
duced cotton seed into Japan, and immediately it spread to
various provinces. Since the time of Keicho (1596-1614) cotton
fabrics were woven for everyday use and there was no province
where cotton was not produced; but the provinces of Kawachi,
Settsu, Kii, Ise, Mikawa, Musashi, Awa, and Shimotsuke were
especially famous."[46] Peasant families grew cotton, spun it into
thread and wove it into fabric for simple everyday use. But their
peasant, self-sufficient economy fell before the onslaught, not of
a native, mechanized textile industry, but of foreign imported
cotton. As we have seen above, the import of cotton fabrics con-
stituted 16.02 per cent of the total value of imports from 1868
to 1872 and 19.53 per cent from 1873 to 1877, and rapidly declined as the Japanese textile industry began to grow and flour-
ish. But the effect of this importation of cotton fabrics was not
so disastrous on peasant economy as was the import of cotton
yarn. Since fabrics are imported for immediate consumption
they do not impinge upon the process of production so directly
as does the import of cotton yarn which is a means of production. Although the domestic or household manufacture of cotton
fabrics competed to a certain extent with the machine-made
imported goods, nevertheless the fabrics turned out by the peas-

[45] *Ibid.*, p. 138.
[46] Yokoi Tokifuyu, *Nihon Kogyo Shi* (History of Japanese Manufacture), Tokyo,
1927, p. 115, in the Kaizo Bunko Edition of 1929, p. 126.

ant were intended primarily for the use of his own household. The effect of imported yarn on domestic spinning industries, which produced yarn both for consumption in the household as well as for the city mills, was decisive. The following table[47] will help to show, by implication, the disastrous effect of imported cotton yarn (as distinct from fabrics) upon the production of domestic yarn.

Year	Price per 100 Kin of Japanese Cotton Yarn	Price per 100 Kin of Imported Cotton Yarn
1874	42.70 yen	29.66 yen
1875	43.54	29.94
1876	40.79	27.42
1877	40.41	26.86

Although in the first three or four years after the Restoration the percentage of total imports held by cotton yarn was slightly less than that held by cotton fabrics, the former rapidly increased in the two decades after the Restoration until in the 1878-82 period it far surpassed imported cotton fabrics. This increase was partly a result of the birth of the Japanese textile industry which, like industrial production in general, was stimulated by the inflation following the Satsuma Revolt, and still further strengthened by the weeding out of backward, under-capitalized industries which took place in the succeeding "deflationary" period. This increased industrial activity, particularly on the part of textile factories, meant that Japanese mills could use greater quantities of cotton yarn to turn into fabric. The old, hand-spinning method could not turn out a standardized product to suit the requirements of the new textile industries equipped with the most up-to-date machinery. Consequently, the Japanese textile industry gave the *coup de grace* to that big sector of domestic handicraft industry, cotton-spinning (and later weaving), which had been fatally wounded in the first place by the imported commodity.[48]

[47] Table taken from Tsuchiya and Okazaki, *op. cit.*, p. 192.

[48] Although not strictly connected with the ruin of "domestic" industry as such, the drastic reduction in the area of land in cotton was also a blow at peasant "self-sufficiency." Though peasants grew cotton to a certain extent for the market they also used it at first for their own home-spun yarn and home-woven fabrics until the overwhelming cheapness of foreign articles discouraged them. In its attempts to become self-supporting and independent of foreign raw materials as far as possible, the Meiji Government encouraged the cultivation of cotton. The agricultural population responded by steadily increasing the amount of raw cotton grown, until by 1887 cotton culture extended over an area of 88,000 *chobu*

Other instances of the ruin of domestic industry can only be cited in passing. In the early Meiji era, sugar stood second in imports to cotton (including yarn and fabric) and had a disastrous effect on Japanese sugar cultivation. The area used for sugar-cane production (chiefly in Sanuki and Ehime) declined by 75 per cent between 1877 and 1882.[49] The import of cheap kerosene used for lighting largely replaced the old wax-tree and rapeseed oil produced formerly by domestic industries. The sudden mushrooming of newspapers and magazines after the Satsuma Revolt required special wood-pulp paper and thus severely dislocated the old hand-made paper industry.[50]

Another calamity for the peasant and his self-sufficient or largely self-sufficient economy was the drastic reduction in the common lands after the Restoration. During the Tokugawa period, the authorities had permitted meadow and woodland to be used for grazing and for the collection of fodder, fertilizer, fuel and timber, in return for the payment of "thank-money" (*unjo* or *myogakin*). Now, however, most of such land became state property. To put it precisely, after the return of the land registers in 1869 and the abolition of fiefs in 1872, those lands which had no clear proof of ownership, particularly lands in the Tokugawa domain, now became state land, regardless of previous "customary usage."[51] The loss to the peasantry of the usufruct of these lands which supplied them with fodder, fertilizer, wood for fuel, and implements, not only undermined still further the disintegrating "self-sufficient" economy, but also compelled the peasant household to purchase on the market

---

(215,600 acres), yielding a total of 39,928,000 *kin* (1 *kin* = 1.32 lbs. av.), Horie in *Keizai Ronso* (cited), p. 139.

Very soon the peasant found it hard to produce raw cotton of sufficiently high quality and low price to compete against foreign raw cotton. So cheap was foreign raw cotton that it soon supplied the Japanese factories with the vast proportion of their raw material and even penetrated into peasant households where it was used as the raw material for hand-spinning and weaving of fabrics to be consumed largely in the household. The effect of the greatly reduced price of Chinese and Indian cotton was decisive in this connection. Horie, *ibid.*, pp. 139-40.

After the removal of the import duty on foreign raw cotton, Japanese cultivation of cotton became negligible.

[49] Mori, *op. cit.*, p. 182.

The value of sugar imported into Japan during the first five years of the Meiji period (1868-72) was 10.67% of total imports. *Ibid.*, p. 178.

[50] These examples come from Horie, *Keizai Ronso* (cited), pp. 140-1.

[51] A detailed account of this annexation of common land by the Meiji Government is to be found in Tsuchiya and Okazaki, *op. cit.*, p. 199 *et seq.*

those commodities which formerly could be obtained from the common lands. With the intensification of agricultural produc-tion accompanying the great pressure on the land, another im-portant item which the peasant now had to buy was phosphate fertilizer (production begun in 1887), which became a necessity despite the continued use of night-soil gathered from neighbor-ing towns and villages.[52]

This condensed account of the ruin of the old domestic hand-icraft industry does not imply the atrophy of *all* household in-dustry as in 18th century England for instance; but it does indi-cate how first of all foreign commodities and later Japanese machine industry, together with such factors as the annexation of commons, forced the peasant to shift from the old type of domestic industry to the new. This was chiefly sericulture, which became the supplementary household industry *par excellence* in Japan—an industry which did not compete with foreign com-modities and fitted in well with Japanese economic develop-ment. With the growth of a stagnant population, the need for such supplementary domestic industry became a matter of life and death for a large section of the peasantry, so that the num-ber of agricultural households engaged in such additional work actually increased at least until shortly after the Great War.[53]

The significance of the ruin of the old domestic industry, and of the consequent divorce of industry from agriculture together with the commercialization of agricultural produce, lies in the part played by these agents in widening the home market for the disposal of manufactured goods. This creation of the home market greatly stimulated Japanese industrial development; but at the same time one must note that the extremely high rent and land tax, which left very little surplus in the hands of the peas-antry, whether tenant or proprietor, the limited extent to which the separation of industry from agriculture was carried out and the existence of the huge, impoverished surplus population all combined to keep this home market relatively narrow. This was revealed in the economic crisis of 1890, when it became

[52] One foreign observer writes that artificial fertilizer alone frequently takes as much as one-fifth the value of the crops on rice land. Buchanan, *loc. cit.*, p. 552.

[53] *Supra*, note 39. Since the Great War there has been a decline in the number of households engaged in supplementary industry. In 1910 the number of purely agricultural households was 3,771,318, and the number of those engaged in addi-tional industry was 1,726,600. The figures for 1937 are 4,180,672 and 1,394,207 respectively. *Norin Tokei* (abridged), 1939, p. 18.

apparent that the very low labor costs, which had been a most important element in the amazing growth of the Japanese textile industry, became a retarding factor (amongst the others just mentioned) in the further expansion of industry in Japan if it looked to the home market alone for its chief maintenance. Consequently, the new textile industry which was the axis of the first industrial revolution in the late eighties, felt the full force of this first economic crisis of modern Japan.

The most characteristic creation of this industrial revolution was the Nihon Boseki Rengo-Kai (Japanese Spinners' Association), formed in 1882 under the guidance of Okada Reiko, formerly the superintendent of the government model spinning-factory in Aichi. In 1890, the year of the crisis, this alert and capably led Association asked the Diet to remove the double import-export tariff on cotton.[54] Late in the same year the Association girded up its loins to fight its way into the foreign market, realizing it would have to export on a big scale or go under. In November an arrangement was made with the Nippon Yusen Kaisha whereby, despite profit or loss, the Association promised to export for five successive years at least 30,000 bales of cotton per year, and the N.Y.K., in return for the exclusive right to transport this cotton, agreed to reduce its freight rates to Shanghai from five to three yen a ton. In this way by breaking into the foreign market, specifically the Chinese market, prompt measures were taken to overcome the glut of surplus goods which threatened to accumulate at home.[55] This one example shows how Japanese industry, partly under the pressure of foreign competition and partly because of the insufficient purchasing power of the home market, had no alternative but to look to the foreign market as the guarantee of future expansion and progress.[56]

[54] The export tariff on cotton thread was removed in 1894, and in 1896 the import tariff on raw cotton, now coming chiefly from Bombay, was lifted. The shift to Indian raw cotton and the abolition of the tariff barrier on its import spelled the doom of raw cotton production in Japan. The details on the activities of the *Boseki Rengo-Kai* are taken chiefly from Tsuchiya and Okazaki, *op. cit.*, pp. 282-4.

[55] The agreement with the N.Y.K. was extended to import trade in raw cotton in Bombay in order to circumvent the P. & O. monopoly, and the N.Y.K. opened its Bombay line for that purpose in 1893. Kobayashi, *op. cit.*, p. 172.

[56] The effect of the Japanese victory over China (1894-95) in giving the cotton industry a much-extended market in Korea and the Yangtze valley is duly recorded in a history of the cotton industry, "Hompo Bosekigyo no Hattatsu" (The Development of the Cotton Industry in Our Country), in *Nihon Sangyo Shiryo*, edited by Mukai and Takimoto, Volume VI, p. 167. On this point see also Chapter VI, pp. 202-3.

CHAPTER VI

PARTIES AND POLITICS

Since it is quite impossible within the compass of this chapter to give even a summary of the political and constitutional history of Japan in the late 19th and early 20th century, what will be attempted here is a brief account of some aspects of Japanese politics which are frequently a source of speculation and possibly misunderstanding among Western observers. The author does not flatter himself by thinking that he can supply a definitive answer to these doubts and queries, but he merely hopes that by centering a discussion upon such subjects as the origin and nature of Japanese liberalism, its relation to political parties and the bureaucracy, and its attitude to foreign policy, he may be able to throw some light on an obscure chapter of Japanese political history.

Agrarian Movement of the Second Period, 1877-83, and Rise of the Liberal Party (Jiyuto)

The stormy politics of the first few years of the Meiji era up to 1877 were typical of any transitional period. The disappearance of the old, pure feudal classes, and the emergence of new social forces were marked by confusion and bitterness, by hopes aroused and too often disappointed. In the time of transition no clear-cut political divisions appear, only the hazy outline of tendencies which later were to become sharply defined as political parties with definite programs. In the third chapter an attempt was made to analyze the position and aspirations of various sections of the nation, the merchants, the old feudal classes (*samurai* and *daimyo*) and the peasantry. It was emphasized that in the first six or seven years following the Restoration, peasant revolt reached an apex of violence and then gradually declined. The peasant movement was one of apparent contradictions, a mixture of reaction and radicalism which gave contemporary Japanese politics the appearance of a tapestry of intricate pattern showing no obvious design, but only a combination of vivid or somber concentrations of light and shade. When led by discontented *samurai*, this agrarian movement, which was the core of early Meiji political life in the broadest sense, represented a desire to return to the old order; when directed against usury, high rent and excessive taxation, it expressed a vague aspiration toward a fuller democracy.[1] The first type of reactionary agrarian revolt, led by discontented elements and directed against the new régime, was gradually extinguished, so that after the suppression of the Satsuma Revolt (1877) it ceased to be important. Thereafter the agrarian movement branched off into three directions. First there was the agitation of the tenant for the reduction of rent. Second was the action of small landed proprietors who were menaced with dispossession and who struggled against usurers and aggrandizing landholders. The third type was the movement of landowners in general against the government policy of favoring the great mercantile and financial houses at the expense of the rural community. Examples of the first two movements are numerous, since agitation for rent reduction and against usury is common to any society which has tenants who pay high rent or small proprietors who fear foreclosure by the local usurer. The situation giving rise to such movements in the early Meiji period has been summarized by Mayet in his introductory letter to Count Yamagata. "The condition of the rural population has during the last years been eminently unsatisfactory. Proofs of this may be seen in the insurrection of peasantry, the feuds between debtors and creditors, the bankruptcy and compulsory sale of (in many cases) hundreds of farming establishments in several provinces and the petitions sent to the Government by several great assemblies

[1] We have already discussed the relation of the early peasant revolts to the democratic or anti-feudal movement. As the nature of these revolts was very complex, even contradictory, one must make generalizations about the democratic character of the agrarian movement with great caution. It might be of interest to see what the most reputable Japanese authorities say about it. Professor Fujii Jintaro, in *Nihon Kempo Seitei Shi*, p. 198, says that the various local uprisings of the early Meiji had nothing to do with the constitutional movement which in the Meiji period was synonymous with the People's Rights movement. Professor Ono Takeo, however, respectfully disagrees with him. See his *Meiji Ishin Noson Shakai Shiron*, p. 59. Rather than enter into controversy with so distinguished a scholar over this subject, Professor Ono contents himself with citing a reference from Professor Fujii himself which would seem to contradict his former statement. In that instance Professor Fujii says "Thus as far as politics are concerned, it is worth the historian's attention to note that the various mass movements which arose then were the fore-runners of the later-arising 'People's Rights movement.'" Quoted in Ono, *op. cit.*, p. 57. It is obvious from Professor Ono's comment that he agrees with this latter view.

of agriculturists for the remission or diminution of the Land-Tax."[2]

A good example of these first two movements is the vigorous activity of the Debtors' Party (*Shakkinto*) in numerous localities—particularly in Izu, Ibaraki, Gumma and other prefectures; and, more specifically, the insurrection in Chichibu (Saitama prefecture) in November 1884, which spread to Nagano and Gumma, having as its object the reduction of rent and interest rates.[3]

But politically the type of agrarian movement represented in the first and second categories was not so important in this period (1877-85). The third, which may be called a protest of landowning agriculturists against the favored position of the financial oligarchy, is the most significant historically. It is from this group that the cry "Liberty and People's Rights" arose most vociferously. Since these landowners were to become the standard-bearers of the constitutional movement, and since also they formed the background of the Liberal Party (*Jiyuto*), we may examine the features of this movement in some detail.

At first sight it might seem incongruous that landowners should form the core of the liberal movement. The word "landowner" at once brings to the mind of the Western reader the English squire and his deep-seated conservatism in all matters relating to society and politics. To explain the Japanese landowner's outlook we must hark back to the analysis of Japanese tenant-landlord relations, as described in the last chapter.

We saw that the Japanese landlord collects rent while the tenant takes the entrepreneur's risks but not his profits. Thus the landlord is interested primarily in converting the rice or other agricultural produce collected as rent into money at the best possible rate. Hence his only concern is the current price of rice. His interest in turning agricultural products into commodities makes the Japanese landlord a small commercial capitalist who invests his money in land or in local domestic industries connected with the land, such as the making of *miso* (bean paste) and brewing of *sake*, or who becomes a rice-broker or

---

[2] Mayet, *op. cit.*, p. 3.

[3] *Ibid.*, pp. 66-7. Mayet gives a list of the various activities both of a peaceful and violent kind aimed at reducing rent and the rate of interest or at securing better terms for debt settlement, etc. *Ibid.*, pp. 65-8. We shall refer to this incident in another connection.

small merchant of artificial fertilizer and the like.[4] A foreigner who several years ago tramped far and wide over the Japanese countryside, making detailed notes on Japanese rural society, wrote in this connection, "When I drew attention to the fact that there (i.e. a village in Nagano prefecture) the manufacture of *sake* and soy seemed to be frequently in the hands of landowners, it was explained to me that formerly this was their industry exclusively." And in another passage, "Before I left the town I had a chat with a landowner who turned his tenants' rent rice into *sake*. He was of the fifth generation of brewers." And again, "All the shopkeepers seem to own their own houses and all but three have some land."[5] Thus as the collector of an exorbitant rent he is a semi-feudal landlord, but he has also the other side, that of the commercial capitalist. It was this commercial capitalist side which drove the Japanese landlord into politics in the period of which we are speaking. This is seen in the active part played by landlord-manufacturers in forming the Liberal party, the *Jiyuto*. In 1880 a Council of *Sake*-Brewers (*Sakaya Kaigi*) was formed under the leadership of a certain Kojima Minoru and rapidly attracted to it great numbers of *sake*-brewers throughout the country.[6] The government, which was then considering a program of naval expansion requiring increased taxation, proposed among other new methods of revenue increase a tax on *zoseki* (a yeast stone used in brewing). Immediately the *Sakaya Kaigi*, at the first conference of the *Jiyuto* in 1881, opposed this tax and raised the slogan "Freedom of Enterprise," worthy of the purest Manchester Liberal in 19th century England. The great popularity of this organization among village and town gentry alarmed the government, so that

[4] A typical example of how even small landowners have also the nature of commercial capitalists appears in the social case-history of a small village studied in great detail by Yoshikawa Sei and entitled "Tezukuri Jinushi no Ikko Satsu," etc. (An Observation on Tezukuri or "Cultivating" Landlords as seen in the Case of Ishida Village of Shimo-Niikawa gori in Etchu), in *Nihon Shihonshugi Shi Ronshu* (Collection of Essays on the History of Japanese Capitalism), by Tsuchiya Takao and others, Tokyo, 1937, pp. 103-33. The author Yoshikawa discovered that between 1887 and 1897 many of these local landlords became commercial capitalists; for instance, one of them became a rice-broker, another a trader in fertilizer, while still another invested in a textile factory, and so forth. *Ibid.*, pp. 128-9.

[5] J. W. Robertson Scott, *The Foundations of Japan*, Notes Made During Six Thousand Miles in the Rural Districts as a Basis for a Sounder Knowledge of the Japanese People, London, 1922, pp. 119, 213, 267.

[6] This and the following facts about the political activity of the *Sakaya Kaigi* appear originally in Itagaki's *Jiyuto-Shi* (History of the Liberal Party), p. 618 *et seq.*, and are related in Hirano, *op. cit.*, pp. 182-3.

in December 1881 the council was dissolved at the order of the governor of Osaka-Fu. Despite the ban the brewers opened their session on a boat in the Yodogawa. The activity of this brewers' council attracted large numbers of landlord-manufacturers and small landlords with commercial interests into the *Jiyuto* and gave it the peculiar coloring described above, that is a Liberal party based on the landlord class. Thus his trading or manufacturing activities made of the Japanese landlord a modest Cobden, but his interests as landlord could make him intensely conservative.

The other concern of the landowning class in general was tax reduction. The government had reduced the land tax from 3 to $2\frac{1}{2}$ per cent to conciliate the landowners and to dampen any sympathy they might entertain for the sporadic *samurai* revolts culminating in the Satsuma Revolt of 1877, which tax-reduction anticipated but did not prevent. Despite this conciliatory gesture, the landowning gentry felt that the weight of taxation was unduly heavy upon them. From 1875 to 1879 the land tax accounted for 80.5 per cent of the revenue, from 1880 to 1884 for 65.6 per cent, and from 1885 to 1889 for 69.4 per cent. Furthermore, the government policy of liquidating inconvertible notes, together with its industrial policy, had caused, so it was believed, a disastrous fall in the price of rice, which was the basic concern of the landlord. At the same time that financial and industrial circles close to the government were receiving subsidies, generous government contracts and trading monopolies, the landowning class saw the price of rice fall steadily from 221 in 1881 (1873 = 100) to 105 in 1888, rising slowly to 154 in 1893.[7] In a word, the agricultural classes felt that the financial and industrial oligarchy enjoyed the exclusive favor and protection of the government while the landowners were paying the bill for industrialization. The feelings of this landowning class were sympathetically interpreted by the forerunners of the liberal movement in a memorial advocating the establishment of a Representative Assembly, and presented to the Emperor in June 1877 by the *Risshisha* (Society of Free-Thinkers). "The taxes of the *fu* and *ken* are collected and sent directly to the *Okura Sho* (Department of Finance). This causes great scarcity of money in the country and cripples its powers of production. The government shows great activity in promoting schemes for

[7] *Supra*, Chapter V, note 15.

agricultural industries, in opening up Yezo and in establishing manufactures, but the officials appointed to take charge of such matters utterly mismanage whatever is entrusted to their care and interfere with the just rights and powers of the merchants. Hundreds of thousands of yen are spent in assisting certain companies, or in founding new ones, but such benevolent acts of the government are confined to certain persons or associations and in no way exercise any benefit for the public good."[8]

Accordingly, the landlords participated in the liberal movement, attacking the bureaucratic governing circle and its financial supporters as small commercial capitalists, interested primarily in rice-brokerage, in trading, in usury and in small local investments. It was this side which made them active champions of "Freedom and People's Rights" and "Freedom of Enterprise," and not the pure landlord side with its semi-feudal conservative character. The somber side of the landlord never disappeared even during the hey-day of liberalism, but lay dormant until later years when it completely overshadowed the "liberal" side. The point to note is that Japanese liberalism had its roots in the countryside, unlike English liberalism which was a movement of the cities especially of the city merchants in opposition to the conservative landed gentry.

The theoretical leaders of the liberal movement were ex-*samurai*, chiefly from the former Tosa and Hizen clans which no longer shared equally in the fruits of office with Satsuma and Choshu. That many of these men were inspired by genuinely liberal ideals is not disputed; their later careers and sacrifices are sufficient testimony to their singleness of purpose. Nevertheless, as two Japanese authorities have pointed out, the abolition of the clans had undermined the economic base of feudalism, leaving many discontented *samurai*, while the failure of the advocates for an expedition to Korea (*Seikan Ron*) had embittered others, and so these ex-*samurai* were drawn into the liberal movement merely because it was *the anti-government movement*.[9] Thus individual place-seeking and jealousy of the *Sat-cho*

---

[8] McLaren, *JGD*, p. 471. A quotation from a Japanese writer supports this view. "The *Go-No* (rich peasants or big landowners) joined them (the ex-*samurai*) in the movement. The *Go-No* felt that the burden of the new financial policy fell unduly upon them and they also resented the new order on general principles. Therefore they were willing to join a movement against the *Sat-cho* group that ruled." Iwasaki, *op. cit.*, p. 87.

[9] Osatake Takeshi and Hayashi Shigeru, "Seiji" (Politics) in *Gendai Nihon Shi Kenkyu* (Study of Contemporary Japanese History), symposium by various authors, Tokyo, 1938, p. 82. See also Chapter III, note 93, *supra*.

monopoly acted as a stimulus for organizing the first political associations in Japan. It was natural that these ex-*samurai* in opposition to the government should become the acknowledged leaders of the movement which demanded a people's assembly. They enjoyed great prestige as members of the *shizoku* class, and above all as leaders in the Restoration of 1868. On this account some Japanese authorities have called them the heirs of the *Kinno* or *Sonno* Party (loyalists who fought against the *Bakufu*) and the true embodiment of the anti-feudal struggle.[10]

But the impelling force of the liberal movement came from the great mass of small peasants, tenants and city poor who rallied to it urging the reduction of taxes, the establishment of representative institutions, even demanding representation in the liberal movement.[11] It was difficult however for the peasants living in outlying, isolated villages to take active part in politics. It was only natural that the most active element in local politics should be the large landowners, while the national leadership tended to be in the hands of ex-*samurai* or of a few large landlord merchants.[12]

This widespread and loosely connected movement of small landowners and peasants under the leadership of former *samurai* and big landlord merchants took national form in the *Jiyuto* (Liberal Party) organized early in 1881. The quality of its leadership inevitably made the political philosophy of the *Jiyuto* a rather softened, conciliatory liberalism, a liberalism which strove primarily for democracy, for people's rights, for freedom of enterprise—all for the respectable classes. This is well brought out in the reply of the liberal leaders, Soyejima, Goto and Itagaki (who were to become the most active members of the *Jiyuto*), to Kato Hiroyuki's argument against representative government in Japan. "Now if this council chamber be established, we do not propose that the franchise should at once be made universal.

---

[10] Fujii Jintaro in *Nihon Kempo Seitei Shi*, pp. 265-6. Osatake and Hayashi, *op. cit.*, pp. 82-3. Another writer says rather naively: "Thus these reactionaries became progressives." Iwasaki, *op. cit.*, p. 86.

[11] Osatake and Hayashi, *op. cit.*, p. 82.

[12] On the landlord leadership of tenants and peasants in the *Jiyuto*, see Ono Takeo, *Ishin Noson Shakai Shiron* (cited), p. 58. Professor Ono mentions there that the overwhelming majority of the participants in the early liberal movement of the eighties were small peasants who had taken part in the innumerable tax-reduction agitations. But he categorically states that the leadership in the Liberal Movement, or to be more accurate the *Jiyuto*, was in the hands of large landlords. *Ibid.*, p. 59.

We would only give it in the first instance to the *samurai* and the richer farmers and merchants, for it is they who produced the leaders of the Revolution of 1868."[13]

Thus from its start Japanese liberalism as embodied in the *Jiyuto* was of a moderate, temporizing quality and later it was to change into its opposite, uncompromising conservatism, when the *Seiyukai* was formed from the ruins of the *Jiyuto* in 1900. We are not discussing here the extreme left-wing of the *Jiyuto*, which later took on almost a revolutionary coloring, but the basic political philosophy of the chief leaders of the *Jiyuto*. Despite any vagueness in its program, the *Jiyuto* before its split into local grouplets with a right and left wing, because of the enthusiastic backing it received from land-hungry tenants and debt-burdened peasant proprietors, had great *élan* and even revolutionary potentialities. For this reason, as we shall see later, the Government in its campaign of suppressing political parties launched its fiercest onslaught against the *Jiyuto*.[14]

Outline of Early Political Societies and Parties

In the eyes of the two Japanese authorities already cited, Japanese liberalism was really a movement for enlightenment and for the dissemination of the abstract doctrine of the natural rights of man.[15] These writers give this judgment in their account of the Aikokukoto (Public Society of Patriots), one of the first political associations to have as its goal the establishment of representative institutions. At this point it might be convenient to make a short digression outlining the programs and history of the first political parties, beginning with the *Jiyuto* which was foreshadowed by the Aikokukoto. The last-named association was formed in 1874 by such well-known figures as Itagaki Taisuke, Goto Shojiro, Yuri Kimimasa, Ogasawara Kan, Eto Shimpei (shortly to be involved in the Sega Revolt and executed for his part in it), and Soyejima Taneomi. Its purpose was to appeal to public opinion in support of the idea of representative institutions, and its program consisted of the following three points. First, to contribute to world civilization; to

---

[13] *JGD*, p. 445.

[14] Comparing the *Kaishinto* and *Jiyuto*, one Japanese historian writes, "The former (*Kaishinto*) was moderate in thought and action, while the latter was radical and sometimes even violent." G. E. Uyehara, *The Political Development of Japan, 1867-1909.* London, 1910, p. 91.

[15] Osatake and Hayashi, *op. cit.*, p. 85.

accomplish this task it was essential to instill throughout the nation a respect for the natural rights of man. Second, to unite the Emperor and his people and thus to bring real prosperity to the realm; this in turn must be realized through the independent and unrestricted development of the rights of the individual. Third, to fulfill this program the signatories swear to endure any trials and difficulties.[16] As our authorities point out, this program created a stir among the intellectuals of the day who were eager to study Western political theory. But it could hardly form the basis for the organization of a genuine political party; consequently it soon died a natural death. Another similar political society was the *Risshisha* (Society of Free Thinkers) organized by the intellectuals of the former Tosa clan (modern Kochi prefecture), upon whom French political thought had made a deep impression. Its leaders were Kataoka Kenkichi, its president, and Itagaki Taisuke. This group also talked of the people's welfare and the individual's rights, attracting to it many of the younger ex-*samurai*, even some members of the Imperial Guard who had returned home; in fact its constitution limited membership to the gentry or *shizoku* class, so it had a feudal character which effectively discouraged any participation of the common people in its councils.[17] The members of this political association together with those of the *Aikokusha* (Society of Patriots, which was the successor to the *Aikokukoto*) were the forerunners and founders of the *Jiyuto*, which was organized as a national political party in 1881 with Itagaki Taisuke as president and Nakajima Nobuyuki as vice-president. Its program was as follows: (1) to broaden liberty, protect the people's rights, increase prosperity, and reform society; (2) to expend its strength in establishing a sound constitutional system; (3) to accomplish its purpose the party must co-operate with others in the country who are striving for the same end.[18] The content of its program differs scarcely one whit from the vague and abstract aspirations of such earlier political groups as the *Aikokukoto* or the *Risshisha*, but the significance of the *Jiyuto* of 1881 lies in the victory of the idea of the right of a political party organized on a national basis to play a legitimate part in the life of the nation.

[16] *Ibid.*, pp. 83-4.
[17] *Ibid.*, pp. 85-7.
[18] *Ibid.*, p. 117.

Another party to be founded at the same time was the *Rikken Kaishinto* or simply *Kaishinto* (Reform Party) led by Okuma Shigenobu. It was composed of groups like the old style bureaucrats centering about Kono Binken, Maejima Mitsu, Kitabatake Harufusa, Yano Fumio and intellectuals of the Keio School, Fujita Shigekichi, Shimada Saburo, Inukai Tsuyoshi, Ozaki Yukio, with lesser known names of two groups, the *Otokai* which overlapped with the first group, and the *Toyo Giseikai*, together with some members of the capital's intelligentsia. Its chief supporters were bureaucrats who were out of office, the city intelligentsia, and some of the larger merchants and industrialists, particularly the Mitsubishi Company. Its principles were based largely on contemporary English liberalism and utilitarianism. Its program was so watered down that by contrast it makes the *Jiyuto* platform revolutionary. The essence of the *Kaishinto*'s political philosophy can best be epitomized in its watchword "*Onken Chakujitsu*," which might be paraphrased as "moderate and sound, slow but steady."

The third political party was the *Rikken Teiseito* (Constitutional Imperial Party) organized in 1882. It was founded as the government party to offset the influence of the other two and was conservative to the core. According to Osatake and Hayashi, the real backers of this party were not its avowed leaders, the bureaucrats Fukuchi Genichiro, Maruyama Sakura and Mizuno Torajiro, but in reality the higher court circles revolving around such luminaries as Ito Hirobumi, Inouye Kaoru and Yamada Akiyoshi, who wished to use this party as a platform for *étatisme* on the German model and also as a counter against the other two parties.[19] But this party proved to be no match for its rivals either in organization or in popular appeal.

Each party had its own organ[20] and held public debates at

[19] *Ibid.*, p. 120.

[20] As far as the more important journals are concerned the liberal view was championed in the *Choya Shimbun* and the conservative or government view was defended in the *Nichi Nichi Shimbun*. McLaren, *A Political History of Japan*, p. 109. The ablest controversialists in the radical camp were Kataoka Kenkichi and Nakae Tokusuke (or Chomin), a materialist philosopher best known for his work *Ichi-nen yu-han* (One year and a half). He had studied in France (1871-74) and was one of the first translators of J.-J. Rousseau. Another left-wing writer was Oi Kentaro, author of *Jiji Yoran* (Guide to Current Problems) and editor of the radical newspaper *Azuma Shimbun*. He was the most active spirit in the abortive attempt to set up a democratic regime in Korea, and later he became a leader of the radical *Toyo Jiyuto* (Eastern Liberal Party).

The spokesman of moderation and English utilitarianism was Fukuzawa

which the most contentious subject was the question of sovereignty. The *Jiyuto* maintained that sovereignty lay with the people and that consequently the constitution should be drawn up by an elective people's assembly. The *Teiseito* bitterly contested this claim, asserting that sovereignty was inalienably attached to the Emperor's person and that accordingly he alone could grant a constitution to the people as a gift. The *Kaishinto* in the best English constitutional style compromised between these two views by asserting that sovereignty lay jointly in the Throne and the people's assembly.

The Government Policy Toward Political Parties

The Government's attitude toward the growth of liberal ideas and the organization of political parties was one of misgiving to say the least. When the demand for representative institutions first began to grow clamorous in the years after the defeat of the *Seikan Ron* in 1874, the Government decided to make concessions in that direction without compromising its own autocratic powers, and devised the local or prefectural assemblies (*Fu-Ken-Kai*) established in 1878.[21] These local assemblies were forerunners of the national assembly or Diet not only in point of time but in constitutional powers. Very little public interest was shown in them since all real power still lay in the hands of the ruling bureaucracy. In the opinion of some authorities, the Government's purpose in this was to reduce the growing pressure for representative institutions and at the same time create an organization, the *Fu-Ken-Kai*, as a training center for a local bureaucracy over which the central oligarchy hoped to extend

Yukichi, founder of Keio University, indefatigable essayist and translator, possibly the greatest publicist in Japanese letters, and master of one of the finest prose styles in the language. His influence on Japanese intellectual and political life was immense.

The cause of the bureaucracy and of Prussian absolutism was championed by Kato Hiroyuki, who replied to the memorial for the establishment of a Representative Assembly in 1874. See *JGD*, pp. 433-9. He wrote numerous articles and books, among which was his statement of political philosophy, the *Kokutai Shinron* (1874), which was the product of his lectures at the *Kunaisho* (Department of Imperial Household). In this work he had some favorable words to say of the republican system of government. In later years when he became a Privy Councilor, he was so embarrassed by this passage that he tried to buy up all the old copies of the work. See Tsurumi Yusuke, *The Liberal Movement in Japan*, New Haven, 1925, p. 68.

[21] For regulations concerning the Prefectural Assembly, see *JGD*, pp. 272-6. For the constitution and powers of the *Fu* and *Ken* governments, see *ibid.*, pp. 276-85.

its control.[22] Whatever purpose the Government hoped this local assembly would serve, it revealed a characteristic precautionary policy (which was to be shown again at critical times) of granting a concession with one hand and taking it back with the other. In this instance, however, it reversed this order by first taking a step which to a large extent stultified the concession that followed. Before the creation of the local assemblies with their high property qualifications for electors, the Government in June 1875 had passed a drastic Press Law, which it used unsparingly in the next few years for smothering any effective criticism of the Government policy.[23] Shortly after the creation of these local assemblies, discontent with the Government's high-handed methods again gathered momentum. When the loosely-knit network of local debtors' parties and liberal societies was organized into national parties (particularly the *Jiyuto*), and when agitation for representative institutions became more violent, the Government decided again to make a concession. Accordingly in 1881 it promised the nation a Diet by the year 1889. But the Imperial Edict of October 12, 1881, promising the establishment of the national assembly, did not put an end to the demand for representative institutions, but added fuel to the democratic movement.[24] This movement, as expressed in the growing popularity and power of political parties, was viewed by the Government with the greatest alarm and it took swift action by launching an attack against these two opposition liberal parties, the *Kaishinto* and *Jiyuto*, first by direct repression and secondly by splitting the liberal movement and winning over to its own camp some sections of the opposition. Having promised a Diet within nine years, the Government in

[22] McLaren, *A Political History of Japan*, p. 132. "In regard to the franchise, the government's policy according to the same authority was to enfranchise the people to as limited an extent as possible sufficient to satisfy the popular demand for representation, but not endangering its own supremacy." *Ibid.*, pp. 132-3.

[23] A leading newspaper of the day had this to say of these strictly enforced Newspaper Regulations. "But in glancing back at the history of any nation whatever, we have never heard of all the editors of a whole city being brought up before the courts for violating the laws or inciting the people during a whole month, nor that, while one editor is on his trial, another is brought up, and before judgment is given against him, before even his trial comes off, another is brought in and no day passes without the trial of an editor." Quoted in Uyehara, *op. cit.*, p. 83, note 2.

[24] Osatake and Hayashi, *op. cit.*, p. 128. See also Professor Ukita Kazutami and Counts Itagaki and Okuma, "History of Political Parties in Japan," in *Fifty Years of New Japan*. Vol. I, p. 148.

1882 passed new regulations in regard to meeting and association, which were far more severe and more rigorously enforced than the previous regulations.[25] The most stringent repression, however, came only after the Government had succeeded in rendering the political movement ineffective either by winning over some of its leaders or by playing off the *Kaishinto* against the *Jiyuto*, and in this way removing some of the ablest political leaders from successful participation in the democratic movement.

Just at the time when the agitation for people's rights and representative institutions seemed to be sweeping victoriously over the country, indicating a crucial struggle in the near future with the Government, the members of the *Jiyuto* were amazed to learn suddenly late in 1882 that their most experienced leaders, Itagaki Taisuke and Goto Shojiro, were sailing for Europe to study Western political institutions at first hand. Rumors emanating from the *Kaishinto* and aired by the Tokyo-Yokohama *Mainichi Shimbun* insisted that the expenses for this trip were met by the Government.[26] Although many of the *Jiyuto* members stoutly denied the charge that their leaders had been virtually bought off by the Government some of them including Baba Tatsui, Oishi Masami and Taguchi Ukichi shortly withdrew from the party in protest. The truth was that the traveling expenses had been furnished by the Mitsui Company, with Goto and Inouye Kaoru acting as intermediaries.[27] This dubious incident and its repercussions stung the *Jiyuto* into bitter recrimination against the *Kaishinto*. Okuma, the leader of the *Kaishinto*, was accused of acting as the political agent of the Mitsubishi Company and of pouring over-generous subsidies

[25] The severity of these police regulations restricting political association can be seen by examining the full decree as it appears in *JGD*, pp. 495-9, and the revised regulations, *ibid.*, pp. 499-501. After many annoying but not insuperable obstacles to political association, there comes the regulation which makes it a criminal offense to advertise a meeting or debate, to induce anyone to attend the meeting, to send out invitations by mail, to establish any local branches of a political party or association, to have any communications between different parties or associations, and to hold open-air meetings. *Ibid.*, p. 496-7. The enforcement of this law was if anything more drastic than its provisions.

[26] Osatake and Hayashi, *op. cit.*, p. 130.

[27] *Ibid.*, p. 130. The full details of this matter are sifted and weighed by Osatake Takeshi in his chapter entitled "Itagaki Taisuke no Seiko Mondai" (The Question of Itagaki Taisuke's Trip Abroad), in *Meiji Seiji Shi Tembyo* (Sketches in Meiji Political History), Tokyo, 1938, pp. 151-79.

and grants into its coffers.[28] This accusation evoked the cry "*Gito Bokumetsu*" (destroy false parties) and "*Umi-Bozu Taiji*" (subdue the sea monsters, *i.e.*, the Mitsubishi Company). Taking advantage of this attack on the Mitsubishi, the Government established its short-lived Kyodo Un'yu Kaisha under the patronage of Shinagawa Yajiro. The Mitsubishi weathered the storm, amalgamated with the Kyodo Un'yu Kainsha to form the N.Y.K., and drew closer than ever before to the government circles, especially when Okuma or his companions were in office. The upshot of this was that rather than combining to attack their common enemy, the absolutist clan government, the two opposition parties fell into the trap set for them by the Government, wrangled bitterly with each other and dissipated their energies in such a way as to discredit political parties and to strengthen the Government.[29] Following its clever maneuvers in playing off one opposition party against another, the Government capped its campaign against the parties by the severe repression mentioned above. Faced with the alternative of carrying on the struggle by illegal methods or of bowing before the Government's will, most of the leaders of the liberal movement chose the latter course. In October 1884, the *Jiyuto* was voluntarily dissolved,[30] while the *Kaishinto* preceded it by a year, dissolving in September 1883.

New Shift of Agrarian Revolt Following Dissolution of Jiyuto in 1884

Even before the dissolution of the parties, with the press effectively muzzled and all political activity stringently suppressed, local branches of the political parties had energetically

[28] Ukita, Itagaki and Okuma, *op. cit.*, p. 155.

[29] Osatake and Hayashi, *op. cit.*, pp. 130-1. The following words are instructive "The strife between the two parties, and the consequent neglect of their main object of attacking the common enemy, encouraged the Government to resort to still more vigorous means of oppressing the political parties." Ukita, Itagaki and Okuma, *op. cit.*, p. 155.

[30] In studying the motives for dissolution, one is struck by the note of unconditional surrender to the Government's policy of suppression. For instance, in the dissolution speech of Itagaki Taisuke delivered in Osaka, on October 29, 1884, he gave as his primary reason for dissolution the enactment of laws regulating public meetings and the publication of newspapers. He also stated that another reason for dissolution was the *violent character of many of the local incidents*, instigated by *Jiyuto* members, which were assuming revolutionary form. See "Josobun" (Memorials or Appeals to the Throne of Itagaki Taisuke) in *Meiji Bunka Zenshu*, Vol. III, pp. 466-7.

The same motives for dissolution are also given by Osatake and Hayashi, *op. cit.*, pp. 132-3.

protested against government suppression and had even turned to insurrection as a means of achieving their end—the overthrow of the autocratic government.[31] Many of the lesser leaders in the *Jiyuto*, angered and bewildered by what seemed to them the defection of their chiefs, often supported these ill-starred uprisings. The historical interest of these local incidents arises from the political and economic demands which motivated the rank and file of the liberal movement and the resolution, however misplaced, with which these demands were backed in comparison to the tergiversations of the leaders. One of the shrewdest observers of Japanese national life, Fukuzawa Yukichi foresaw as early as 1881 the tendency for the rank and file in the liberal movement to display a violent impatience with government policy. In writing to Okuma, he says, "The *Minken Ron* (Advocacy of People's Rights) seems to be more and more favoring direct action. If it goes on in that direction, the antagonism between the government and people will become increasingly embittered, and in the end I fear it will mean unfortunate bloodshed."[32]

[31] On the activity of these local parties which sprang up all over the country following the suppression of the great national parties and the ban on political association, see Osatake and Hayashi, *op. cit.*, pp. 128-9.

One of the most interesting examples of these left-wing derivatives of the liberal movement was the *Toyo Shakaito* (Eastern Social Party), first organized in May 1882 in a Buddhist temple, the Kotoji at Shimabara in Hizen. (The site of Shimabara is rather interesting since one of the last great uprisings against Tokugawa domination took place there in the early 17th century. The Shimabara Revolt was generally regarded as inspired by Christians who refused to capitulate to the anti-Christian decrees of the regime.) The leaders of this party were Tarui Tokichi and Akamatsu Taisuke. Its program was as follows: (1) Ethical standards were to guide the speech and conduct of the party members. (2) Equality was to be its guiding principle. (3) The greatest happiness of the masses was to be its goal. It was even hoped that its activities would be extended to Korea and China. Its manifesto closed with the words, "We will not make anybody our enemy, but if there are some obstacles in our way, we are even willing to give our lives to achieve our purpose." When this party's existence was brought to the attention of the Home Minister, he ordered its dissolution, but it continued to exercise influence over some of the local parties for some time to come. These details are taken from a memorandum describing the formation of the party in *Meiji Bunka Zenshu*, Vol. II, pp. 434-5.

Professor Abe Isoh considers this effort of Tarui Tokichi to organize a left-wing of the *Jiyuto* as the first attempt to introduce socialism into Japan. Its failure postponed the first successful effort until the end of the century, when the rise of great industries gave the basis for a socialist party, the Social Democratic Party of Japan, founded in 1901. See Abe Isoh, "Socialism in Japan," in *Fifty Years of New Japan*, Vol. II, p. 505.

[32] Letter of Fukuzawa to Okuma Shigenobu, dated October 1, 1881, in *Zoku Fukuzawa Zenshu* (Supplement to the Collected Works of Fukuzawa), edited by the Keio Gijuku, Tokyo, 1933, Vol. 6, p. 248.

Fukuzawa's forebodings were only too accurate. The first of these revolts broke out in 1882 in Fukushima prefecture. Indignation at the arbitrary action of the prefectural governor, Mishima Tsuyo, in over-riding the prefectural assembly of Fukushima was the spark which kindled the uprising in that province. The leader was Kono Hironaka, a man of extreme views and resolute character. After the suppression of the revolt he and his associates were arrested and sentenced to imprisonment.[33] Almost at the same time an uprising broke out in Takada of Niigata prefecture in which the leaders were accused of plotting to assassinate the government leaders.[34] An insurrection occurred in Chichibu (Saitama prefecture) in 1884 in which the *Shakkinto* or local debtors' party played a leading role as did also a radical group from the local *Jiyuto*. These political leaders were alleged to have stirred up bad feeling among the peasantry and village poor against the local landlords, and when police arrived on the scene the peasants had resisted them forcibly.[35] We have noted this uprising in another connection, but what is of interest for our immediate purpose is that this Chichibu uprising symbolizes the great divide in the history of the *Jiyuto* or Liberal Party. We have already seen that leadership in this party was in the hands of landowners who were merchants or manufacturers as well; it was this commercial side of their nature which drew them into politics. However, as government repression became intensified to meet the mounting demand for greater democracy, these local branches, which were often in more radical hands than was the national leadership, stirred up such violent popular sentiment not only in favor of representative institutions but also for rent reduction that it terrified many of the more cautious leaders, bringing out the conservative landlord side of their nature, and thus made party dissolution by no means as unpalatable as it might otherwise have been. As one authority writes, "The *Jiyuto* and *Kaishinto*

[33] These details on the Fukushima uprising are taken from Fujii Jintaro and Moriya Hidesuke, "Meiji Jidai" (The Meiji Period), being Volume XII, of *Sogo Nihon Shi Taikei*, Tokyo, 1934, p. 83.
The manifesto of the rebels is translated into English in Uyehara, *op. cit.*, p. 98. note 2.
[34] Fujii Jintaro, *Nihon Kempo Seitei Shi* (cited), pp. 268-9.
[35] The extent of the political organization in Chichibu preparatory to the uprising is seen by the wide circulation of posters and pamphlets which took place in the vicinity. The details on the Chichibu Revolt are taken from *Meiji Bunka Zenshu*, Volume III, pp. 469-70.

were more or less directly connected with the exhibition of violence in the provinces, though it is not likely that the leaders of either countenanced the measures adopted. To clear itself of the stigma of inciting to rebellion, the *Jiyuto* at a general meeting held on October 20, 1884, in Osaka, resolved to disband and wait for an opportunity when society will be prepared for its reconstitution."[36]

After the dissolution of the *Jiyuto*, local uprisings such as those just described, usually led by the extremist followers of the *Jiyuto* or its offshoots, took on a most violent and bloody character. Without going into further details, we can merely list the better known uprisings: the Nagoya riots of 1884 in which the local *Jiyuto* played the leading part; the Kabasan (Ibaraki prefecture) insurrection of 1885; the Iida (Aichi prefecture) incident of the same year; and the Shizuoka rising of 1886.[37] Most curious of all the conspiracies and armed revolts of this period was the plot of Oi Kentaro and his confederates, mostly from the *Jiyuto* and all greatly influenced by French revolutionary concepts.[38] Foiled in their political activity by government repression, they planned to go to Korea, spread their political doctrine there, establish a democratic régime in that peninsula and thence conduct liberal agitation in Japan. They were about to sail from Osaka with arms and ammunition when they were seized by police on November 23, 1885.[39]

[36] McLaren, *Political History*, p. 163.

[37] Fujii, *op. cit.*, pp. 269-71. See also Uyehara, *op. cit.*, p. 99, and Ukita, Itagaki and Okuma, *op. cit.*, p. 157.

[38] The political philosophy of the extremist wing of the *Jiyuto* was greatly influenced by French and Russian revolutionary thought. The *Contrat Social* of Rousseau, popularized by Nakae Chomin (see note 20, *supra*), was an important influence in Japanese liberalism. The heady doctrines of Russian nihilism and of the *Narodniki* also found a welcome hearing among the more intrepid followers of the early *Jiyuto*. Translations of French and Russian revolutionary novels and treatises, particularly the works of Kropotkin, circulated in those times. See Fujii and Moriya, *op. cit.*, pp. 875-80. Such men as Nakae Chomin and Oi Kentaro, whose radicalism stemmed from French revolutionary thought and who were the theoretical guides of the left-wing of the *Jiyuto*, became the spiritual fathers of Japanese socialism. Among their followers was Kotoku Shusui, executed in 1908 on a charge of high treason. See Asari Junshiro, "The Development of the Social Movement and Social Legislation in Japan," in *Western Influences in Modern Japan*, Japanese Council, Institute of Pacific Relations, Tokyo, 1929, Paper Number 4, Volume II, p. 3.

[39] Uyehara, *op. cit.*, p. 90, note 1. Also Ukita, Itagaki and Okuma, *op. cit.*, p. 157. Oi Kentaro was arrested in Osaka and his confederates, Arai Shojo and Inagaki Shimetsu, were arrested in Nagasaki, whence they were sailing to join Oi and his group in Korea. See A. H. Lay, "Political Parties in Japan, *TASJ*, Volume XXX, 1902, p. 394, Note 2.

Thus ends the first chapter in the history of Japanese liberalism. Most instructive in this history is the evidence of the fundamental weakness in a liberalism which stemmed *from the countryside*. In other countries victorious liberalism, whether of the Independents or rather the London Presbyterians during the Cromwellian era or of revolutionary Paris, was essentially an urban movement which could draw on the immense financial power of the city merchant and could be propelled by the highly centralized political organization of the city masses. Above all, English and French liberalism, though led by wealthy merchants, lawyers or even country gentry, was reinforced by the presence in the metropolis of a large and comparatively articulate urban citizenry. This is, of course, equally true of 19th century English liberalism after the Reform Act of 1832, when the Liberal Party drew its strength almost exclusively from the city classes. But in Japan a liberalism based on the countryside with its isolated villages, where local issues often absorbed the attention of the neighboring population to the exclusion of all else and where conditions differed widely from one locality to another, inevitably brought inner clashes and final failure. Furthermore the antagonism between the landlord leadership of the *Jiyuto* and the rank and file peasant following was bound to force a split in the party. We have seen how this leadership of the *Jiyuto* succumbed more easily to the government offensive after the startling incidents described above, when peasants voiced among other cries the demand for rent reduction. Deprived of all central leadership, the local branches of the *Jiyuto* under various names and for various local issues often resorted to violence in order to weaken the grip of government repression. These attempts were too scattered and sporadic, in a word *too local in character* both geographically and politically, to be crowned with even partial success. The government won out all along the line, thanks to the unity of the ruling bureaucracy and its autocratic methods on the one hand, and to the disunity and confusion of the opposition on the other.

The *Jiyuto* was reconstituted again with the opening of the Diet in 1890. But the series of successive splits by which the most radical groups within it had been gradually sloughed off, and the very high property qualifications for the electorate (payment of at least fifteen yen in direct national taxes) made the reformed *Jiyuto* a chastened and moderate party. Its transformation through various intermediate stages into the *Seiyukai* (1900), the party of the landlords, indicates the triumph of that semi-feudal landlord aspect in the leadership of the original *Jiyuto*.

Strengthening of the State: The Constitution of 1889

Liberalism did not die with the dissolution of the political parties in 1883-4. Nevertheless, after that first flush of political enthusiasm and fruitless energy it was to become a still more restrained and compromising movement. We have not the time here to trace the quick shifts and ephemeral coalitions of the various liberal factions led by Itagaki and Okuma;[40] but while these factions intrigued for some share in the rewards of office, the government quietly went on strengthening its defenses against the sort of storm which swept the country from 1880-4. It also effected much needed administrative reforms which gave it greater flexibility and efficiency. The most energetic spirit in this government activity was Ito Hirobumi, who had been sent to Europe in 1882 to study constitutions of Western nations preparatory to drafting the Japanese constitution. His first act

[40] The question of treaty revision served as a pretext for many of the old war-horses in the *Jiyuto* and *Kaishinto* to emerge from their obscurity. Followers of dissolved political parties were invited to form the *Daido Danketsu* (Union at Large), founded by Goto. In the words of Japanese authorities, "the question of Treaty Revision which had been absorbing the people's minds so much was not one between rulers and ruled, as had been the case in previous disputes; it concerned the interests of the country as a whole. Appreciating the real nature of the problem, and anxious to placate the inimical sentiments of the people, the Government invited Count Okuma to take the head of the Department of Foreign Affairs in February 1888." Ukita, Itagaki and Okuma, *loc. cit.*, pp. 160-1.

This indicates a growing tendency for former political opponents to sink, not just old quarrels, but their distinctive principles as well, and to join in the scramble for office with little regard for basic political issues. Thus Goto followed Okuma by a few days into the Kuroda Cabinet as Minister of Communications, and thus killed his own *Daido Danketsu*. It is rather an ironic fact that Okuma's new political chief, Premier Kuroda, was the man whom he had attacked for the scandal in connection with the sale of government properties in Hokkaido to private hands at a price far below their value (July 1881).

Another blow was given to the newly reformed political associations by the Peace Preservation Regulations of December 25, 1887, which forbade any political leader from approaching closer than three *ri* (about eight miles) to the capital. (For its measures see Uyehara, *op. cit.*, p. 104.) With the opening of the Diet in 1890, political parties participating in parliamentary life, and depending as they did on a narrow electorate with high property qualifications became less and less the champions of democratic rights and more and more the agents of business and landed interests whose task it was to bargain with the bureaucracy over details in incidence of taxation and share of government subsidy, etc.

after his return in August 1883 was to rehabilitate the nobility (July 1884) by creating the new orders of prince, marquis, count, viscount and baron. The new nobility was made up of the former *kuge* (court nobility), *daimyo* (feudal nobility) and those who had distinguished themselves by conspicuous services during or after the Restoration. This step assured strong support from the aristocratic and official classes for Ito and his policies. His next move was to reform the cabinet system (December 1885) so that in the new cabinet (*Naikaku*) unlike the old Council of State (*Dajokan*) there would be a clear division of departmental work coördinated by the Minister President (*Naikaku Sori Daijin*), who in his powers closely resembles the chancellor of former Imperial Germany. (The office technically termed *Naikaku Sori Daijin* is generally rendered in English as prime minister). The Civil Service was now based upon an examination system, in this way removing official appointments from political favoritism. This reform helped to strengthen the bureaucratic system composed of efficient and usually disinterested civil servants whose loyalty was not attached to any political party or patron but to the bureaucracy as a whole.

At the same time reforms in the educational system had been taking place which were symptomatic of the political philosophy of the government. In 1880 absolute state control of elementary and secondary schools was established. In the following year, the chief center of Japanese higher education, Tokyo University (later Tokyo Imperial University), was reorganized in such fashion as to make it the instrument for training the future bureaucracy.[41] By this reform the entire staff of the University was placed under government control, subject to all the responsibilities and restrictions of government officials, and given places in the bureaucratic hierarchy. The old loose and rather independent departmental organization was now changed to a rigidly centralized control wielded by a President who had to answer only to the Minister of Education who in turn was directly responsible to the Emperor. Thus professors were no longer primarily scholars but government officials, and in this capacity they had to take new oaths to the government. These reforms were undertaken partly under the supervision of that

[41] Tokyo Imperial University, *Tokyo Teikoku Daigaku Goju Nen Shi* (History of Fifty Years of Tokyo Imperial University), Tokyo, 1932, Volume I, pp. 505-6.

champion of autocracy Kato Hiroyuki,[42] who at this time was re-appointed President. Unquestionably the teaching and intellectual atmosphere at Tokyo University would henceforth adhere closely to the ideals of the ruling oligarchy.[43]

Meanwhile to guard against a threat from political parties which showed signs of reviving, and to prevent any criticism of its attempts to revise the treaty system, the government passed the Peace Preservation Law (*Hoan Jorei*) on December 25, 1887, which some historians have considered to be the most repressive measure since the Restoration.[44]

The greatest single innovation of this period was the creation of the Constitution. Ito had been working on this Constitution since 1884, when the *Seido Torishirabe Kyoku* (Bureau for Investigation of Constitutional Systems) was established with Ito at its head together with Marquis (later Prince) Tokudaiji, Inouye Tsuyoshi, Kaneko Kentaro and Ito Miyoji. This bureau was attached to the Imperial Household Department, thereby becoming sacrosanct and completely removed from any outside influence. One Japanese authority expressed surprise that this department was selected rather than the Senate (*Genro-In*), (which was the chief legislative organ of the government at the time), or the Department of Justice. He answers his own query as follows, "The reason seems to have been to guard the work of framing the Constitution from any contact with public opinion."[45]

[42] *Supra*, note 20.

[43] *Tokyo Teikoku Daigaku Goju-nen Shi* (cited), p. 512.
In the first clause of the Act of March 1886, establishing the Tokyo Imperial University (before known as Tokyo University), the purpose of the University is stated to be the following: "The purpose of the Imperial University is to teach and investigate those mysteries of science and learning, of arts and crafts, *which are of practical service to State necessity.*" (Italics mine E. H. N.). *Ibid.*, Vol. I, p. 932.
The changes embodied in the Act of 1886 provided, among other measures, that the President of the University should also act as the Dean of the Faculty of Law. This Faculty was the citadel of conservatism in the University, and especially after the promulgation of the Constitution in 1889 it was deemed essential that the political philosophy of the nation's highest seat of learning should conform closely to the ideas of the prevailing *étatisme*. *Ibid.*, pp. 993-4.

[44] See Uyehara, *op. cit.*, p. 104. The full regulations which restricted the holding of public meetings and the publishing of newspapers and books are given in JGD, pp. 502-4.

[45] Uyehara, *op. cit.*, p. 118. The same writer, using an article by Baron Kaneko in the magazine *Taiyo* (March 8, 1909, p. 85) as authority, says: "Kaneko, one of the prominent people concerned, tells us that while the Constitution was framing, the people were intensely eager to know what Constitution they would be·

In 1888 the Privy Council was created through the initiative of Ito Hirobumi, who was its first president. Its function originally was to pass critical judgment on the Constitution, which was nearing completion. But after the promulgation of the Constitution in 1889, the Privy Council remained as the watchdog of autocratic rule. Its own composition and its power to decide any conflict of opinion which may arise between the different organs of government regarding the interpretation of the Constitution have made it the last stronghold of conservation.[46]

We cannot enter here into an analytical discussion of the Constitution itself. This omission however is not serious in view of the excellent studies devoted to this subject which have already appeared in English.[47] We might note in passing that it was Ito's express opinion, which has been honored ever since, that the Constitution was a gift of the Emperor to his people not a concession to the demand of the people for a Constitution. Only the Emperor can initiate amendments to the Constitution which have to be approved by the Upper and Lower Houses, and its interpretation lies with the courts of the country and, in the last analysis, in the hands of the Privy Council.[48] It was conceived in a spirit of benevolent autocracy and has remained as the inflexible instrument of absolutism.

Since any attempt to amend the Constitution by popular fran-

---

granted, for they doubted the Constitutional ideas of Ito, knowing the influence of Bismarck, and therefore every possible precaution was taken to guard against popular interference and the invasion of public opinion." *Id.*

It may be of interest to students of comparative government to learn that Baron Kaneko received his inspiration for the idea of strict secrecy in framing the Constitution from his study of accounts describing the Constitutional Convention in Philadelphia in 1787 and written by Madison and Jefferson. See Kaneko Kentaro, *Nihon Kempo Seitei no Yurai* (The Origin of the Establishment of the Japanese Constitution), in *Shigaku Zasshi* (Journal of Historical Study), Tokyo, October, 1911, Vol. XXII, pp. 1168-9. This reference comes from Yanaga, *op. cit.*, pp. 272-3.

[46] See R. K. Reischauer, *Japan: Government and Politics*, New York, 1939, pp. 87-9.

[47] Some of the more important studies on the Constitution are to be found in the following works: Ito Hirobumi, *Commentaries on the Constitution of the Empire of Japan*, translated by Ito Myoji, second edition, Tokyo, 1906; G. E. Uyehara, *Political Development of Japan 1867-1909*, New York, 1910; H. S. Quigley, *Japanese Government and Politics*, New York, 1932; T. Takeuchi, *War and Diplomacy in the Japanese Empire*, New York, 1935, Part One; McLaren, *Political History of Japan During the Meiji Era*, London, 1916; R. K. Reischauer, *Japan Government and Politics*, New York, 1939.

The text of the Constitution is printed in *JGD*, pp. 134 *et seq.*

[48] Reischauer, *op. cit.*, p. 77.

chise, court decision or vote of either house separately or both together would put the initiator beyond the pale of legality, the greatest constitutional struggles in modern Japan have been fought over the question of suffrage, which was deliberately excluded by Ito from the Constitution and hence left open to legislative change.[49] For this reason many groups and parties sometimes not represented in the Diet, and more often parties associated with the Labor movement, have been active in the campaign to extend the franchise.

A brief account of the franchise in Japan will show the progress made in this direction. Under the original election law of 1890 the vote was restricted to those who paid a direct national tax (land, business or income tax) of not less than fifteen yen for a period of at least one year previous to the time when the electors lists were drawn up. At that time the electorate numbered 460,000. In 1900 the electoral reform lowered property qualifications for the voter to the payment of ten yen in direct national taxes (it was lowered to five yen in 1899 but raised to ten in 1900). The electorate was then increased by approximately three times its original number. This reform could be carried out by the existing political parties because, by extending the electorate in this way, it strengthened parliamentary rule and enhanced the position of political parties. But the further extension of the franchise to the non-propertied members of the community was a step rather too sweeping to be encouraged by any but the more radical members of the Diet or of some labor groups outside the Diet. A pioneer in this movement was Oi Kentaro,[50] one of the early radical members of the *Jiyuto*; as leader of the left-wing split of the Liberal Party, the *Toyo Jiyuto*, he was one of the first spokesmen for universal suffrage. This extra-parliamentary movement for universal suffrage is inextricably associated with the names of those who were most active in the labor and socialist movement, like Nakamura Tahachiro, Kinoshita Naoye, Katayama Sen and Abe Isoh. This agitation became most vocal toward the end of

---

[49] In his commentaries on the Constitution, Ito wrote, "The provisions relating to elections are, as stated in the present article, passed over to those of a special law, so as to make it easy, when the necessity for it arises in the future, to make additions or alterations in the mode of carrying out elections. It is therefore undesirable that the constitution should enter into minutiae on the subject." Ito Hirobumi, *Commentaries on the Constitution of Japan*, Tokyo, 1931 edition, p. 67.

[50] *Supra*, note 20.

the Meiji period. During Katsura's third and final Government (winter 1912-13) large-scale rioting and police suppression indicated the tension between government and people in regard to this question.[51] It was not until after the Great War, however, and after the famous Rice Riots (1918) had badly shaken the prestige of the Terauchi Cabinet that the stage was set for the next reform in the franchise. In 1920 the property qualifications were reduced from ten to three yen, thus increasing the electorate to something over three millions. It will be seen that the non-propertied classes were still excluded from the vote. The final electoral reform of 1925 (first election, 1928) brought universal manhood suffrage, marking the highest point in parliamentary democracy yet reached in Japan.

Political Parties and the Diet

To return to political parties at the end of the 19th century, it became apparent that with the opening of the Diet in 1890 the former *Jiyuto* and *Kaishinto* were now content to play a more passive part in the political life of the nation. Acceptance of Ito's handiwork—the newly fashioned governmental apparatus, including the Diet with the far-reaching limitations on its legislative and even financial powers[52]—reduced these opposition parties to the condition where their only function was to develop their nuisance value sufficiently for them to receive some share in the actual government or some of the spoils of office. Rather than make common cause against the government which was universally acknowledged to be autocratic in its methods, the opposition parties were only too prone to fight among themselves, allowing the dominant bureaucracy to drive a wedge between them. Thus despite the overwhelming number opposed to the government in the Diet, this opposition was usually divided and ineffective. Henceforth, although there were to be many issues on which the opposition parties bitterly attacked the government and impeded it so as to force repeated adjournments of the House, nevertheless on matters of fundamental importance to the government, such as its plan for military and naval expansion, the parties had little stomach for serious opposition. This was made clear in the very first session

---

[51] These riots are graphically described by A. Morgan Young in *Japan in Recent Times, 1912-16*, New York, 1929, pp. 25-30.

[52] See Quigley, *op. cit.*, p. 185; pp. 188-193; 231.

of the Diet when the stage for similar compromises in later sessions was set. It has been described by a Japanese commentator: "At the first session (1890) of the Diet the opposition parties cut the budgetary expenditure of ¥80,000,000 by approximately ten per cent, the reason assigned for this retrenchment being that the financial capacity of the nation must be restored. Mutsu Munemitsu, Minister of Agriculture and Commerce, who was given the task of manipulating the Diet, effected a 'compromise' with Itagaki, and, winning over to his side one section of the *Jiyuto* group in the Lower House, succeeded in passing the budget with a reduction of only ¥6,500,000 to the infinite relief of the bureaucratic dignitaries in power. This compromise was most ominous in the history of Japanese constitutional government, for it was the first, though remote, cause of the corruption and fall of the political parties in subsequent years."[53]

The next Government of Matsukata, viewing the preceding Yamagata Cabinet's tactics as being too considerate of the hated political parties, determined to adopt a policy of bureaucratic intransigence. The Diet insisted on reducing the budget by ¥7,900,000, whereupon the Government dissolved the Diet. The ensuing election was among the most violent in Japanese political history. The Minister of Interior, Shinagawa Yajiro ordered the police to see to it that all hostile candidates were defeated. Nation-wide rioting resulted in 25 killed and 388 wounded.[54] National indignation demanded an end to the brow-beating methods of Shinagawa who was forced to resign. Ito, who joined in the universal condemnation of government coercion in electioneering, accepted the premiership for the second time in 1892. He was faced with the same problem as his two immediate predecessors of a Diet asking for reduction in government expenditures. He avoided the cynical policy of corruption used by the first Yamagata Government and the savage police terror of the Matsukata ministry and adopted a method that effectually silenced even the whisper of opposition on this vital question of naval and military expenditure. Ito forthwith secured an Imperial message to be read in the Lower House which left it with no alternative but to bow to the Government's

[53] Iizawa Shoji, *Politics and Political Parties in Japan*, The Foreign Affairs Association of Japan, Tokyo, 1938, p. 17. See also Iwasaki, *op. cit.*, p. 90.
[54] Uyehara, *op. cit.*, p. 222.

will.[55] The Imperial message showed displeasure with the partisanship which had prompted the appeal to the Throne and urged harmonious co-operation between the Government and the parties in the interests of the nation. At the same time it announced an Imperial donation of ¥300,000 annually to be raised by reducing the Imperial household expenses and to be given for six successive years for naval expansion and commanded at the same time all officials to contribute 10% of their salaries for the same purpose. "In obedience to this mandate, the Lower House receiving the Government's promise to adjust its affairs and reduce current expenses before the next session, passed the Budget with only such reductions as the Government was willing to accede to."[56]

Following the compromise of the opposition parties of which the *Jiyuto* was the strongest, a charge of corruption directed against the *Jiyuto* stalwart and President of the Lower House, Hoshi Toru, led to his impeachment and expulsion, splitting the *Jiyuto* into two parts. One of the resulting splinter groups showed a desire to join the government camp, with the result that eventually Itagaki entered the Cabinet as the Minister of Interior in April 1896. All serious opposition to the government had ceased by 1894, when the Diet unanimously approved the Budget of ¥150,000,000. This marked the complete triumph of the bureaucracy over the opposition parties. In the meantime, the Sino-Japanese war of 1894-5 welded all parties together in common agreement with the Government. By 1898, so little fear had the ruling bureaucracy of the leaders of political parties that Itagaki and Okuma were permitted to form a government which lasted a few months. The immediate issue on which the Government resigned was a speech by its Minister of Education, Ozaki Yukio, in which he deplored the power of wealth in politics. In a lecture before the Imperial Education Association he had said, "Suppose that you dreamed Japan had adopted a republican system of government, a Mitsui or a Mitsubishi would immediately become the presidential candidate."[57] At once he was subjected to the harshest criticism for even hypothetically stating that Japan might be a republic, and so the Government resigned. However, the real interest in his remark lies not in his

[55] Iizawa, *op. cit.*, p. 18; McLaren, *Political History*, etc., pp. 220-1; Uyehara, *op. cit.*, p. 224.

[56] Ukita, Itagaki and Okuma in *Fifty Years of New Japan*, Vol, 1, p. 169.

[57] Uyehara, *op. cit.*, p. 239.

unfortunate slip, but in his testimony regarding the growing power of wealth in Japanese politics.

Following the Sino-Japanese war of 1894-5, Yamagata had greatly strengthened the position of the bureaucracy as opposed to the parties by his Civil Service Appointment Ordinance and his Government Service Retirement Ordinance, which were intended to keep party men without previous experience from becoming officials.[58] At the same time he strengthened the position of the military by his decree of 1895, which limited Ministers of War and Navy to the ranking generals and admirals on the active list, and also by the creation of the Supreme Military Advisory Council in January 1898. Ito now became alarmed at the increasing power of Yamagata and his clique and seriously attempted to recapture his once dominant position in the government. For that purpose he decided to found a party which was to act as a check upon Yamagata's influence. By this step Ito had not ceased to be a bureaucrat, nor did he show a desire of initiating any fundamental reforms. His real purpose seems to have been to effect some administrative reforms in order among other aims to block the further advance of the Yamagata clique. In looking about him for a party following, he chose the *Kenseito*, which had been an amalgamation of *Jiyuto* and *Kaishinto* elements from which Okuma had broken away to head his own *Kenseihonto*. Out of the amorphous elements loosely grouped around the *Kenseito* made up of decomposed groups from the old *Jiyuto*, which despite its inner antagonism was the most vigorous exponent of liberalism in early Japanese politics, the *Seiyukai* was formed. This represents the final metamorphosis of the old Liberal Party into a party of big landlords headed by a powerful bureaucrat, with a program which was the very antithesis of the early *Jiyuto* platform.[59] This shows clearly how the two-sided nature of the *Jiyuto*, made up as it was of both landlords and peasantry, set up a contradiction which ended in the complete victory of the former element. For the next decade or so Japanese politics consisted of the back-stage maneuvering of the Yamagata wing of the bureaucracy led by Katsura against the more moderate group headed by Saionji, who succeeded Ito as the leader of the *Seiyukai*. So little fundamental difference

[58] Takekoshi Yosaburo, *Prince Saionji*, Tokyo, 1933, p. 162.

[59] In McLaren (*Political History, etc.*, pp. 263-7) there appears a long verbatim report of Ito's remarks on the founding of the *Seiyukai*.

separated these two camps that the period between the Russo-Japanese War and the World War has often been termed the years of the Katsura-Saionji compromise, with Katsura personifying the bureaucracy and the *Seiyukai* representing landed and business interests.

Foreign Policy and International Relations

We turn now to foreign policy and international relations, a topic which is so closely related to internal affairs that the last few pages describing the compromise of the political parties with the bureaucracy, particularly over the question of military and naval expansion, makes a natural transition to this subject.

Despite her scarcity of natural wealth, Meiji Japan had made the most of those few assets she possessed, namely comparative geographic isolation from the Great Powers, the patient industry of her people and the unconquerable will to learn and adapt to her own uses those arts and sciences which were necessary for the fashioning of a modern society. The slogan of the Meiji Reformers *"Sonno Joi"* (Revere the Emperor and expel the barbarian) had served as an excellent rallying-cry in the struggle to shake off the heavy hand of feudal incompetence as well as the grip of foreign capital before it became the constricting vise which was already pressing so heavily upon China. After the downfall of the *Bakufu* that slogan had been discarded in favor of the new cry *"Fukoku Kyohei"* (A rich country and a strong defense). This slogan became a reality through the government policy of state control over industry and rapid industrialization by means of subsidy, together with jealous care for armaments and the strategic industries. Furthermore, the chiefs of the armed forces in new Japan were not laggard in fulfilling their duties to the state. With the historical background of a warrior *élite* class ever present in the minds of the people, and the dangers to which the country had been exposed in the last decades of feudalism still fresh in their memory, it was unthinkable that the ablest leaders of the enlightened bureaucracy recruited from the *samurai* class should neglect the task of creating a modern army and navy.

The Japanese army until 1872 had consisted in a skeleton form of garrisons located in the larger cities and the Imperial Guard stationed at the capital. These troops were made up exclusively of former *han samurai* mostly of the anti-Tokugawa camp. This army was just strong enough to protect the young government from overthrow by *coup d'état* or civil war. Its ability in this direction to suppress peasant or *samurai* revolts was enhanced by the reforms following upon universal conscription first enforced in 1873.[60] This re-invigorated army met its first real test in suppressing the Satsuma Revolt of 1877, a victory for a conscript army of all classes aided by modern arms and equipment (such as the telegraph) over a stubbornly resisting, but outmoded and inevitably doomed, feudal levy of *samurai*. After this revolt no serious internal armed attack against the government was to be expected. Thus the complete re-organization and expansion of the armed forces from 1882 to 1884 and the revision of the conscription law in 1883 were designed to place the army in readiness for some crisis or contingency other than an internal one. This reform of 1882, which went into full effect in 1884, indicates a most remarkable advance in comparison with the strength of the standing army previous to the reform. The army of 1879 consisted of the following: infantry, 16 *rentai* (regiments); cavalry, 1 1/3 *daitai* (battalions); field artillery, 10 *daitai*; engineers' corps, 3½ *daitai*; army service corps, 1 *chutai* (company) and 2 *shotai* (squadrons). The plan of 1882 provided for the following: infantry, 28 *rentai*; army service corps, 14 *chutai*, or 7 *daitai*. In addition there were to be *tonden-hei* (military colonists or frontier militia), which had not hitherto been used. This consisted of infantry, four *daitai*; cavalry, one *tai* (corps); artillery, one *tai*; and engineers, one *tai*.[61]

[60] That this army with a total strength of 400,000 was strong enough only to guard against civil wars is explicitly stated by Major-General T. Kono, "The Japanese Army," in *Western Influences in Modern Japan,* Japanese Council, Institute of Pacific Relations, Tokyo, 1929, Vol. II, No. 18, p. 6.

[61] Izu Kimio and Matsushita Yoshio, *Nihon Gunji Hattatsu Shi* (History of Japanese Military Development), Tokyo, 1938, pp. 196-7. On military expansion and revision of the conscription law, see Yamagata Aritomo, "The Japanese Army" in *Fifty Years of New Japan,* Vol. 1, pp. 207-9.

A convenient glossary of Japanese military terms is given in J. C. Balet, *Le Japon Militaire,* Yokohama and Paris, 1910, p. 100 *et seq.* Some of the more relevant terms are given for the reader's convenience.

Gundan: armée, unité de circonstance, de composition variable.

Shidan: division; unité supérieure autonome, comprenant toutes les armes et tous les services.

Ryodan: brigade; élément secondaire pouvant convenir, en l'état présent, à l'infanterie, à certaines unités de la cavalerie et de l'artillerie de campagne ou lourde.

Rentai: régiment; élément tertiaire, subdivision de la brigade en 2 ou 3 fractions.

The quarter in which possible action might arise was suggested in the words of the greatest figure in Japanese military history, Field Marshal Yamagata. "In the meantime the high-handed attitude of the Chinese towards Korea, which was antagonistic to the interests of Japan, showed our officers that a great war was to be expected sooner or later on the continent; and made them eager to acquire military knowledge, for they were as yet quite unfitted for a continental war."[62]

At the same time commenced the period of feverish naval expansion. The naval expansion plan of 1882 provided for the laying of 48 keels in 8 years. But this was considered to be too slow a pace, so in 1886 it was possible by floating naval bonds to increase the number to 54 vessels.[63] These facts show that the Meiji leaders clearly understood the historical situation and the tasks arising from it. For generations Korea had been the constant source of friction between China and Japan. The appearance in 1884 of another contestant for Korean hegemony, namely Russia, which had concluded a commercial treaty with Korea that year, and the still more important "Overland Commercial Treaty" of 1888, heightened Japanese anxiety over the final destiny of the peninsula.[64] The advocates of the Korean expedition in 1872-3 had been defeated in their plan because the men at the helm realized that Japan was not ready for such expansion since she still lacked a modern army and navy and a mature industry capable of supplying a war-machine or of bringing in foreign exchange through a large export trade. When these prerequisites were called into existence, and when the foreign powers, Great Britain in particular, were willing to remain benevolently neutral if not actually giving technical aid, some of those who had opposed the Korean expedition twenty years earlier now saw the possibilities of defeating the effete Ch'ing Dynasty without serious risk. Their calculations proved to be correct, even to the anticipation of some such obstacle as

---

Daitai: bataillon d'infanterie, du génie, du train, des chemins de fer, et groupe d'artillerie.
Chutai: compagnie d'infanterie, escadron de cavalerie, batterie d'artillerie.
Shotai: section d'infanterie, peloton de cavalerie, fraction de batterie d'artillerie.
    Ibid., p. 100.

[62] Yamagata Aritomo, in *Fifty Years of New Japan,* Vol. I, p. 208.

[63] A detailed summary of this expansion is to be found in the article by Count Yamamoto Gombei. "The Japanese Navy," *ibid.,* p. 226.

[64] Soyeshima Taneomi, "Japan's Foreign Relations." *ibid.,* Volume I, p. 109.

the Three-Power Intervention of 1895[65] by Germany, Russia and France, when these Powers forced Japan to relinquish the Liaotung Peninsula.

How the Struggle for National Independence Inevitably Led to Expansion

National consciousness, which had been awakened in the struggle for the Restoration and by the threat of foreign encroachment, gradually permeated all layers of society in the early years of the Meiji and was sharpened by the arduous attempts at revision of the unequal treaties which were finally crowned with success in 1899. In the meantime, Japanese capitalism had passed through its formative stage, deprived from the first of tariff autonomy and hence forced to labor simultaneously on two fronts. *Internally* its task was to hasten industrialization and the development of a home market, and *internationally*, to win recognition as a Great Power—a consummation which would automatically bring treaty revision, better trading privileges, even alliance with some of the Great Powers. These two problems, the internal and external, were so closely interwoven that it does violence to historical science to discuss them independently with no attempt to inter-relate them, as if such and such a foreign policy could have been arbitrarily adopted or discarded according to the fancies or ambitions of statesmen and generals. Actually the evolution of Japan's social organization, together with the constant pressure of international power politics, compelled Japan in the 19th century to expand in search of the foreign markets so desperately needed to realize the profits which could not be obtained from the narrow home market, and in search of cheap essential raw materials which were denied her through the accident of geography. Thus those nations which had compelled Japan during the turbulent years of the Restoration to put her house in order, to look after her defenses first and last as a guarantee of her own independence, and to build up around these defenses industries which were to become the blood and sinews of a modern military system, now had to witness her emergence from incipient colonial subjection to a position of demanding equal status with themselves. Having once entered upon the path of modernization and industrializa-

[65] H. B. Morse, *International Relations of the Chinese Empire*, London and New York, 1918, Volume III, p. 47.

tion, the molders of Japanese policy saw that if they were to escape the fate of China or Egypt, they must adopt the political methods and economic policy of those powers who had been responsible for Japan's rude awakening and for the partial colonization of China. History is a relentless task-master, and all its lessons warned the Meiji statesmen that there was to be no half-way house between the status of a subject nation and that of a growing, victorious empire whose glory, to paraphrase that gloomy realist Clemenceau, is not unmixed with misery.

Consequently the primary task in Japanese foreign policy during the first thirty years of the Meiji period was to abolish that symbol of a nation destined for foreign domination, the unequal treaties.[66] To turn back before they had reached the status of an independent power would spell humiliation, disaster, and possibly submission to foreign rule, while to continue along the course so brilliantly charted by the Meiji leaders meant expansion in the only direction permitted by history and geography, namely the Asiatic mainland where half-awakened peoples were stirring uneasily under the menace of the Western Powers. The leaders of Meiji Japan saw no reason to abstain from the scramble for the partition of China, and if economic pressure, a narrow home market and scarcity of essential raw materials are to be considered as justification, Japan had more of it than the other powers.[67] So through a complex set of motives, including the necessity for foreign markets and raw materials, the fear of the uncomfortable proximity of Russian influence, and the desire to gain status as a Great Power, Japan successfully emerged from this first trial of strength as a modern nation.

That there was no halting place mid-way between a conquering and conquered nation, as far as Japan at any rate was concerned, and that the bitter struggle for national independence logically led to expansionism is strikingly shown by the fact that Japan acquired extraterritorial rights in China before she had shaken herself free of similar foreign privileges on her own land. Viewed from another point of view, this brings into sharp relief

[66] That the revision of the unequal treaties which were signed at the end of the *Bakufu* was the chief task of Meiji diplomacy is the contention of most Japanese historians. A notable example is to be found in the chapter on the revision of the treaties by the eminent authority on Japanese diplomatic history, Watanabe Ikujiro, *Nihon Kinsei Gaiko Shi* (Diplomatic History of Modern Japan), Tokyo, 1938, pp. 35-42.

[67] *Infra*, p. 203.

another thesis of this study, that the *lateness* of Japan's entry into the comity of Great Powers left indelible marks on her national structure, her society and government, and hence upon her foreign policy. A modern state was established, and industries were started on the foundation of a very narrow home market at a time when other nations, having long reaped the profits of the old mercantile-colonial period, had progressed through the early morning of *laissez-faire* trading capitalism and were now entering the noontide of an imperialist epoch marked by the acquisition of colonies and spheres of influence. We have seen how Japan telescoped a whole century or more of her development as a capitalist power, passing from her restricted type of town-against-country mercantilism to a social organization compounded of monopoly control in private industry and state control of vital industries, thus permitting no economic freedom of the *laissez-faire* variety and consequently very little political freedom. There were circumstances over which the leaders had only partial control; too much had been conditioned by the preceding, complex history of Japan for them to attempt a point of departure parallel to the development, for instance, of the United States or the Scandinavian countries. Entering the race for empire with all the disadvantages of th late comer, Japan had to prove to the Western Powers her own abilities to undertake the responsibilities and tasks expected ot great powers. Hence the struggle for the revision of treaties was an integral part of the struggle for recognition as a world power and for the fruits which such recognition brings. The Sino-Japanese War of 1894-5 was the first overt step in a direction which had been apparent before then. "In 1894 Japan had gone to war with China ostensibly over Korea, but really as a necessary step in her internal and external development. By this it must not be understood that the Chinese War of 1894-1895 was a war of mere adventure or spoliation; it was a violent movement desired and pushed forward by the whole nation, both as a practical demonstration of power and as an economical necessity."[68]

The national consciousness which had been forced into existence by events surrounding the Restoration, matured in the heated struggle for treaty revision, was to be strengthened a hundred-fold by the famous Triple Intervention, of April 23,

[68] B. L. Putnam Weale, *The Coming Struggle in Eastern Asia*. London, 1909, p. 401.

1895 (six days after the signing of the Treaty of Shimonoseki)
Although intervention did not come as a complete surprise to
the government, it aroused a feeling of national humiliation
which was turned into rage by the unnecessary brutality of the
German Minister at Tokyo who openly threatened war if Japan
did not comply with the *démarche* of the East Asiatic *Dreibund*
(Russia, France and Germany). Aside from the immediate sequel
to this intervention, which was the retrocession of the Liaotung
Peninsula and the imposition of a heavy indemnity in its place,
the effect in Japan was to make national sentiment hyper-sensi-
tive to foreign actions. Thus the adoption of a strong foreign
policy came to be not only feasible but popular.

The war of 1894-5, therefore, marked a definite turning-point
in Japanese foreign policy along the path of expansion, and
enormously strengthened the position of the advocates of such
a policy. Despite the Three Power Intervention the rewards
from the war were such as to strengthen the arguments of these
same advocates. The cession of the rich island of Formosa and of
the Pescadores, the indemnity of 230 million Kuping taels
(about 36 million pounds sterling) which became the basis for
introducing the gold standard into Japan, these tangible results
together with the diplomatic prestige which Japan gained were
rich prizes for a nation which twenty short years earlier had
just emerged from feudal isolation. The full recognition of
Japan as a power on equal terms with the other nations automatically followed. Thus in 1899 the Anglo-Japanese agreement
to abolish consular jurisdiction became the signal for other
countries to reach a similar agreement. The participation of
Japanese troops with those of the Great Powers in the suppression of the Boxer uprising in 1900 symbolized this entry of
Japan into the ranks of the imperialist powers, and the Anglo-
Japanese Alliance of 1902 signified that Japan had been singled
out by the most experienced Empire builder, Great Britain, as
the most effective counter-balance to its rival, Imperialist Russia.
It is indisputable that this Anglo-Japanese Alliance, while bene-
fiting England in its attempts to block Russian monopolistic
ambitions in Manchuria and North China, was at the same time
an invaluable diplomatic weapon in Japan's victory over Russia
Following this victory Japan replaced Russia as the greatest
power either actual or potential in Eastern Asia. These rapid
steps leading to the recognition of Japan as a world power were

a logical outcome of Japan's victory in the war of 1894-5. What twenty years of peaceful negotiation had failed to do was accomplished forcefully almost overnight. This was at least the superficial explanation of success which greatly strengthened the prestige of the expansionist camp.

The Position of a Liberal Opposition and the Question of "Military versus Civil" in the Japanese Government

This leads us to the question, what was the attitude of those outside the government toward this policy? Although this has been partly answered already, it might be well to conclude this outline of Japanese foreign policy by looking into the matter at greater length.

With some writers on political affairs it has become axiomatic that liberalism is inimical to a policy of expansion. Historically this is very difficult to prove either in the case of Japan or of other nations. It will be recalled that between 1871 and 1873 great pressure was brought to bear upon the government by a group favoring a campaign against Korea. This group was made up of three elements, one of which was to become the constitutional or liberal opposition to the clan government. It was not a liberal group which blocked this premature attempt at military adventure, but on the contrary the more conservative and cautious leader Okubo. It is true that in the eighties the extreme left wing of the liberal party with such local groups as the *Toyo Shakaito*[69] showed a rather vague tendency to extend a fraternal hand to Korea and China. But this left wing was disavowed by the leaders of the liberal movement and promptly suppressed by the government, so that it scarcely survived long enough to influence public opinion or government policy. The opposition parties, as re-constituted after the opening of the Diet of 1890, showed, as we have already noted, no inclination to struggle against the steady increase in armament expenditure which was the key question of the day. The opposition which the government faced between 1890 and the outbreak of the war had been weakened in the first instance by corruption. The police terror of Shinagawa had dangerously roused the whole country against the government so that Ito stepped in to mend the damage by invoking the Imperial message and effectively silencing opposition. But as the opposition faded away, the trend of foreign

[69] *Supra*, note 31.

policy had become apparent. As a contemporary observer of Japanese politics wrote, "Even therefore before the war with China something very near to the militarist spirit had become apparent in administrative circles. . . . It became clear to all attentive observers that henceforth the existence of a militarist party in the country was a factor to be reckoned with in any estimate of the future course of Japanese policy. The leading exponents of this militarist policy were, of course, to be found among naval and military officers, but their views were shared by the Japanese statesmen who had taken a prominent part in military reforms."[70] The turn toward a policy of expansion was not initiated by a handful of Hotspurs who dragged a reluctant government after them, but by the most far-sighted statesmen of the day, notably Ito, who twenty years previously had stood in opposition to the advocates of the Korean expedition.[71] Some would interpret this as a conversion of Ito to a policy of expansion. Some writers suggest it was a move deliberately undertaken by Ito to distract public attention from the hurly-burly of domestic politics.[72] While this may have played a part in Ito's strategy,[73] and may even have affected the precise moment for the outbreak of hostilities, it seems too narrow an explanation for the government policy. The author prefers to regard it not so much as a change in Ito's mind since the days of the *Seikan Ron*, as a change in the circumstances of the relative positions of Japan, China and the Powers which now definitely indicated that the decadent Ch'ing Dynasty could be removed from control over Korea without serious danger to Japan. In fact there is evidence that several years before the war broke out, the need for Japanese expansion was recognized by Ito himself in his negotiations with Li Hung-chang in 1885. He

[70] J. H. Gubbins, *The Making of Modern Japan* (cited), pp. 223-4.

[71] "It is then impossible to declare that the Sino-Japanese war was caused by the intrigue of chauvinistic groups." E. E. N. Causton, *Militarism and Foreign Policy in Japan*, London, 1936, p. 106.

[72] Freda Utley, *Japan's Feet of Clay*, New York, 1937, p. 255.

[73] The most convincing evidence on this point came, strangely enough, from official quarters. In explaining the war to Secretary of State Gresham, the Japanese Minister at Washington said: "Our situation at home is critical and war with China would improve it by arousing the patriotic sentiment of our people and more strongly attaching them to the government." Quoted in W. L. Langer, *The Diplomacy of Imperialism*, New York 1935, Volume 1, p. 173. Professor Langer himself accepts this explanation. For a critical estimate of the authority on which this view is based, see Payson J. Treat, "The Cause of the Sino-Japanese War of 1894" in *Pacific Historical Review*, June 1939, Vol. VIII, No. 2, pp. 151-2

is reported to have given the following argument: "The claims of China over Corea were historical only, i.e. as the history of China reckons Corea among her tributaries . . . The claims of Japan over Corea were economical, i.e. she did not claim any legal authority over Corea, but, from her geographical position and the necessity of providing for her constantly increasing population, she was intent on utilizing Corea as the best source from which the defect in the home produce of rice was to be supplied: as well as the nearest field in which the future sons of Japan might find employment."[74] This statement was made almost a decade before the war; after it, further indication of this same need for expansion was expressed in an editorial in the semi-official *The Far East*. "Moreover, the trade with Korea which previously had been in the hands of Chinese merchants became ours; though recent events have served in some degree to darken its prospects. When it is remembered that this trade amounts to six million yen a year, it will be acknowledged that this acquisition alone is not an insignificant step in the progress of Japanese commerce."[75]

The outbreak of war found all members of the former liberal opposition in complete agreement with the government. In view of the earlier activity and philosophy of these liberal leaders there is nothing strange in this. Twenty years before many of them were most vociferous in calling for a punitive expedition against Korea. Although bitterly opposed to the monopoly of government exercised by the Satsuma-Choshu clique, the liberal leaders who were mostly former *samurai* had never ex-

---

[74] Ariga, in *Japan by the Japanese* (cited), p. 197.

[75] The editorial is called "The Commerce and Industry of Japan as Affected by the War." *The Far East* (February-December), 1896, Vol. I, No. 3, p. 10.

A Japanese scholar writes of the Sino-Japanese clash of trading interests over Korea. "In Korea, whence the Chinese merchants withdrew during the China-Japan war of 1894-5 and were replaced by Japanese traders, it is Japan alone of all trading nations which enjoys a large share both in the import and export trade. . . ." K. Asakawa, "The Russo-Japanese Conflict: Its Causes and Issues," Boston and New York, 1904, pp. 14-5.

Since clear instances of trade rivalry between China and Japan in Korea are somewhat difficult to discover, one further example might be cited. "In 1889 the Korean Government, without previous notice, issued a decree prohibiting the export of beans to Japan. This act resulted in a loss of 140,000 yen to Japanese merchants, who had made advances to the Korean producers. Japan immediately demanded damages, but the claim was not discharged until 1893, owing to the interference of the Chinese Commission at Seoul, *who controlled the custom-houses in Korea* (Italics mine E.H.N.). S. G. Hishida, *The International Position of Japan as a Great Power*, New York, 1905, p. 169.

pressed any difference of opinion with government leaders on questions of foreign policy. Rather what difference there was in this regard arose from the impatience of this liberal opposition at the passivity and slowness of the government in foreign policy. That there was nothing peculiarly Japanese about a liberal opposition which could be comparatively radical on domestic problems and more aggressive than the government in foreign policy is seen from such examples as the careers of Lloyd George in England and Theodore Roosevelt in America. Furthermore, after the victory of the bureaucracy over the opposition parties in the early eighties, Japanese parliamentary liberalism could be accurately epitomized in the words of Goto and his *Daido Danketsu: "Daido Sho-i"* (difference in small things, similarity in great things). This motto has served as the beacon for Japanese parliamentary liberalism (as well as for most other brands). Thus in years to come the parliamentary opposition might fight over the increase in land tax or business tax, but with rare individual exceptions it seldom showed its teeth on basic issues such as military expenditure or universal suffrage. Even in peace times the heaviest budget could be pushed through by a skillful mixture of brow-beating and the tactful use of the government slush fund. Thus the budget for the fiscal year 1907-8, which amounted to upward of six hundred million yen, several times as great as any pre-war budget, was passed unanimously by the House of Representatives in less than three hours of debate.[76]

These remarks should not be interpreted as implying any moral criticism of Japanese liberalism. The future course of Japanese liberalism was charted in the early eighties when its leaders, dismayed by the violent enthusiasm of their own followers and disheartened by government repression, retired to their tents and left the government in solitary command of the field. A few years later when Ito's handiwork was completed, the political leaders took their place in a Diet which had suffered emasculation in regard to such vital questions of government as control of the purse and power to amend the constitution. They had to participate in parliamentary government on terms which excluded all but negative power to block legislation or constitutional amendment initiated from above. Parliamentary leaders could at best be little more than spokesmen of public opinion or, to be more precise, spokesmen for

[76] Weale, *op. cit.*, 367.

some important section of the community. This role of tribune of the people has been honorably played by many Japanese parliamentarians, notably Ozaki Yukio, Abe Isoh, Inukai Tsuyoshi, Tagawa Daikichiro and other lesser figures. At worst, members became political careerists who by perfecting the art of obstruction could compel the government to silence them either by promotion or bribery.

Opposition to the Government has not been confined merely to politicians sitting in the Diet. Since the beginning of the 20th century opposition to the government of the most effective type, despite the severe Peace Preservation Act of 1900, came from labor and socialist parties, and in recent years from various military or fascist groups. The former have agitated for the radical extension of democracy through universal suffrage and improved labor legislation while the latter have urged the complete eradication of democracy on the ground that it favors corruption, inefficiency and national disunity. To take but one example, the only intransigent opposition to the Russo-Japanese war came from the small Socialist Party.[77] Similarly the movement for the extension of the suffrage followed on the heels of Japan's greatest social upheaval in recent times—the Rice Riots of 1918.[78]

If then there is no unbridgeable gulf between the parties and the bureaucracy, is there a cleavage between the "military" and "civil" camps within the government? The neat division of the Japanese governing circles into military and civil despite its conveniences is an oversimplified if not unreal manner of speaking. Historically there have been conflicting opinions among Japanese leaders on both foreign and domestic problems, but these differences do not necessarily arise from two unalterably opposed camps labeled "military" and "civil." Even among the military leaders differences have cropped up, as the public becomes dimly aware when these are illuminated by lightning flashes of violence like the assassination of Lieutenant-General Nagata in August 1935, or the February 26th incident of 1936. There are also, of course, divisions within non-military groups. The role of the bureaucracy lies not in opposing the military

[77] Abe Isoh, "Socialism in Japan" in *Fifty Years of New Japan*, Volume II, pp. 506-7.

[78] Two of the most convenient summaries of these rice riots are to be found in A. Morgan Young, *op. cit.*, pp. 116-8, and in Kobayashi Ushisaburo, *The Basic Industries and Social History of Japan 1914-1918*, New Haven, 1930, pp. 272-4.

from some abstract "civilian" viewpoint, but in the steadying influence they exert upon the whole administrative machine. "The appearance of exercising political power next to that of the militarists is represented by a group of bureaucratic civil officers, who are turning to their own advantage the diminishing confidence of the nation in the political parties and the ardent desire of the militarists to effect reforms; a desire, which the technical knowledge possessed by the bureaucrats, but lacking in the militarists, is able to do much to satisfy. Such bureaucrats have no national support behind them, nor do they constitute any material influence. They are 'a fox in the position of aping the dignity of a lion' as an old Japanese saying goes. Their *raison d'être* in this connection is that they are the possessors of technical information concerning social and economic problems which are ever increasing in complexity; and therefore, they are qualified, as a steadying influence in the administrative machinery, to carry out whatever control of the national economy the real power behind them commands."[79]

With the huge military state enterprises as their material foundation which gives them a very real purpose and means of self-perpetuation, the bureaucracy acts as a shock-absorber in Japanese political life. As stated in Chapter IV, they act as mediators who reconcile the conflicts between the military and financial or industrial groups, shifting their weight now to one side and now to the other in order to prevent the complete domination of the military clique and to check big business from controlling politics in its exclusive interest. As it shuttles back and forth from the military to the financial camp, or from the court circles to political parties, this almost anonymous but experienced bureaucracy has gradually snuffed out all signs of genuine democratic activity, but on the other hand it has blocked the victory of outright fascist forces. The result has been to make the Japanese political scene the despair of foreign commentators. Contemporary Japan has some of the earmarks of fascism, but it lacks the distinctive full-blown features of a fascist dictatorship. This is not the place to enter into a full discussion of this fascinating but elusive subject, yet it might not be an exaggeration to say that the key to understanding Japanese political life is given to whoever appreciates fully the historical role and actual position of the bureaucracy.

[79] Iizawa Shoji, *op. cit.,* pp. 44-5.

CONCLUSION

This study has been carried down analytically and topically, rather than chronologically, to the period of the Russo-Japanese War.

The Treaty of Portsmouth signalized the entry of Japan into the ranks of the Great Powers. For our purpose this symbolic milestone in Japan's progress makes a convenient point at which to conclude. We leave a Japan flushed with victory, yet wary of difficulties ahead; sensitive of past humiliations such as the Tripartite Intervention, but a Japan conscious for the first time of her role as a Great Power. This same nation scarcely half a century earlier was racked by the factional strife of feudal jealousies; poor in all forms of material wealth; threatened and even attacked by the gunboats of Western Powers. This rapid transformation has earned for Japan the ungrudging praise of an astonished world and, for obvious reasons, of the Asiatic world in particular. Much has been written to express the delighted amazement of Western traveler, journalist or diplomat, as he warms to this spectacle of a nation so quick in learning the industrial arts of the Occident, so precocious in mastering the diplomacy of the Christian Powers. This often condescending admiration whose object is worthy of a more understanding if less effusive appreciation, becomes at times quite fatuous in its talk about the "miracle" of Japan as if, somehow, Japanese development had transcended all the laws of history and nature. Implicit throughout the foregoing study has been the assertion that Japan's spectacular rise was not a miracle certainly, but the result of highly complex and as yet only partly explored phenomena, still demanding to be analyzed and interpreted.

Returning to the thesis presented in the first pages, it is emphasized again that to explain in the first instance the speed of transition from a feudal to a modern state, one must bear in mind the fortuitous concurrence of two processes: (1) the death agony of feudalism and (2) the pressure exerted on Japan by the Western nations. The conjunction of the internal with the external crisis greatly hastened the change to a modern society. The rapidity of growth which characterized the next stage of

207

development, namely the advance from a nation of untried strength, still dependent on an agricultural economy, to a power of the first rank, was contingent upon the social and political nature of the Meiji settlement. The policy of the Meiji Government was to initiate strategic industries, to endow lavishly the defense forces, to subsidize generously a narrow and comparatively weak merchant-banking class in order to encourage its entry into the field of industry. The reverse side of this policy was marked by a disproportionately heavy tax burden on the agricultural classes, by the stinting of enterprises less vital than those connected with defense, and by a general impatience at any sign of unrest or democratic protest which might precipitate a domestic crisis and so hinder or retard the task of reconstruction. Nevertheless, it was this policy which succeeded in the very speedy creation of industries, a merchant marine, an overseas market, and an efficient navy.

Looking at it from another viewpoint, the tempo of Japanese progress (once the political revolution of 1868 had been carried out) was increased by the fact that those nations which Japan had singled out as a model or instructor had already proceeded a great distance along the road of technological improvement and economic organization. Japanese industry thus stood to profit from the experience of others.[80] But this very process of industrial acclimatization was far from easy; technical illiteracy, scarcity of certain essential materials, and a late start in the race for the pre-emption of markets and for the arrogation of raw materials increased the difficulties of Japanese industrialization. These disabilities of an inherent nature, together with those difficulties arbitrarily created by the pre-existing balance of world economic forces, contributed to the formation, at a comparatively early stage, of cartels and, more particularly, of monopoly control in trade and industry, a trend emphasized on the one hand by government subsidy of the powerful merchant-banking houses, and, on the other, by the interlocking of banks and industries (Mitsui, Mitsubishi, Yasuda, Sumitomo). This lateness in modernization, or to be more exact, in the process of industrialization, hastened the tendency toward trustification, toward monopoly which was in turn bound to have certain political repercussions. These latter may best be described as a sensitivity on the part of government and political parties to

[80] This is particularly noticeable in the Japanese textile industry.

the lobbying pressure exerted by one or more of the great *Zaibatsu*. But these great financial houses can pursue their interests only after taking into consideration the attitude of the landlords (represented chiefly in the *Seiyukai*), of the Army, Navy, and bureaucracy, whether it be on a matter relating to taxation, monetary policy, or foreign affairs. Generally speaking, all these groups can work harmoniously together, but occasionally the delicate equilibrium of these multiple forces is temporarily upset (as for instance during the last Katsura Government of 1913); it is possible at such moments to hear *Vox Populi* clamoring in thick accents for such ideals as universal suffrage, purification of political life, and even on rare occasions (Navy Scandal of 1914 and the aftermath of the Siberian campaign of 1921-2) for a more effective control of the armed forces.

It may be well to close this study with the picture just outlined above, suggesting the complexity of modern Japanese society; a society of which it is easier to describe some characteristic feature than it is to explain its significance to the whole. It is not so difficult to present a brief account, for example, of the bureaucracy, of the financial houses, of the armed forces, or of the political parties, but to ascribe to each group its own proper position, its relation to other parties of society, to judge between any of these groups and say this one is master and that one servant, this would be something of a Sisyphean task, but one which none the less ought to be shouldered. If, in reading this study, it becomes apparent that more questions are raised than answered, it may not be altogether a matter for disappointment, for it will convey to the reader some inkling of the richness, the bewildering variety and sharp contrasts revealed in the history of Japan in recent times

SELECTED BIBLIOGRAPHY ON MEIJI JAPAN

Works mentioned in this bibliographical note, but not specifically referred to within the body of the book, are marked by an asterisk *. English translations of Japanese titles are given only on first citation.

The very propinquity of that half century which embraces the Meiji Era is at once a help and a drawback to the historian of to-day. An enormous mass of historical material has been collected and much of it published. But the period is so recent that its history has not yet been systematically charted and widely explored as the period of the French Revolution, for example, has been to a remarkable extent by such scholars as Aulard, Mathiez, Lefebvre and their disciples. Despite the excellent monographic studies on Meiji history which are constantly appearing in Japan, and despite the growing volume of collected and published source materials, it seems as if the time has not yet come for a monumental work or series of works which would gather together, evaluate and synthetize the history of the Meiji Era.

General surveys of Japanese history are not few, but the standard work is by Professor Kuroita Katsumi, *Kokushi no Kenkyu* (A Study of Our National History), Tokyo, 1937 (revised), 3 vols. Although it has no direct bearing on the subject of the Meiji Era, it is, however, a most convenient and, needless to say, reliable source of reference on pre-Restoration history. It has a most useful general bibliography in the first volume, as well as a less valuable bibliography of Western works on Japan in the third.

It is axiomatic that for a study of Meiji history, at least a general knowledge of Tokugawa society is necessary. For a student interested in delving into the primary sources, the collection edited by Professor Takimoto Seiichi and known as the *Nihon Keizai Taiten* (A Cyclopedia of Japanese Political Economy) Tokyo, 1928, 55 vols., is invaluable. This collection of 55 volumes contains a rich and variegated assortment of nearly 600 works of Tokugawa and even earlier periods, covering political thought, law, administration, agriculture, trade, economic problems, as well as belles-lettres, essays and miscellanies (*zuihitsu*). The wealth of this source collection may be estimated by a glance at the bibliography appended to Miss Takizawa Matsuyo's study *The Penetration of Money Economy in Japan*, New York, 1927, where there appears a selection of titles from the *Nihon Keizai Taiten* (which she cites as

Bibliotheca Japonica Aeconomiae Politicae) with a brief description of the contents of each. To be precise, the collection mentioned by Miss Takizawa is entitled *Nihon Keizai Sosho** (Japanese Economic Series), Tokyo, 1914-17, which was later absorbed or enlarged into the *Nihon Keizai Taiten.* The Western student will find that this collection presents formidable difficulties of style; thus it would be a great service to Far Eastern studies if some of the shorter, more important treatises were translated into English. In addition to the *Nihon Keizai Taiten* there are other collections of great value, notably the *Kinsei Shakai Keizai Sosho** (Modern Social and Economic Series), Tokyo, 1926-7, 12 vols., edited by Honjo, Tsuchiya, Nakamura and Kokusho, in which is included (Vol. 1) the justly famous Tokugawa work, the *Seji Kemmon Roku* (Record of Worldly Affairs) written in 1816, with an introduction by Buyo Inshi.

Professor Ono Takeo has written numerous and learned studies on Tokugawa society, particularly on the key question of agrarian relations, such as *Ei-kosaku Ron* (Discussion of Permanent Tenancy), Tokyo, 1927; *Nihon Sonraku Shi Gairon* (Outline History of the Japanese Village Community), Tokyo, 1936; and *Noson Shakai Shi Ronko* (Discussions on the History of Agricultural Society), Tokyo, 1935. These studies, together with *Nihon Shakai Shi* (A Social History of Japan), Tokyo, 1935, by Professor Takigawa Masajiro, and shorter studies by Professor Tsuchiya Takao and collaborators, entitled *Nihon Shihonshugi Shi Ronshu* (Collections of Essays on the History of Japanese Capitalism), Tokyo, 1937, especially the essay "Shinjinushi Ron no Saikento" (A Further Criticism on the Subject of the New Landlord), can be recommended as interpretative works on Tokugawa society.

Those who do not read Japanese, yet who wish to make some effort to understand the forces undermining Tokugawa feudalism, will not find any one work devoted to this subject. Yet a survey of the relevant chapters in G. B. Sansom, *Japan: A Short Cultural History,* New York and London, 1931; A. R. La Mazelière, *Le Japon, Histoire et Civilisation,* Paris, 1907, 8 vols.; and James Murdoch, *A History of Japan,* London, 1925-6, New York, 1926, 3 vols., should give a general outline of the political, cultural and administrative aspects of Tokugawa rule. A precise account of the mechanism of Japanese feudal practice, the management and descent of feudal profits or rights (*shiki*) is to be found in the Introduction to Professor K. Asakawa's *Documents of Iriki,* New Haven and Oxford, 1929. On economic and social history there is Miss Takizawa's work already referred to; also the three-volume abridged translation of the twelve-volume Japanese original of Takekoshi Yosaburo's *Nihon Keizai Shi* (Economic History of Japan), Tokyo, 1935 edition,

12 vols. The organization and presentation of the English translation—*The Economic Aspects of the History of the Civilization of
Japan*, London and New York, 1930, 3 vols.—make this an extremely difficult work to use, but in the present state of Japanese
studies in the West, even so cumbrous a history can be used to advantage. Professor Honjo's work *The Social and Economic History
of Japan*, Kyoto, 1935, is rich in quotations from Japanese sources,
especially from authors in the *Nihon Keizai Taiten* and the *Kinsei
Shakai Keizai Sosho*. Professor Tsuchiya Takao's popular work in
the Iwanami series entitled *Nihon Keizai Shi Gaiyo** (An Outline
Economic History of Japan), Tokyo, 1933, gives a convenient,
straightforward account of Japanese economic development up to
the Meiji Restoration. It has been translated into English for the
Transactions of the Asiatic Society of Japan, Tokyo, December
1937, Vol. XV (Second Series), under the title "An Economic History
of Japan." The translation leaves something to be desired, but
at the end of each chapter there are useful though brief bibliographical references to Japanese secondary sources. Just recently a second
companion volume by Professor Tsuchiya has appeared, entitled
Zoku Nihon Keizai Shi Gaiyo* (Supplement to the Outline Economic History of Japan), Tokyo, 1939, published, in the same
popular series as the preceding volume, by the Iwanami Shoten.
This work covers Meiji economic history and, in view of the scarcity
of such works in English, it is to be hoped a translation will shortly
be forthcoming.

Dr. Hugh Borton's thorough study entitled "Peasant Uprisings
in Japan of the Tokugawa Period," *Transactions of the Asiatic
Society of Japan*, Tokyo, May 1938, Vol. XVI (Second Series), helps
to throw light on one aspect of the agrarian problem and it provides
the reader with a select bibliography of both Japanese and Western
works bearing on this special subject. Professor Asakawa's long
article "Notes on Village Government in Japan after 1600," *Journal
of the American Oriental Society*, New Haven, 1910-11, Vols. 30-1,
has, in addition to a wealth of detail on village administration under
the Tokugawa, a long, selected bibliography (Vol. 30) of Japanese
sources on the social and institutional history of late feudalism. At
the time of its writing, however, many of the best collections referred to above were not yet published.

On the subject of pre-Meiji trading and cultural relations between Japan and various parts of the Asiatic mainland the standard
work has been Professor Tsuji Zennosuke's *Kaigai Kotsu Shiwa*
(Lectures on Intercourse Beyond the Seas), Tokyo, 1930 (revised
and enlarged edition). This study, however, has been partially
superseded by the recently published *Ni-shi Koshoshi no Kenkyu*
(A Study of the History of Intercourse Between Japan and China),

Tokyo, 1939, by Professor Akiyama Kenzo, which draws upon important fresh sources. The basic source material utilized by Professor Akiyama and hitherto neglected for studies in this field consists of 1) the *Ko Min Jitsu Roku* (The Authentic Records of the Ming Dynasty), a day-to-day court record from which the dynastic history was compiled; 2) *The Ri-cho Jitsu Roku* (The Authentic Record of the Court of Li), a similar official record of the famous Korean dynasty of which there are very few available copies; and 3) the *Rekidai Hoan*, the name for the chronological record kept by Chinese merchants and agents in the Ryukyu Islands.

Turning to Western works on the subject of contemporary European comment on Tokugawa Japan, we should perhaps refer first to the actual records of travelers and traders who were permitted to enter Japan during the epoch of exclusion. One of the celebrated works describing Japan at the end of the 17th century was written by the physician to the Dutch East India Company, Doctor Engelbert Kaempfer (1651-1716). The best English version is entitled *History of Japan 1690-92*, translated by J. G. Scheuzer, Glasgow, 1906, 3 vols. Covering a wider field is the work of another doctor, P.-F. von Siebold (1796-1866), written a few decades later than Kaempfer's; it is entitled *Nippon; Archiv zur Beschreibung von Japan,** Leyden, 1832, English edition, *Nippon,** London, 1841. There is also a French translation, *Voyage au Japan, éxécuté pendant les années 1823 à 1830,* edited by A. de Montry and E. Fraissinet, Paris, 1838-40, 5 vols. It is a veritable mine of information on subjects ranging from natural history to customs of the people. In passing, one might mention earlier and slighter works which reveal as much about the European mind as about Japanese feudal society. One of the more interesting books, the observations of a factor in the Dutch East India Company, François Caron (†1655 or 6) and his colleague Joost Schouten, is *A True Description of the Mighty Kingdoms of Japan and Siam,** reproduced from the English edition of 1633 with Introduction and Notes by C. R. Boxer, London, 1935. One item of special interest in this work is a list of the *daimyo* in Japan together with their rice revenues, based most probably on the *Edo Kagami** (The Edo Mirror), a kind of blue-book published in Edo twice a year down to the 19th century. This work of Caron's was the "standard" on Tokugawa Japan until the publication of Kaempfer's history. The views of another agent of Dutch trade, Isaac Titsingh (1745-1811) have been edited and related by the same authority, C. R. Boxer, in Chapter VII of his work on Dutch influence in Japan, *Jan Compagnie in Japan 1600-1817*, The Hague, 1936. A description of pre-Meiji Japan by an American. Richard Hildreth, *Japan as It Was and Is,* Boston, 1855, contains an interesting appendix, "Products of Japan" by S. Wells Williams, the interpreter to the Perry expedition.

A detailed monograph on European contacts with pre-Meiji Japan has been written by M. Paske-Smith, *Western Barbarians in Japan and Formosa in Tokugawa Days 1603-1868,* Kobe, 1930. This study together with the researches of C. R. Boxer, especially his *Jan Compagnie in Japan,* have partially superseded an earlier monograph by N. Yamasaki, *L'Action de la Civilisation Européenne sur la Vie Japonaise avant l'Arrivée du Commodore Perry,* Paris, 1910. This work is arranged conveniently by nations (i.e., Dutch, Portuguese, etc., influences) and by topic (military sciences, medicine, art, music, mathematics and so on).

As for the historiography of the Meiji Restoration and the settlement following it, the author's bibliographical knowledge is too sketchy, and both the source material and special studies too extensive; consequently it will not receive here any methodical or exhaustive analysis, but rather a selective treatment.

On questions relating to early industrialization, the land tax, finance, economic policy of the government and the like, perhaps the most indispensable collection of source material is the *Meiji Zenki Zaisei Keizai Shiryo Shusei* (Collection of Historical Material on Finance and Economy in the Early Years of the Meiji Era), edited by Tsuchiya Takao and Ouchi Hyoei, Tokyo, 1931, 20 vols. It contains official documents concerning the organization of trade and industry, records of industrial undertakings, accounts of local enterprise, etc., often written by leading contemporary figures. Another collection, smaller because treating of only one problem. namely, public finance, and compiled under official auspices, is the *Meiji Zaisei Shi* (A History of Meiji Finance), compiled and edited by the Meiji Zaisei Shi Hensan Kai (Committee for the Compilation of the History of Meiji Finance), Tokyo, 1904, 15 vols. Strictly speaking this is not so much a collection as a history, narrated topically and chronologically, embodying in full all of the important official documents relating to the subject. It is of particular value on the reform of the land tax. For a detailed description of Meiji technological and industrial development, the *Meiji Kogyo Shi* (A History of Meiji Industry), edited by Tanabe Sakuro and others. Tokyo, 1925-31, 10 vols., is a convenient collection since it is arranged according to industry, locality and then chronology. Another larger series which gives very full histories of industries and their organization, of the development of trade and commerce, and which extends into a later period than the source collection of Ouchi and Tsuchiya, is the *Nihon Sangyo Shiryo Taikei* (Series in the Historical Materials for Japanese Industry) edited by Takimoto Seiichi and Mukai Shikamatsu, Tokyo, 1926-7, 13 vols., including one index volume. It contains, *inter alia*, a study by Paul Mayet, a German adviser on agricultural insurance to the Japanese Government. This work is especially valuable because it is one of the few treatises by a scientifically trained observer which covers in detail the agrarian problem in the early Meiji period. It appears in this collection (Vol. II) as "Nihon Nomin no Hihei oyobi sono Kyuji Saku" (The Impoverishment of the Japanese Peasantry and a Policy for Its Remedy); as far as could be ascertained it is not available except in this Japanese translation. However the same authority, P. Mayet, wrote a book on his special subject, *Agricultural Insurance,* translated from the German by Rev. Arthur Lloyd, London, 1893. To illustrate his thesis the author scattered here and there a considerable amount of factual material illumined by pithy comment and interpretation.

Professor Ono Takeo's studies on the agrarian problem dominate the field for the Meiji as well as for the Tokugawa period. His work *Meiji Ishin Noson Shakai Shiron* (An Historical Treatise on Agricultural Society at the Restoration), Tokyo, 1932, is particularly helpful for an understanding of the problem of land ownership, land tax reform, village administration and the peasant movement in the years after the Restoration. A chronicle of peasant unrest in the early Meiji period based on a wide collection of source materials has been compiled by Professors Ono Michiyo and Tsuchiya Takeo, entitled *Meiji Shonen Nomin Sojo Roku* (Chronicle of Peasant Uprisings in the Early Years of the Meiji Era), Tokyo, 1931. The source materials are arranged geographically. A short survey of peasant revolt in this same period by Professor Kokusho Iwao, "Meiji Shonen Hyakusho Ikki" (Peasant Revolts at the Beginning of the Meiji Era), appears as a chapter in a volume of studies on Meiji economic history edited by Professor Honjo Eijiro, entitled *Meiji Ishin Keizai Shi Kenkyu* (A Study of the Economic History of the Meiji Restoration), Tokyo, 1930. This symposium also has interesting chapters on early Meiji trade and commerce, on the economic role of Osaka, on religious uprisings in the early Meiji, on technological development and on the reactionary trends in Meiji political thought, by members of the Department of Economics, Kyoto Imperial University. A recent study of considerable value for the investigation of such social problems as stagnant population in the Japanese village, the position and significance of female labor, all related to the central problem of government social policy, has been written by Kazahaya Yasoji, *Nihon Shakai Seisaku Shi* (History of Japanese Social Policy), Tokyo, 1937.

For general surveys and interpretations of Meiji social and economic history, the following monographs are both informative and suggestive: Hirano Yoshitaro, *Nihon Shihonshugi Shakai no*

Kiko (The Mechanism of Japanese Capitalist Society), Tokyo, 1934; Horie Yasuzo, *Nihon Shihonshugi no Seiritsu* (The Formation of Japanese Capitalism), Tokyo, 1938; Kobayashi Yoshimasa, *Nihon Sangyo no Kosei* (The Structure of Japanese Industry), Tokyo, 1935; Tsuchiya Takao and Okazaki Saburo, *Nihon Shihonshugi Hattatsu Shi Gaisetsu* (Outline History of the Development of Japanese Capitalism), Tokyo, 1937.

Before leaving the general topic of modern Japanese economic history, reference should be made to a work of the greatest convenience to a student of the subject. It is by Professor Honjo Eijiro and is entitled *Nihon Keizai Shi Bunken** (A Bibliography of Japanese Economic History), Tokyo, 1933. This work gives not only the author and title, but a brief summary of each work cited; its usefulness is further enhanced by an index (unfortunately too great a rarity in Japanese learned publications) and by a list of studies relating to prefectural and local histories. It also has a short bibliography of European works on Japanese economic history.

As regards works in Western languages on Meiji economic history, there is really no book which is entirely devoted to that particular subject. The relatively antiquated and cumbersome work by Karl Rathgen, *Japans Volkswirtschaft und Staatshalt,* in *Staats und Sozialwissenschaftliche Forschungen,* edited by Gustav von Schmoller, Leipzig, 1891, Vol. XLV, No. 10, gives a surprisingly large amount of detail but is weak in organization and interpretation. This is not the place to select works in which only a chapter or two is devoted to Meiji economic history. Any study which describes the economic aspect of modern Japanese life often throws light on earlier years. In this connection studies by such writers as Professors John E. Orchard (*Japan's Economic Position,* New York, 1930) and G. C. Allen (*Modern Japan and Its Problems,* New York and London, 1928) and Henry Dumolard (*Le Japon Politique, Economique et Social,* Paris, 1905) should be mentioned. Except for Dumolard, they deal only incidentally with the Meiji period, and none of them has made any extended use of Japanese material. Articles on Japanese economic history which are English translations, often abridged, from *Keizai Shi Kenkyu* (A Study of Economic History) published by the Department of Economics, Kyoto Imperial University, are to be found in the *Kyoto University Economic Review.* Professor Horie frequently contributes articles to this *Review* on Meiji economic development, and Professor Honjo deals with late Tokugawa economic problems; many of the latter's earlier articles were incorporated into his *Social and Economic History of Japan* (see above). Thus the field lies open both in Japanese and in Western languages for an authoritative work on the economic history of modern Japan.

On the political and constitutional history of the Meiji Era, several notable works in Japanese have recently been published. Of course in this field greater advances have been made than in others, since the collection and publication of government documents and of the numerous diaries and letters of Meiji statesmen has been proceeding slowly but steadily for several years.

One of the older but still very useful collections of source material for Meiji political and cultural history is the *Meiji Bunka Zenshu* (Collection of Works on Meiji Culture) edited by Yoshino Sakuzo, Tokyo, 1930, 24 vols. In it are to be found some of the earliest accounts of Meiji political history (Vol. III), written in many instances by active participants in the political arena; also a generous selection of memorials, essays, *livres de circonstance* and pamphlets of the period. Its bibliographical data is especially valuable, listing and often describing as it does the earliest newspapers, journals and the first translations of Western literature into Japanese. Its subject matter extends even to the history of manners and costumes. Starting from the opening of the Diet in 1890, Imperial messages, Government decrees and ordinances, texts of treaties, ministerial statements, etc., are printed in the *Kampo** or Official Gazette, Tokyo, 1890–. This Gazette is therefore of considerable value to a student of later Meiji or modern Japanese political history. It might be of interest to American students to know that a file of it is available in the Library of the Harvard Law School. This same Library houses another valuable source for Japanese political history, namely, a complete file of the *Giji Sokkiroku** (Records of Parliamentary Proceedings), Tokyo, 1890–.

Among the more authoritative studies of Meiji political history is *Meiji Jidai Shi* (History of the Meiji Period), by Professors Fujii Jintaro and Moriya Hidesuke, being Vol. XII in the *Sogo Nihon Shi Taikei* (The Synthesis of Japanese History Series), Tokyo, 1934. This work is in part an expansion of the lectures of Professor Fujii, *Meiji Ishin Shi Kowa* (Lectures on the History of the Meiji Restoration), Tokyo, 1929. The *Meiji Jidai Shi* is very handy for quick reference since it has been edited with paragraph headings. A distinguished Japanese scholar, Mr. Osatake Takeshi, has written a series of essays in Meiji political history under the general title *Meiji Seiji Shi Tembyo* (Sketches in Meiji Political History), Tokyo, 1938, dealing in masterful style with such controversial problems as the famous European trip of Itagaki Taisuke and Goto Shojiro in 1882. A standard work by the same author on Meiji constitutional theory and history is *Ishin Zengo ni okeru Rikken Shiso*

(Constitutional Thought at the Time of the Restoration), Tokyo, 1929, 2 vols.

A popular work in the Iwanami series on political and economic thought at the time of the Restoration has recently been written by Kada Tetsuji, *Ishin igo no Shakai Keizai Shiso Gairon* (An Outline of Social and Economic Thought since the Restoration), Tokyo, 1934. The *Meiji Ishin Shi Kenkyu* (Researches into the History of the Meiji Restoration), edited by the Shigakkai (Historical Society), Tokyo, 1936, is a collection of essays on Meiji political history of rather uneven quality. A more erudite collection of studies on roughly the same topic but confined to the years just before and after the Restoration is *Meiji Boshin* (*Boshin* is the cyclical year-name for 1868), edited by Ichijima Kenkichi, Tokyo, 1928. This work contains a long and learned essay by Mr. Osatake Takeshi on the background of the famous five-point Imperial Oath of April 6, 1868.

We are fortunate in possessing an English version of selected documents illustrating early Meiji rule, from 1868 to 1889, called *Japanese Government Documents* edited by W. W. McLaren, originally published in *Transactions of the Asiatic Society of Japan*, Tokyo, 1914, Vol. XLII, Pt. 1, with a very suggestive introduction by the editor. The same writer has given what is still one of the fullest accounts of Meiji political history, *A Political History of Japan during the Meiji Era 1867-1912*, New York, 1916; although some readers may consider it marred by the author's tendency to moralize, it is nevertheless a penetrating description of Meiji public life. J. H. Gubbins, a British diplomat, wrote two books on Japanese politics, *Progress of Japan, 1853-1871*, Oxford, 1911, and *The Making of Modern Japan*, London, 1922, which despite the early date of their composition contain much that is still fresh and illuminating. The former is concerned mostly with the complexities and political intrigues at the end of the Tokugawa period and with the confusion of the first years of the new regime; the latter, covering a wider period extending up to the turn of the century, is necessarily less detailed in its treatment of political events. The last three volumes (especially Vol. IV) of Mazelière's work, mentioned above, is still of value since it furnishes a surprisingly full account of Meiji politics and social problems. The collection entitled *Fifty Years of New Japan*, edited by Okuma Shigenobu, London, 1910, 2 vols., translated from the Japanese, ought not to be overlooked. It consists of studies on various special topics covering almost all aspects of Japanese life, with excellent sections on political parties, foreign affairs, cultural development and the like; each chapter is written by some eminent Japanese authority.

Works of minor significance written half a century ago but covering subjects which are scarcely touched elsewhere are A. H. Mounsey, *Satsuma Revolt: An Episode of Japanese History*, London, 1879, and Charles Lanman, *Leading Men of Japan*, Boston, 1883. Lanman's book gives a brief outline biography of fifty-eight leading personalities of the early Meiji period.

Without attempting to estimate the relative merits of each book, at least a short list of the more reliable, solid studies on Meiji political and constitutional development should be given. These studies are Ito Hirobumi, *Commentaries on the Constitution of the Empire of Japan*, translated by Ito Myoji, Tokyo, 1906 (second edition), a standard treatise on the constitution written by its chief architect; G. E. Uyehara, *Political Development of Japan 1867-1909*, New York, 1910, rich in quotations from contemporary Japanese journals; H. S. Quigley, *Japanese Government and Politics*, New York and London, 1932, one of the most detailed works; Takeuchi Tatsuji, *War and Diplomacy in the Japanese Empire*, New York and London, 1935. Part 1 of this last study, "Constitutional Organisation," describes the functions and workings of each organ of state, and Part 3, "The Conduct of Foreign Relations," explains the source and mechanism of the treaty-making power, the war power and the formulation of foreign policy. McLaren's study has been commented upon above. R. K. Reischauer's *Japan: Government and Politics*, New York, 1939, is one of the clearest, most succinct summaries of modern Japanese politics, from the early Meiji up to the present. The books by Ito, Takeuchi and Quigley and the documents edited by McLaren, all give the text of the Japanese Constitution.

In this bibliography it is impossible even to scratch the surface of a vast corpus comprising memoirs, diaries and biographies of Meiji statesmen. Such collections as the *Kiheitai Nikki* for example, describing in diary or epistolary form the activities of the *Kiheitai* ("shock troops"—the name for the Choshu volunteers who fought the Tokugawa armies on the eve of the Restoration) are written in a difficult old-fashioned Japanese style presenting the Western student with formidable problems. The importance of this collection lies in the fact that many of the Choshu *Kiheitai* became leaders in the Meiji Government.

The writings of the great publicist and educationalist Fukuzawa Yukichi offer the careful student a storehouse of interpretation and observation upon current trends. His *Autobiography*, translated by E. Kiyooka, Tokyo, 1934, makes exciting reading. However, those who can read Japanese will be rewarded by taking even a cursory glance into his selected correspondence, which appears in *Zoku Fukuzawa Zenshu* (Supplement to the Collected Works of

Fukuzawa) edited by the Keio Gijuku, Tokyo, 1933, 7 vols. His style is straightforward and clear when compared to that of many of his great contemporaries, and his comments always shrewd and penetrating, as befitted one of the most politically-minded men of the day. Takekoshi Yosaburo's *Prince Saionji*, Kyoto, 1933, ought to be a storehouse of information and instruction, but constrained perhaps by the limitations of his subject, the author has not made of it the vivid and rich work it deserved to be. Nevertheless, it should be consulted by any student of Meiji public life.

The journals and memoirs of Western diplomats in Japan, from its opening until shortly after the Restoration, are often of great importance in supplying contradictory or corroborative evidence on some problem relating to early Meiji policy or diplomacy. Among the more outstanding of such records are those associated with the names of Townsend Harris, Sir Ernest Satow, Sir Rutherford Alcock, and Lord Elgin. These works are *The Complete Journal of Townsend Harris** edited by Dr. Mario Emilio Cosenza, New York, 1930; Sir Ernest Satow, *A Diplomat in Japan,** London, 1921; Sir Rutherford Alcock, *The Capital of the Tycoon: A Narrative of a Three Years' Residence in Japan,* London, 1863, 3 vols.; Laurence Oliphant, *A Narrative of the Earl of Elgin's Mission to China and Japan in the Years 1857-58-59,* New York, 1860. Since Americans played so prominent a part in the opening of Japan, mention should be made of a standard work on early American-Japanese relations by Professor Payson J. Treat, *Diplomatic Relations of the United States and Japan 1853-1865,** Baltimore, 1917.

Finally, a collection of great value to the student of Japanese diplomatic history is the *Dai Nihon Gaiko Bunsho** (Documents of Japanese Diplomacy), Tokyo, 1936, 7 vols. This source material is being currently published by the Nihon Kokusai Kyokai (International Society of Japan) and compiled by the Nihon Gaimusho Chosa-bu (the Inquiry Section of the Japanese Foreign Office). It consists of a generous selection of diplomatic notes, *aide-mémoires* and so forth (mostly in Japanese but a great number in the original European languages) exchanged between the Japanese and foreign governments since the opening of Japan. Publication began in 1936 and the latest volume to appear in the series is the seventh, covering the period from January to December 1874 in detail. For a secondary work on Japanese diplomacy there is an excellent study, recently published, by the eminent authority Mr. Watanabe Ikujiro, entitled *Nihon Kinsei Gaiko Shi* (Diplomatic History of Modern Japan), Tokyo, 1938.

For accounts in Western languages of Meiji diplomatic history one can do no better than to refer to the work of Professor Takeuchi, already mentioned in another connection, and to the masterly chapter (Vol. II) on the Anglo-Japanese Alliance in Professor William Langer's *Diplomacy of Imperialism*, New York, 1935, 2 vols., where there appears at the end of the chapter a critical bibliography; there is an equally valuable chapter (Vol. I) on an earlier crisis in Japanese foreign policy, "The Sino-Japanese War and the Far Eastern Triplice," also followed by selected bibliography. For a well documented and formal treatment of the Anglo-Japanese Alliance a study by Alfred L. P. Dennis, *The Anglo-Japanese Alliance,** Berkeley, California, 1923, should be consulted.

These somewhat random notes on a few of the sources which one might use in preparing a study on Meiji Japan may be of service, it is hoped, to fellow-students of Japanology. They may also serve to awaken the reader (if he is not yet aware) to a realization of the immensity of the fertile field called Meiji history which lies fallow and awaiting cultivation both by the Japanese and, more especially, by the Western historian.

WORKS IN WESTERN LANGUAGES

AKAGI, R. H. *Japan's Foreign Relations 1542-1936.* Tokyo. 1936.

ALCOCK, SIR RUTHERFORD. *The Capital of the Tycoon: A Narrative of a Three Years Residence in Japan.* London. 1863. 2 vols.

ALLEN, G. C. *Modern Japan and Its Problems.* New York and London. 1928.

ANDRÉADÈS, ANDRÉ. *Les Finances de l'Empire Japonais et Leur Evolution.* Paris. 1932.

ASAKAWA, K. *Documents of Iriki.* New Haven and Oxford. 1929.

———. *The Russo-Japanese Conflict: Its Causes and Issues.* Boston and New York. 1904.

BALET, J. C. *Le Japon Militaire.* Yokohama and Paris. 1910.

BIENSTOCK, GREGORY. *The Struggle for the Pacific.* London and New York. 1937.

BLAND, J. O. P. and BACKHOUSE, E. *China Under the Empress Dowager.* London. 1912.

BORTON, HUGH. *Peasant Uprisings in Japan of the Tokugawa Period.* Transactions of the Asiatic Society of Japan. Second Series. Vol. XVI. Tokyo. May 1938.

BOXER, C. R. *Jan Compagnie in Japan 1600-1817.* The Hague. 1936.

CABINET IMPÉRIAL DU JAPON. *Résumé Statistique de l'Empire du Japon.* No. 2. Tokyo. 1888.

CARR-SAUNDERS, A. M. *World Population.* Oxford and New York. 1936.

CAUSTON, E. E. N. *Militarism and Foreign Policy in Japan.* London. 1936.

COURANT, MAURICE. *Okubo.* Paris. 1904.

———. *Les Clans Japonais sous les Tokugawa. Conférences faites au Musée Guimet.* Paris. 1903-5. Part 1, Vol. XV.

CROCKER, W. R. *The Japanese Population Problem.* New York and London. 1931.

CURTLER, W. H. R. *The Enclosure and Redistribution of Our Land.* Oxford. 1920.

DENNETT, TYLER. *Americans in Eastern Asia.* New York. 1922.

DOBB, MAURICE. *Political Economy and Capitalism: Some Essays in Economic Tradition.* London. 1937; New York. 1939.

DULLES, FOSTER RHEA. *Forty Years of American-Japanese Relations.* New York and London. 1937.

DUMOLARD, HENRY. *Le Japon Politique, Economique et Social.* Paris. 1905.

FUKUDA, TOKUZO. *Die Gesellschaftliche und Wirtschaftliche Entwicklung in Japan.* Münchener Volkswirtschaftliche Studien. Stuttgart. 1900.

FUKUZAWA, YUKICHI. *Autobiography.* Translated by E. Kiyooka. Tokyo. 1934.

GRIFFIS, W. E. *The Mikado: Institution and Person.* Princeton. 1915. 2 vols.

GUBBINS, J. H. *The Making of Modern Japan.* London. 1922.

————. *Progress of Japan. 1853-1871.* Oxford. 1911.

HABBERTON, WM. *Anglo-Russian Relations Concerning Afghanistan 1837-1907.* Illinois Studies in the Social Sciences. Vol. XXI, No. 4. Urbana, Illinois. 1937.

HAMMOND, J. H. and BARBARA. *The Rise of Modern Industry.* London. 1925.

HART, SIR ROBERT. *These from the Land of Sinim. Essays on the Chinese Question.* London. 1901.

HECKSCHER, ELI F. *Mercantilism.* London. 1935. 2 vols.

HILDRETH, RICHARD. *Japan as It Was and Is.* Boston. 1855.

HISHIDA, S. G. *The International Position of Japan as a Great Power.* New York. 1905.

HONJO, EIJIRO. *The Social and Economic History of Japan.* Kyoto. 1935.

HSU, SHUHSI. *China and Her Political Entity.* New York. 1926.

HUDSON, G. F. *The Far East in World Politics.* Oxford and New York. 1937.

IIZAWA, SHOJI. *Politics and Political Parties in Japan.* Foreign Affairs Association of Japan. Tokyo. 1938.

IKEMOTO, KISAO. *La Restauration de l'Ere de Meiji et sa Repercussion sur les Milieux agricoles japonais. 1867-1930.* Paris. 1931.

IMPERIAL JAPANESE COMMISSION TO LOUISIANA PURCHASE EXPOSITION. *Japan at the Beginning of the Twentieth Century.* Tokyo. 1904.

INSTITUT INTERNATIONAL DE STATISTIQUE. *Bulletin de l'Institut International de Statistique.* Tome XXV, 2ème livraison. Tokyo. 1931.

ISHII, RYOICHI. *Population Pressure and Economic Life in Japan.* London and Chicago. 1937.

ITO, HIROBUMI. *Commentaries on the Constitution of the Empire of Japan.* Translated by Ito Myoji. Tokyo. 1906.

IWASAKI, UICHI. *Working Forces in Japanese Politics (1867-1920).* New York. 1921.

KAEMPFER, ENGLEBERT. *History of Japan 1690-1692*. Glasgow. 1906. 3 vols.

KANTOROVICH, ANATOLE. *Amerika v Bor'be za Kitai* (America in the Struggle for China). Moscow. 1935.

KIERNAN, E. V. G. *British Diplomacy in China 1880-1885*. Cambridge University Press. 1939.

KINOSITA, YETARO. *The Past and Present of Japanese Commerce*. New York. 1902.

KLAPROTH, J. *San Kokf* (sic) *Tsou Ran to Setsu; ou aperçu des trois royaumes*. Paris. 1832.

KOBAYASHI, USHISABURO. *Military Industries of Japan*. New York and London. 1922.

———. *Basic Industries and Social History of Japan 1914-1918*. New Haven and London. 1930.

KNOWLES, L. C. A. *The Industrial and Commercial Revolutions in Great Britain during the Nineteenth Century*. London. 1921.

LANGER, W. L. *The Diplomacy of Imperialism*. New York. 1935. 2 vols.

LATOURETTE, K. S. *The Development of Japan*. New York. 1938. Fourth edition.

MAYET, PAUL. *Agricultural Insurance*. Translated by Rev. Arthur Lloyd. London. 1893.

DE LA MAZELIÈRE, ANTOINE ROUS. *Le Japon, Histoire et Civilisation*. Paris. 1907. 8 vols.

McLAREN, W. W. *A Political History of Japan during the Meiji Era. 1867-1912*. New York. 1916.

———. *Japanese Government Documents*. Transactions of the Asiatic Society of Japan. Vol. XLII, Part 1. Tokyo. 1914.

MIKI, SHOZABURO. *The Labour Problem in Japan*. Unpublished MS. in Columbia University Library. 1900.

MITSUI, HOUSE OF. *A Record of Three Centuries*. Tokyo. 1937.

MOGI, S. and REDMAN, VERE. *The Problem of the Far East*. London. 1935.

MORSE, H. B. *The Trade and Administration of China*. London. 1920. Third edition.

MOUNSEY, A. H. *The Satsuma Rebellion; An Episode of Japanese History*. London. 1879.

MURDOCH, JAMES. *A History of Japan*. London. 1925-6. New York. 1926. 3 vols.

NASU, S. *Land Utilization in Japan*. Japanese Council, Institute of Pacific Relations. Tokyo. 1929.

NAUDEAU, LUDOVIC. *Le Japon Moderne*. Paris. (No date; *circa* 1910.)

NITOBE, I. (editor). *Western Influences in Modern Japan*. Institute of Pacific Relations. Tokyo, 1929; Chicago, 1930. 2 vols.

OGAWA, GOTARO. *The Conscription System in Japan*. New York and London. 1921.

OKUMA, SHIGENOBU (editor). *Fifty Years of New Japan*. London. 1910. 2 vols.

OLIPHANT, LAURENCE. *A Narrative of the Earl of Elgin's Mission to China and Japan in the Years 1857-58-59*. New York. 1860.

ONO, YEIJIRO. *The Industrial Transition in Japan*. Publication of The American Economic Society. Baltimore. January 1890. Vol. II, No. 1.

ORCHARD, JOHN E. *Japan's Economic Position*. New York. 1930.

OZAKI, YUKIO. *The Voice of Japanese Democracy*. Yokohama. 1918.

PASKE-SMITH, M. *Western Barbarians in Japan and Formosa in Tokugawa Days, 1603-1868*. Kobe. 1930.

PETIT-DUTAILLIS, C. *The Feudal Monarchy in France and England*. London. 1936.

POOLEY, A. M. *Japan at the Cross Roads*. London. 1917.

QUIGLEY, H. S. *Japanese Government and Politics*. New York and London. 1932.

RAFFLES, SIR STAMFORD. *Report on Japan to the Secret Committee of the English East India Company. 1812-1816*. Edited by M. Paske-Smith. Kobe. 1929.

RATHGEN, KARL. *Japans Volkswirtschaft und Staatshalt;* in Staats und Sozialwissenschaftliche Forschungen. Vol. XLVI. Leipzig. 1891. Edited by D. Schmoller.

REISCHAUER, R. K. *Japan: Government and Politics*. New York. 1939.

SANSOM, G. B. *Japan: A Short Cultural History*. New York and London. 1931.

SATOW, ERNEST (translator). *Kinse Shiriaku. A History of Japan from the First Visit of Commodore Perry in 1853 to the Capture of Hakodate*. By Shozan Yashi (pseudonym?). Yokohama. 1873.

SCOTT, ROBERTSON J. W. *The Foundations of Japan*. London. 1922.

SMITH, N. SKENE (editor). *Materials on Japanese Social and Economic History: Tokugawa Japan*. Transactions of the Asiatic Society of Japan. Second Series. Vol. XIV. Tokyo. June 1937.

STEAD, A. (editor). *Japan by the Japanese. A Survey by Its Highest Authorities*. London. 1904.

TAINE, HIPPOLYTE. *Les Origines de la France contemporaine* (Vol. I: "L'Ancien Régime"). Paris. 1878.

TAKEKOSHI, YOSABURO. *The Economic Aspects of the History of the Civilization of Japan*. London and New York. 1930. 3 vols.

TAKEKOSHI, YOSABURO. *Prince Saionji.* Kyoto. 1933.

TAKEUCHI, TATSUJI. *War and Diplomacy in the Japanese Empire.* New York and London. 1935.

TAKIZAWA, MATSUYO. *The Penetration of Money Economy in Japan.* New York. 1927.

TANIN, O. and YOHAN, E. *Militarism and Fascism in Japan.* London, 1935; New York, 1934.

——. *When Japan Goes to War.* London and New York. 1936.

TAWNEY, R. H. *The Agrarian Problem in the Sixteenth Century.* London. 1912.

TSUCHIYA, TAKAO. *An Economic History of Japan.* Transactions of the Asiatic Society of Japan. Second Series. Vol. XV. Tokyo. December 1937.

TSURUMI, YUSUKE. *The Liberal Movement in Japan.* New Haven. 1925.

UTLEY, FREDA. *Japan's Feet of Clay.* New York, 1937; London, 1936.

UYEHARA, S. *The Industry and Trade of Japan.* London. 1936 (revised edition).

UYEHARA, G. E. *Political Development of Japan 1867-1909.* New York. 1910.

VEBLEN, THORSTEIN. *Essays in Our Changing Order.* New York. 1934.

WATARAI, TOSHIHARU. *The Nationalization of Railways in Japan.* New York. 1914.

WEALE, B. L. PUTNAM. *The Coming Struggle in Eastern Asia.* London. 1909.

WILENKIN, GREGORY. *The Political and Economic Organization of Modern Japan.* Tokyo. 1908.

YAMASAKI, N. *L'Action de la Civilisation Européenne sur la Vie Japonaise avant l'Arrivée du Commodore Perry.* Paris. 1910.

YANAGA, CHITOSHI. *Theory of the Japanese State* (Doctoral thesis. University of California. 1936).

YOUNG, A. MORGAN. *Japan in Recent Times.* New York. 1929. (The English edition is entitled: *Japan under Taisho Tenno.* London. 1926.)

COLLECTIONS AND MONOGRAPHS IN JAPANESE

AKIYAMA, KENZO. *Ni-shi Koshoshi no Kenkyu* (A Study of the History of Intercourse Between Japan and China). Tokyo. 1939.

AZUMA, TOSAKU. *Meiji Zenki Nosei Shi no Sho-Mondai* (Various Problems in the History of Agrarian Policy in the First Part of the Meiji Era). Tokyo. 1936.

FUJII, JINTARO. *Nihon Kempo Seitei Shi* (A History of the Establishment of the Japanese Constitution). Tokyo. 1929.

———. *Meiji Ishin Shi Kowa* (Lectures on the History of the Meiji Restoration). Tokyo. 1929.

FUJII, JINTARO and MORIYA, HIDESUKE. *Meiji Jidai Shi* (A History of the Meiji Period). Vol. XII of the *Sogo Nihon Shi Taikei* (The Synthesis of Japanese History Series). Tokyo. 1934.

FUKUZAWA, YUKICHI. *Zoku Fukuzawa Zenshu* (Supplement to the Collected Works of Fukuzawa). Edited by the Keio Gijuku. Tokyo. 1933. 7 vols.

Gendai Nihon Shi Kenkyu (A Study of Contemporary Japanese History). A Symposium. Tokyo. 1938.

HIRANO, YOSHITARO. *Nihon Shihonshugi Shakai no Kiko* (The Mechanism of Japanese Capitalist Society). Tokyo. 1934.

HONJO, EIJIRO. *Tokugawa Bakufu no Beika Chosetsu* (The Regulation of the Price of Rice during the Tokugawa Bakufu).

HONJO, EIJIRO (editor). *Meiji Ishin Keizai Shi Kenkyu* (A Study of the Economic History of the Meiji Restoration). Tokyo. 1930.

HORIE, YASUZO. *Nihon Shihonshugi no Seiritsu* (The Formation of Japanese Capitalism). Tokyo. 1938.

———. *Waga Kuni Kinsei no Sembai Seido* (The Monopoly System in Our Country in Modern Times). Tokyo. 1935.

ICHIJIMA, KENKICHI (editor). *Meiji Boshin* ("Boshin" is the cyclical name for the year 1868). Tokyo. 1928.

IIDA, TADAO. *Iwasaki Yataro* (Life of Iwasaki Yataro). Tokyo. 1938.

IZU, KIMIO and MATSUSHITA, YOSHIO. *Nihon Gunji Hattatsu Shi* (History of Japanese Military Development). Tokyo. 1938.

KADA, TETSUJI. *Ishin igo no Shakai Keizai Shiso Gairon* (An Outline of Social and Economic Thought since the Restoration).

KANNO, WATARO. *Osaka Keizai Shi Kenkyu* (A Study in the Economic History of Osaka). Tokyo. 1935.

KAZAHAYA, YASOJI. *Nihon Shakai Seisaku Shi* (History of Japanese Social Policy). Tokyo. 1937.

Keizai Gaku Jiten (A Dictionary of Economic Studies). Tokyo (4th printing). 1935. 6 vols.

Kiheitai Nikki (Kiheitai Diaries). Edited by the Nihon Shiseki Kyokai. Tokyo. 1918. 4 vols.

KOBAYASHI, YOSHIMASA. *Nihon Sangyo no Kosei* (The Structure of Japanese Industry). Tokyo. 1935.

KOKUSHO, IWAO. *Hyakusho Ikki no Kenkyu* (A Study of Peasant Revolts). Tokyo. 1928.

KUROITA, KATSUMI. *Kokushi no Kenkyu* (A Study of our National History). Tokyo. 1937 (revised). 3 vols.

MATSUYOSHI, SADAO. *Shinden no Kenkyu* (A Study of Reclaimed Lands). Tokyo. 1936.

Meiji Boshin. Edited by Ichijima Kenkichi. Tokyo. 1928.

Meiji Bunka Zenshu (Collection of Works on Meiji Culture). General editor, Yoshino Sakuzo. Tokyo. 1930. 24 vols.

Meiji Ishin Keizai Shi Kenkyu (A Study of the Economic History of the Meiji Restoration). Edited by Honjo Eijiro. Tokyo. 1930.

Meiji Ishin Shi Kenkyu (Researches into the History of the Meiji Restoration). Edited by the Shigakkai (Historical Society). Tokyo. 1936.

Meiji Kogyo Shi (A History of Meiji Industry). Edited by a committee under the chairmanship of Tanabe Sakuro. Tokyo. 1925-31. 10 vols.

Meiji Taisho Noson Keizai No Hensen (Changes in Agricultural Economy in the Meiji and Taisho Periods). Compiled and edited by Takahashi Kamekichi, Yamada Hidevo and Nakahashi Motokane. Tokyo. 1926.

Meiji Zaisei Shi (A History of Meiji Finance). Compiled and edited by the Meiji Zaisei Shi Hensan Kai (Committee for the Compilation of the History of Meiji Finance). Tokyo. 1904. 15 vols.

Meiji Zenki Zaisei Keizai Shiryo Shusei (Collection of Historical Material on Finance and Economy in the Early Years of the Meiji Era). Edited by Tsuchiya Takao and Ouchi Hyoei. Tokyo. 1931. 20 vols.

MORI, KIICHI. *Nihon Shihonshugi Hattatsu Shi Josetsu* (Introduction to the History of the Development of Japanese Capitalism). Tokyo. 1934.

Nihon Keizai Jiten (Dictionary of Japanese Political Economy). Tokyo. 1936-8. 9 vols.

Nihon Keizai Taiten (A Cyclopaedia of Japanese Political Economy). Edited by Takimoto Seiichi. Tokyo. 1928. 55 vols.

Nihon Nogyo Nenkan (The Agricultural Year Book of Japan).

Nihon Sangyo Shiryo Taikei (Series in the Historical Materials for Japanese Industry). Edited by Takimoto Seiichi and Mukai Shikamatsu. Tokyo. 1926-7. 13 vols.

NIHON SHISEKI KYOKAI (editor). *Kiheitai Nikki* (Kiheitai Diaries). Tokyo. 1918. 4 vols.

Nihon Teikoku Tokei Nenkan (Statistical Year Book of the Japanese Empire).

Norin Tokei (Statistics for Agriculture and Forestry). Published by the Statistical Bureau for the Ministry of Agriculture and Forestry. Tokyo. 1939 (abridged edition).

NUMAZAKI, HIDENOSUKE. *Hyakusho Ikki Chosa Hokokusho* (Reports and Investigations of Peasant Revolts). Mimeographed. Kyoto. 1935.

OHARA, KENJI. *Saigo Takamori* (Life of Saigo Takamori). Tokyo. 1938.

ONO, MICHIYO and TSUCHIYA, TAKAO. *Meiji Shonen Nomin Sojo Roku* (Chronicle of Peasant Uprisings in the Early Years of the Meiji Era). Tokyo. 1931.

ONO, TAKEO. *Ei-kosaku Ron* (Discussion of Permanent Tenancy). Tokyo. 1927.

―――. *Meiji Ishin Noson Shakai Shiron* (An Historical Treatise on Agricultural Society at the Restoration). Tokyo. 1932.

―――. *Nihon Sonraku Shi Gairon* (Outline History of the Japanese Village Community). Tokyo. 1936.

―――. *Noson Shakai Shi Ronko* (Discussions on the History of Agricultural Society). Tokyo. 1935.

Osaka-Shi Shi (History of the City of Osaka). Compiled by the Osaka-Shi Sanji Kai. Osaka. 1913. 5 vols.

OSATAKE, TAKESHI. *Ishin Zengo ni okeru Rikken Shiso* (Constitutional Thought at the Time of the Restoration). Tokyo. 1929. 2 vols.

―――. *Meiji Seiji Shi Tembyo* (Sketches in Meiji Political History). Tokyo. 1938.

OSATAKE, TAKESHI and HAYASHI, SHIGERU. Section entitled "Seiji" (Politics) in *Gendai Nihon Shi Kenkyu,* q.v.

SHIGAKKAI. *Meiji Ishin Shi Kenkyu* (Researches into the History of the Meiji Restoration). Tokyo. 1936.

SHIRAYANAGI, SHUKO. *Nihon Fugo Hassei Gaku* (A Study of the Origins of Japanese Plutocrats). Tokyo. 1931.

TAKAHASHI, KAMEKICHI; YAMADA, HIDEYO; and NAKAHASHI, MOTO-KANE. *Meiji Taisho Noson Keizai No Hensen* (Changes in Agricultural Economy in the Meiji and Taisho Periods). Tokyo. 1926.

TAKEKOSHI, YOSABURO. *Nihon Keizai Shi* (An Economic History of Japan). Tokyo. 1935. 12 vols.

TAKIGAWA, MASAJIRO. *Nihon Shakai Shi* (A Social History of Japan). Tokyo. 1935.

TAKIMOTO, SEIICHI (editor). *Nihon Keizai Taiten* (A Cyclopaedia of Japanese Political Economy). Tokyo. 1928. 55 vols.

TAKIMOTO, SEIICHI and MUKAI, SHIKAMATSU (editors). *Nihon Sangyo Shiryo Taikei* (Series in the Historical Materials for Japanese Industry). Tokyo. 1926-7. 13 vols.

TANABE, SAKURO. *Meiji Kogyo Shi* (A History of Meiji Industry). Tokyo. 1925-31. 10 vols.

TOBATA, SEIICHI. *Nihon Nogyo no Tenkai Katei* (The Process of the Development of Japanese Agriculture). Tokyo. 1936 (revised and enlarged edition).

Tokyo Teikoku Daigaku Goju-nen Shi (History of Fifty Years of Tokyo Imperial University). Tokyo Imperial University. Tokyo. 1932. 2 vols.

TSUCHIYA, TAKAO and OTHERS. *Nihon Shihonshugi Shi Ronshu* (Collection of Essays on the History of Japanese Capitalism). Tokyo. 1937.

TSUCHIYA, TAKAO and OKAZAKI, SABURO. *Nihon Shihonshugi Hattatsu Shi Gaisetsu* (Outline History of the Development of Japanese Capitalism). Tokyo. 1937.

TSUCHIYA, TAKAO and ONO, MICHIYO. *Meiji Shonen Nomin Sojo Roku* (Chronicle of Peasant Uprisings in the Early Years of the Meiji Era). Tokyo. 1931.

TSUCHIYA, TAKAO and OUCHI, HYOEI (editors). *Meiji Zenki Zaisei Keizai Shiryo Shusei* (Collection of Historical Material on Finance and Economy in the Early Meiji). Tokyo. 1931. 20 vols.

TSUJI, ZENNOSUKE. *Kaigai Kotsu Shiwa* (Lectures on Intercourse Beyond the Seas). Tokyo. 1930 (revised and enlarged edition).

WATANABE, IKUJIRO. *Nihon Kinsei Gaiko-Shi* (Diplomatic History of Modern Japan). Tokyo. 1938.

YOKOI, TOKIFUYU. *Nihon Kogyo Shi* (History of Japanese Manufacture). Tokyo. 1927 and 1929.

YOSHINO, SAKUZO (editor). *Meiji Bunka Zenshu* (Collection of Works on Meiji Culture). Tokyo. 1930. 24 vols.

PERIODICAL ARTICLES IN WESTERN LANGUAGES

ALLEN, G. C. "Concentration of Economic Control in Japan." *Economic Journal.* London. June 1937.

ANONYMOUS. "L'Arsenal de Yokosuka." *The Far East* (English edition of *Kokumin-no-Tomo*). Tokyo. Vol. II, No. 11. November 1897.

———. "The Commerce and Industry of Japan as Affected by the War." *The Far East.* Tokyo. Vol. I, No. 3. 1896.

———. "Development of Navigation in Japan." *The Far East.* Tokyo. Vol. I, No. 6. 1896.

ASAKAWA, K. "Notes on Village Government in Japan after 1600." *Journal of the American Oriental Society.* New Haven. Vol. XXX-XXXI. 1910-11.

ASTON, W. G. "Russian Descents into Saghalin and Itorup." *Transactions of the Asiatic Society of Japan*. Tokyo. Vol. I, Part I.

BORTON, HUGH. "Peasant Uprisings in Japan of the Tokugawa Period." *Transactions of the Asiatic Society of Japan*. Tokyo. Vol. XVI (Second Series). May 1938.

———. "A Survey of Japanese Historiography." *American Historical Review*. New York. Vol. XLIII, No. 3. April 1938.

BRATTER, HERBERT M. "Subsidies in Japan." *Pacific Affairs*. New York. Vol. III. May 1931.

BUCHANAN, DANIEL H. "Rural Economy in Japan." *Quarterly Journal of Economics*. Harvard University. Vol. XXVII. August 1923.

DUMOULIN, HEINRICH. "Yoshida Shonin (1830-1859): Ein Beitrag zum Verständnis der Geistigen Quellen der Meijierneuerung." *Monumenta Nipponica*. Tokyo. Vol. I, No. 2. July 1938.

EVRARD, F. F. "Coup d'Oeil sur le Situation Financier du Japon." *The Far East*. Tokyo. Vol. II, No. 2. September 1897.

GRINNAN, T. B. "Feudal Land Tenure in Tosa." *Transactions of the Asiatic Society of Japan*. Tokyo. Vol. XX, Part 1.

GUBBINS, J. H. "The Hundred Articles and the Tokugawa Government." *Transactions and Proceedings of the Japan Society*. London. Vol. XVII. 1918-20.

HONJO, EIJIRO. "Japan's Overseas Trade in the Closing Days of the Tokugawa Shogunate." *Kyoto University Economic Review*. Kyoto. Vol. XIV, No. 2. April 1939.

———. "Léon Roches and the Administrative Reforms in the Closing Years of the Tokugawa Regime." *Kyoto University Economic Review*. Kyoto. Vol. X, No. 1. 1935.

———. "A Survey of Economic Thought in the Closing Days of the Tokugawa Period." *Kyoto University Economic Review*. Kyoto. Vol. XIII, No. 2. October 1938.

HORIE, YASUZO. "An Outline of the Rise of Modern Capitalism in Japan." *Kyoto University Economic Review*. Kyoto. Vol. XI, No. 1. July 1930.

LAY, A. H. "Political Parties in Japan." *Transactions of the Asiatic Society of Japan*. Tokyo. Vol. XXX. 1902.

ORCHARD, JOHN E. "Contrasts in the Progress of Industrialization in China and Japan." *Political Science Quarterly*. Columbia University. New York. March 1937.

PARKER, E. H. (translator). "From the Emperor of China to King George the Third." *Nineteenth Century*. London. Vol. XL. July 1896.

RAMMING, M. "Die Wirtschaftliche Lage der Samurai am Ende der Tokugawa Periode." *Mitteilungen der Deutschen Ge-*

sellschaft für Natur- und Volkerkunde Ostasiens. Tokyo. Band XXI, Teil A. 1928.

ROYAMA, MASAMICHI. "Problems of Contemporary Japan." *Occasional Papers of the University of Hawaii.* No. 24. Honolulu. January 1935.

SAKATANI, Y. "Introduction of Foreign Capital." *The Far East.* Tokyo. Vol. II, No. 9. September 1897.

SAWADA, SHO. "Finàncial Difficulties of the Edo Bakufu." (Translated by H. Borton.) *Harvard Journal of Asiatic Studies.* Harvard University. November 1936.

SMITH, N. SKENE (editor). "Materials on Japanese Social and Economic History: Tokugawa Japan." *Transactions of the Asiatic Society of Japan.* Tokyo. Vol. XIV (Second Series). June 1937.

SPURR, WILLIAM A. "Business Cycles in Japan Before 1853." *Journal of Political Economy.* Chicago. Vol. XLVI, No. 5. October 1938.

STUMPF, FRITZ. "Ninjutsu." *Yamato: Zeitschrift der Deutsch-Japanischen Arbeitsgemeinschaft.* Berlin. July-October 1929.

TAYLOR, GEORGE E. "The Taiping Rebellion: Its Economic Background and Social Theory." *The Chinese Social and Political Science Review.* Peiping. Vol. XVI, No. 4. January 1933.

TOKUTOMI, IICHIRO. "Life of Shoin Yoshida." (Translated by Horace E. Coleman.) *Transactions of the Asiatic Society of Japan.* Tokyo. Vol. XLV (Second Series), Part I. September 1917.

TREAT, PAYSON J. "The Causes of the Sino-Japanese War of 1894." *Pacific Historical Review.* Berkeley, California. Vol. VIII, No. 2. June 1939.

TSUCHIYA, TAKAO. "Economic History of Japan." *Transactions of the Asiatic Society of Japan.* Tokyo. Vol. XV (Second Series). December 1937.

UCHIDA, MINORU. "Japan as a Totalitarian State." *Amerasia.* New York. May 1938.

WITTFOGEL, K. A. "Foundations and Stages of Chinese Economic History." *Zeitschrift für Sozialforschung.* Paris. Vol. IV, No. 1. January 1935.

YOSIO, HONYDEN. "Der Durchbruch des Kapitalismus in Japan." *Weltwirtschaftliches Archiv* (Industrialisierung Japans). Jena. Band 46, Heft 1. July 1937.

CHINESE MONOGRAPH

KUO, MO-JO. *Mo-jo Chin Chu* (Recent Writings of Kuo Mo-jo). Shanghai. 1937.

PERIODICAL ARTICLES IN JAPANESE

HORIE, YASUZO. "Meiji Shoki no Koku-nai Shijo" (The National Market in the Early Years of the Meiji Era). *Keizai Ronso* (Economic Review). Kyoto. Vol. XLVI, No. 4. April 1938.

KANEKO, KENTARO. "Nihon Kempo Seitei no Yurai" (The Origin of the Establishment of the Japanese Constitution). *Shigaku Zasshi* (Journal of Historical Study). Tokyo. Vol. XXII. October 1911.

MAKI, KENJI. "Meiji Shonen ni okeru Tochi Eitai Kaikin" (The Removal of the Ban on the Permanent Alienation of Land in the Early Years of the Meiji Era). *Rekishi to Chiri* (History and Geography). Tokyo. Vol. XX, No. 6. December 1927.

MATSUYOSHI, SADAO. "Tokugawa Jidai no Shinden Kaihatsu toku ni Osaka, Kawaguchi no Keiei" (The Opening Up of Reclaimed Land in the Tokugawa Period, Especially the Plan for Kawaguchi, Osaka). *Keizai Shi Kenkyu* (Study of Economic History). Kyoto. Vol. II, No. 7.

OKA, YOSHITAKE. "Ishin-go ni okeru Joiteki Fucho no Zanson" (Survivals of the Anti-Foreign Trend after the Meiji Restoration). *Kokka Gakkai Zasshi* (or *Zassi*) (The Journal of the Association of Political and Social Science). Tokyo Vol. LIII, No. 5, Pt. 2. May 1939.

OWATARI, JUNJI. "Kokuyu Rin no Mondai" (The Problem of State Forests). *Kaizo* (Reconstruction). Tokyo. Section 2. January 1936.

TAKASU, YOSHIJIRO. "Bakumatsu Sui-han Seiyo Bummeiyun'yu Hanashi" (The Story of the Introduction of Western Culture into the Mito Clan at the End of the Bakufu) *Bungei Shunju* (Annals of Art and Literature). Tokyo Vol. XVIII, No. 5. March 1939.

TSUCHIYA, TAKAO. "Bakumatsu Doran no Keizaiteki Bunseki" (An Economic Analysis of the Unrest at the End of the Bakufu). *Chuokoron* (The Central Review). Tokyo. Vol. XLVII, No. 11. October 1932.

————. "Bakumatsu Shishi no Mita Shina Mondai" (The Problem of China as Seen by Loyalists at the End of the Bakufu) *Kaizo* (Reconstruction). Tokyo. July 1936.

GLOSSARY OF JAPANESE TERMS AND PHRASES

Aikokukōtō "Public Society of Patriots"—one of the first political clubs aiming at the establishment of representative government.

Aikokusha "Society of Patriots." Successor to the above and one of the forerunners of the *Jiyūtō* (Liberal Party).

Bakufu Lit. "Tent Government," the term for Army Headquarters in the feudal period, hence, derivatively, the Government of the *Shōgun*.

Bōseki Rengō Kai The Spinners' Association (of Japan), founded 1882.

Buke-Hatto Code of laws for regulating the military class, enunciated by Tokugawa Ieyasu and amplified by his successors.

Bukeji Term for the real property in Edo, where the military class had their houses.

Bushi Warrior or *samurai* class.

Chian Saibansho Early Meiji name for justices of the peace, whose activities were centered in the local *Ku-saibansho*, q.v.

Chiken Certificates of landownership which were issued to landowners by the Government during the transitional period of land tax reform.

Chō A land measurement of 2.45 acres.

Chōbu The same as *chō*.

Chōji Commoners' land; real property in Edo, where *chōnin* built their houses.

Chōnin Commoners, as contrasted to the military class of *bushi*. This term was generally applied to the merchant class during the Tokugawa period.

Chutai A company of infantry; a cavalry squadron; an artillery battery.

Daichō Registers kept in the *Ku-saibansho* (sub-district court) in which landownership was recorded.

Daidō-danketsu "Union at Large." A loose and temporary coalition of parties organized by Goto Shojiro in October 1888.

"Daidō-Shōi" "Similarity in great things, difference in small." Goto's slogan for his *Daidō-danketsu*.

Daimyō A feudal lord, ruling a fief or clan (*han*).

Daitai A battalion.

Dajōkan The Council of State; superseded in 1885 by the Cabinet (*Naikaku*).

235

Edo (or *Yedo*)   Modern Tōkyō. It was the seat of the administrative government (*Bakufu*) of Tokugawa Japan.

Ei-kosaku   "Permanent Tenancy." One of the forms of peasant land tenure.

Eta   The vulgar but widely used term for the Japanese outcasts.

Ezo (or *Yezo*)   Former name for *Hokkaidō*.

Fu   An urban prefecture, of which there are three, comprising the city and environs of Tōkyō, Osaka and Kyōto.

Fudai   A *daimyō* or feudal lord in hereditary vassalage to the Tokugawa family, as contrasted to the semi-autonomous *tozama*, q.v.

Fudasashi   Rice-brokers. in Edo serving the *hatamoto* and corresponding to the Osaka *kakeya*.

Fuhei   "City-guards." The term applied to the Tōkyō prefectural police which were formed in 1869, later changed to *Rasotsu*.

Fu-Ken Kai   The Prefectural Assembly.

"Fukoku Kyōhei"   "A rich country and a strong defense"—a slogan of the early Meiji.

Fuku-Kochō   Assistant village headman (modern). See *Kochō*.

Gichō   President of the Assembly (or Chamber). This, together with the following three terms, and *Han-Giin*, were used to describe the organs of fief government in the Toba clan, just before the Restoration.

Giin-Kanji   Secretary of the Assembly.

Gimin   People's Assembly; a constituent part of the *Han-Giin*, q.v.

Gimin-chō   President of the People's Assembly.

Goyōkin   A benevolence or forced loan, usually from wealthy merchants to the feudal government and, in its first years, to the Meiji Government.

Gō-nō (or *Gōnō*)   A wealthy farmer; landed gentry.

Gonin-gumi   Team of five. The basic administrative unit in the village under the feudal regime, probably introduced originally from China (cf. the Indian Punchayet).

Goyōnin   See *Yōnin*.

Haihan-Chiken   Abolition of fiefs and establishment of prefectures, 1871.

Han   A fief or clan, the territorial division ruled by a *daimyō* or feudal lord.

Han-Giin   The assembly of the fief (Toba clan).

Hanseki-Hokan   Return of the land-registers by the *daimyō* to the Emperor in 1869.

Hatamoto   Banner Warriors, direct, military vassals of the Tokugawa.

Haze   The wax-tree; *rhus succedanea*.

Heimin   Commoners; the plebs; more precisely, in the early Meiji era, the class of people who did not belong to the former military or aristocratic classes.

Hoan Jōrei   Peace Preservation Regulation (or Act). One of the most stringent of these was passed in 1887.

Honke   The head or main family (in contrast to branch or junior family).

Jiyūtō   The first Liberal Party in Japan, founded in 1881 by Itagaki and others.

Kabu Nakama   Federation of Craft Guilds (Tokugawa period).

Kachi   A name, in the Tokugawa period, given to those who head the procession as a bodyguard.

Kaimeitō   Party of the Enlightened View. A radical party in the Chōshu clan in the years before the Restoration, which defeated the conservative *Zokurontō*.

Kaishintō (or *Rikken Kaishintō*)   The Progressive Party, rival of the more radical *Jiyutō* and founded by Ōkuma in 1882.

Kakeya   Financial agents of the *daimyō*, mostly in Ōsaka.

Kama dome   Another term for *tori kata no kinshi*, q.v.

Kamme (or *Kwamme*)   See Kan.

Kan   A measurement of weight, 3.75 kilograms or 8.27 lbs. Av.

Kanjō-bugyō   The official who administered the finances or accounts of the feudal government.

Karō   A principal retainer; senior minister to a *daimyō*.

Katori (*kataku-ori*)   Tightly woven cloth.

Kawase Kaisha   "Exchange Company." These companies played an important part in the exchange and credit operations during the first few years of the Meiji era.

Kazoku   The peerage, consisting mostly of former *daimyō* and *kuge*, established in a hierarchy of titles in 1884.

Ken   A prefecture.

Kenseihontō   The Genuine Constitutional Party, one of the many splinter groups from the old *Kaishintō*, led by Ōkuma.

Kenseitō   The Constitutional Party, formed out of the fragments from the *Jiyutō* and *Kaishintō* and transformed into Ito's party, the *Seiyukai*, in 1900.

Kiheitai   "Shock Troops." The name of a military organization in Chōshu, led by Takasugi Shinsaku.

Kin   A measurement of weight, 600 grams or 1.32 lbs. Av.

Kinkoku-Suitōsho   Revenue office of the early Meiji Government.

Kinnō   "Revere the Emperor." A term applied to the Loyalists or supporters of Restoration.

Kiri-sute-gomen   "Permission to cut down and leave." The privilege of the sword-wearing military class in Tokugawa Japan to cut down a commoner with impunity.

Koban   A gold coin of the Tokugawa period, roughly equivalent to one *ryō*, q.v.

Kōbu-Gattai   Union of the Imperial Court and the Military. One of the first political leagues, representing members of the *daimyō* and *kuge* classes, to work for the Restoration.

Kōbusho   Department of Industry, dissolved in 1885.

Kochō   A uniform term used after municipal and prefectural reforms of 1872 to designate the village headman or chief village magistrate. (Later designated as *chō-chō*)

Koku   A measurement of capacity, differing according to the period and locality, but standardized at 4.96 English bushels, or 5.12 American bushels, or 1.80 hectolires.

Kokugakusha   Term applied to "Nationalist" Tokugawa scholars who emphasized the native cultural heritage in contrast to the dominant Chinese influence.

Kosaku kabu no toriage   The landlord's right to terminate tenancy at his own desire.

Kuge   Court nobles (in contrast to the feudal nobles, the *daimyō*), who in pre-Restoration times resided with the Emperor's court in Kyōto.

Kunaisho   Department of the Imperial Household.

Kuramoto   Commercial agents of the *daimyō*, usually in Ōsaka, attached to the *kurayashiki*, q.v.

Kurayakunin   Direct representatives of the *daimyō* (therefore a *samurai*) in charge of warehouses.

Kurayashiki   The warehouse, often in Ōsaka, where the rice or other sources of income of the *daimyō* and lesser feudatories was kept, awaiting conversion into money by the *kurayakunin*.

Ku-saibansho   District (or Sub-district) Court.

"Mabiki"   Lit. "Thinning"—colloquial expression for infanticide.

Meiji Ishin   The Meiji Restoration, 1867-8. Formally, this Restoration was signalized by the recognition on the part of the last *Shōgun*, Tokugawa Keiki, that the Emperor was the *de facto* as well as *de jure* ruler of the nation.

Meiji Jidai   The Meiji Era—extending from 1868 to 1912.

Metsuke   "Censors." Officials of the Tokugawa Government in charge of morals and espionage.

Minken-ron   Agitation for People's Rights.

Minken-undō   The Movement for People's Rights, a general term for the democratic movement in the early Meiji period.

Miso   Bean-paste.

Momme   A measurement of weight, in modern times equal to 1325 ounces or 3.7565 grams. In pre-Meiji times used as a measurement of coinage, 60 silver *momme* making one gold *ryō*, q.v.

Myōga-kin   A tax or fee levied by the feudal authorities on merchants in return for trading privileges, with no official or fixed rates (cf. *goyōkin* and *unjō*).

Naikaku   The Cabinet, established in 1885 to replace the *Dajōkan*, q.v.

Naikaku Sori Daijin   "Minister President of the Cabinet," usually rendered into English as the *Premier*.

Nanushi   One of the many pre-Meiji names for a village headman, used in eastern Japan (*Kantō*), while *Shōya* was used in western Japan (*Kansai*).

Okurasho   Treasury, or Department of Finance in the Meiji Government.

"Onken Chakujitsu"   Freely, "Cautious but sound, slow but steady," the watchword of the *Kaishintō*.

Ōtokai   A political club led by Ono Azusa, Takada Sanae *et al.*, which with others went to form the *Kaishintō*.

Rasotsu   "Patrol men"—a name for the police of Tokyo as reorganized in 1871.

Rentai   A regiment.

Rikken Teiseitō (or just *Teiseitō*)   Constitutional Imperial Party founded in 1882 as the government party.

Risshisha   "Society of Free Thinkers," an embryonic liberal association, composed chiefly of Tosa men, and absorbed by the Liberal Party (*Jiyūtō*).

Rōju   Counselor to the *Bakufu*.

Rōnin   Wandering or vagrant swordsmen; *samurai* who for economic, political, or personal reasons no longer owed fealty to a lord.

Ryō   A monetary unit in pre-Meiji Japan. It was made equal to one yen in 1871.

Ryōgaeya   Exchange-brokers; small-scale money-changers and usurers found in towns and villages of pre-Meiji Japan.

Sakaya Kaigi   Council of *Saké* Brewers, founded in 1800, by Kajima Minoru and active (till its suppression) in the *Jiyūtō*.

Saké   Rice wine.

Sambutsu-kaisho   The name for the *han* (clan) organ of monopoly over staple industries.

Samurai   Feudal warrior or knight, owing fealty to *daimyō*, and paid in return by his lord in rice.

Sankin-kōtai   "Alternate attendance" of *daimyo* at the *Shogun's* court. By this system, the *daimyō* was compelled to spend several months a year at Edo, leaving his wife and family behind as hostages on his return to his own fief.

Se   A land measurement, of 119 sq. yds. or .992 acres; 1/100 of a *chō*.

Seido Torishirabe Kyoku "Bureau for the Investigation of Constitutional Systems," headed by Prince Ito Hirobumi, to draft the Japanese Constitution.

Sei-i-tai-Shōgun "Barbarian-Subduing-Generalissimo," the full title of *Shōgun,* q.v.

Seikan Ron Advocacy of a Korean Expedition.

Seiyukai "Society of Political Friends," a party of conservative hue founded in 1900 out of fragments of earlier political parties by Prince Ito Hirobumi, and led afterwards by Marquis (later Prince) Saionji.

Shakkintō Debtors' Party, a local political association formed in the early Meiji era, to protect the interests of small tenants and peasants.

Shichiji-kosaku Tenancy of land held in pawn or mortgage by money lender, etc.

Shichū torishimari "Town Constable," early (1868) name for city police, changed in 1869 to *Fuhei.*

Shi-gakkō Military or *samurai* schools—the name given to training centers for Satsuma *samurai,* organized by Saigo Takamori.

Shiki Lit. "Offices"—the term for feudal profits and rights arising from the exploitation of feudal privileges (cf. the somewhat analogous *seisin* of feudal England).

Shi-kō roku-min Lit. "Four (parts) to the lord, six to the people," this phrase was used to express the customary division of rice between the people and the feudal ruler. In the later feudal period the proportion going to the lord was higher.

Shimpeitai The Imperial Life-Guards; the term was used in the early Meiji era, before general conscription, to describe the standing army of the Government.

Shimpūren "The Band of the Divine Wind." The name of a secret society of discontented ex-*samurai* which provoked an uprising in Kumamoto in 1876.

Shinjinushi "New landlords"—term used with reference to the class of merchants or usurers who became landlords during the late Tokugawa period.

Shizoku The military class or the gentry; a generic term applied to former *samurai* families after the Restoration.

Shōgun Generalissimo, or Commander. This title, an abbreviation of *Sei-i-tai-Shōgun,* was given by the Emperor (who until 1868 lived in Kyōto in virtual retirement) to the military dictator of feudal Japan.

Shōhōshi The first name for the Commercial Bureau, established in 1868, and replaced by the *Tsūshōshi.*

Shōtai A section; a squad; a battery.

Shōya One of the pre-Meiji names for village headman.

Shōyu Soy sauce.

Sonnō-Jōi "Exalt the Emperor, expel the barbarian." The rallying cry of the anti-Tokugawa forces in the years before the Restoration.

Sotsu A private; or more technically, the name for a lesser *samurai* shortly after the Restoration.

Sukegō One of the most onerous forms of the *corvée*; by it horses and men were requisitioned for courier and postal service in the Tokugawa period.

Tachi gekari Another term for *tori kata no kinshi*, q.v.

Tai A company (of troops); a corps.

Tan A land measurement, .245 acres; 1/10 of a *chō*.

Tetsudō Kaigi Council for Railways, instituted by the Meiji Government to supervise railway construction.

Tezukuri jinushi "Cultivating landlords," i.e., landlords who farmed or engaged in "domestic" industry.

Tokugawa Name of the ruling feudal family which dominated Japan from the very beginning of the seventeenth century until the Restoration of 1868. The head of the family governed from Edo as the *Shōgun*.

Tokumi Donya (or *Don-ya*) The Ten Federated *Tonya*, or great monopoly wholesale trading guilds in Edo during the Tokugawa period.

Tonden-hei Militia or, to be more precise, military colonists used in border regions or unsettled areas.

Tonya (or *Ton-ya*) A wholesale house.

Tori kata no kinshi A phrase designating the landlord's privilege of prohibiting a defaulting tenant from harvesting his crop.

Toshiyori An elder, hence a counselor; also one of the many pre-Meiji names for village headman.

Tōyō Giseikai Name of a political club led by Yano Fumio, Inukai Tsuyoshi *et al.*, which with others went to form the *Kaishintō*.

Tōyō Jiyūtō Eastern Liberal Party—the name of a radical splinter from the original *Jiyūtō*, led by Oi Kentaro.

Tōyō Shakaitō Eastern Social Party. One of the earliest and typically ephemeral left-wing parties, founded in 1882 by Tarui Tōkichi and Akamatsu Taisuke.

Tozama Lit. "Outside lord"—a *daimyō* who owed nominal, in contrast to hereditary (*fudai*) vassalage to the Tokugawa family. It was these strong, semi-autonomous lords who combined to overthrow the Tokugawa.

Tsūshō kaisha Commercial companies, formed in the first years of the Meiji era by the initiative of the government in order to promote trade and commerce.

Tsūshōshi   Commercial Bureau, established in 1869 replacing the preceding *Shōhōshi*.

Uchi-harai rei   Decree of the *Bakufu*, promulgated in 1825, commanding the attack and pursuit of foreign ships approaching Japanese waters.

Uchi-kowashi   "House-smashing," city-riots in feudal times directed usually against the high price of rice and against the clan monopoly system.

Uji   Clan; the patriarchal unit of ancient Japan, to be distinguished from the *han*, the fief or clan of a *daimyō*, which was a territorial unit.

Ukiyo-e   A *genre* of painting during the Tokugawa period which depicted "modern," everyday life.

Uikyo-soshi   Popular novels of the Tokugawa, describing common people or more often the *demi-monde*.

Unjō   One of the numerous kinds of "thank-money" paid by merchants in the Tokugawa period to the feudal authorities as a kind of enterprise tax at definite rates (cf. *myōga-kin*).

Yōnin   Chamberlain or adviser, usually in financial matters, to a *daimyō* or *hatamoto*.

Yoriki   A class of retainer attached to important personages in the *Bakufu*.

Zaibatsu   The financial oligarchy, consisting of the greatest houses, such as Mitsui, Mitsubishi, Sumitomo, Yasuda.

Zokurontō   The Vulgar View Party, the conservative faction in the Chōshu clan, defeated by the *Kaimeitō*.

Zōseki   Yeast stone, used in brewing *saké*.

Zuihitsu   A *genre* of writing, meaning, literally, to follow the brush, hence stray notes, fugitive essays, a miscellany.

INDEX